THE MAKING OF BARNSLEY

'THE MAKING OF ...' Series

'The Making of ...' series is a new collection of local histories, brought to you by Wharncliffe Books. This series is not intended to be a chronological account of each area, but instead highlights the prominent factors, which bring to life the development and character of a town, city or area. These highly illustrated books contain illuminating snapshots captivating the history and growth of each locality.

The Making of Manchester, Mike Fletcher • 1 903425 32 8 • £9.99

The Making of Huddersfield, George Redmonds • 1 903425 39 5 • £9.99

The Making of Liverpool, Mike Fletcher • 1 903425 53 0 • £9.99

The Making of the South Yorkshire Landscape, Melvyn Jones • 1 871647 53 6 • £9.95

The Making of the West Yorkshire Landscape, Anthony Silson • 1 903425 31 X • £9.99

The Making of Sheffield, Melvyn Jones • 1 903425 42 5 • £9.99

'ASPECTS' Series

With over 32 books currently available in Series, *'Aspects'* books are unique in that they allow many local authors and historians to contribute articles to each volume. Articles are made up from a collection of nostalgic and historical pieces relevant to an area, each of which is highly illustrated.

Aspects of Sheffield, Melvyn Jones • 1 871647 40 1 • £9.95

Aspects of Barnsley 7, Brian Elliott • 1 903425 24 7 • £9.99

Aspects of Rotherham 2, Melvyn Jones • 1 871647 32 0 • £9.95

Aspects of Wakefield 3, Kate Taylor • 1 903425 06 9 • £9.99

'FOUL DEEDS AND SUSPICIOUS DEATHS' Series

Each book will take the reader into the darker side of their town or region; covering stories that once shocked, horrified and captivated the people who lived there. From the strange to the macabre, to murder and mystery, the authors examine those cases, analysing both motive and consequence, alongside the social conditions prevalent at the time.

Foul Deeds and Suspicious Deaths in Blackburn & Hyndburn, Stephen Greenhalgh
1 903425 18 2 • £9.99

Foul Deeds & Suspicious Deaths In and Around Chesterfield, Geoffrey Sadler
1 903425 30 1 • £9.99

Foul Deeds & Suspicious Deaths In and Around Rotherham, Kevin Turton
1 903425 18 2 • £9.99

Foul Deeds on the Yorkshire Coast, Alan Whitworth
1 903425 01 8 • £9.99

Foul Deeds & Suspicious Deaths In and Around The Tees, Maureen Anderson
1 903425 07 7 • £9.99

Foul Deeds & Suspicious Deaths in Wakefield, Kate Taylor • 1 903425 48 4 • £9.99

Foul Deeds and Suspicious Deaths In Leeds, David Goodman
1 903425 08 5 • £9.99

Foul Deeds and Suspicious Deaths In and Around Durham, Maureen Anderson
1 903425 46 8 • £9.99

Foul Deeds and Suspicious Deaths in Nottingham, Kevin Turton
1 903425 35 2 • £9.99

More Foul Deeds and Suspicious Deaths in Wakefield, Kate Taylor
1 903425 48 4 • £9.99

Please contact us via any of the methods below for more information or a catalogue.

The Making of BARNSLEY

Brian Elliott

Series Editor
Brian Elliott

Wharncliffe Books

First Published in Great Britain in 2004 by
Wharncliffe Books
an imprint of
Pen and Sword Books Ltd.
47 Church Street
Barnsley
South Yorkshire
S70 2AS

First Edition 1986
Second Impression 1990
Third Impression 1992
Revised Edition 2004

ISBN: 1-903425-90-5

A CIP catalogue record for this book is available from the British Library.

Typeset in 10/12pt Plantin by Mac Style Ltd, Scarborough.

Printed and bound in England by
CPI UK.

Pen and Sword Books Ltd incorporates the Imprints of Pen & Sword Aviation, Pen & Sword Maritime, Pen & Sword Military, Wharncliffe Books, Pen & Sword Select, Pen and Sword Military Classica and Leo Cooper.

For a complete list of Pen & Sword titles please contact
PEN & SWORD BOOKS LIMITED
47 Church Street
Barnsley
South Yorkshire
S70 2BR
England
E-mail: enquiries@pen-and-sword.co.uk
Website: www.pen-and-sword.co.uk

Cover Illustration: *The east side of Market Hill as it may have appeared in c. 1890.* (anon)

Contents

FOREWORDS

(1) The Lord Mason of Barnsley

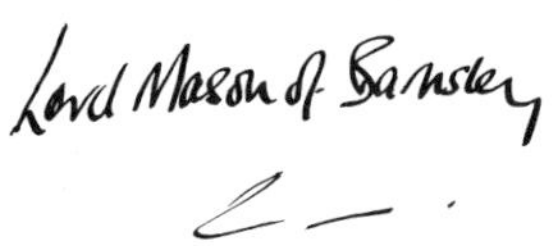

Even going back to its linen-manufacturing days, it's too easy to think of Barnsley – the hard-working, mining, glass and other manufacturing town we all know and love – as simply a child of the Industrial Revolution. That just isn't true.

Our original name (Berneslai) alone shows our Anglo-Saxon origins, and the 1086 Domesday Book lists no fewer than 34 districts of modern Barnsley.

In his *Barnsley Folk of Yore* series in the *Barnsley Chronicle*, scholar Brian Elliott – who has researched Barnsley from original sources – did not go back that far. Much more importantly, he demonstrated just what a thriving area Barnsley was immediately before the Industrial Revolution. This could easily have become a dry-as-dust list of statistics and tables but, being as good a writer as he is a scholar, Mr Elliott related his researches to the heroes, villains and just plain people of the period, bringing our past back alive for us.

As someone who was born and bred in the district, and has spent most of my life representing it in Parliament, I have been fascinated by his stories. Here they are, in book form.

Reading Mr Elliott's history of a dynamic phase in Barnsley's life has been a pleasure: recommending it to you, the reader, is a privilege.

(2) Professor David Hey

Local and family history has never been so popular. In South Yorkshire, as in towns and villages throughout the land, people are keen to know about the history of their everyday surroundings, to understand how places have come to be what they are today, and to find out who their ancestors were and how they lived. This sort of history has an immediate appeal. It is about people and places with whom we have a strong connection.

Writing local history is no easy task. We are soon dissatisfied with books which rely on nostalgia or which recycle old information. An author needs to base his or her work on scholarly research, but at the same time needs to make it interesting to a wide audience. The success of earlier impressions of this book shows that Brian Elliott has struck the right balance. The scholarly basis was achieved by a MPhil thesis at the University of Sheffield; the opportunity to write for a wider audience came with a series of articles for the *Barnsley Chronicle*.

There is a great deal in this book that has never appeared in print before. Our knowledge of Barnsley and its surroundings is greatly enhanced. Many of the documents that are housed in collections in York, London, Wakefield, Leeds and Sheffield, as well as Barnsley Library, have not been seen by previous writers. Nor has anyone paid so much attention to the visual evidence of the past in and around the town. The approach is a modern one which uses every piece of information of what has gone before us. The book has deservedly done well. I have no doubt that it will stand the test of time and continue to delight new readers.

INTRODUCTION

Some people believe that Barnsley had no history before the Industrial Revolution. Even today the area tends to be either ignored by the national media or focused upon for sensational or 'joke' reasons. David Hey in his writings on South Yorkshire history has shown that there is a wealth of interest on our doorstep. There are important archaeological sites and countless historic buildings in the Barnsley area. Excavations and new research are constantly changing the picture. A great deal of discussion has recently taken place about changing the 'image' of Barnsley; images, because they originate mainly from outsiders, are not easy to shake off. But Barnsley people should be proud of their rich heritage; in the nineteenth century, local workers were producing some of the best linen in England and Barnsley Coal – at great human cost – was developing a world-wide reputation.

An important aim of this book, however, is to show that our town was also an important place before it 'became industrial'. Documentary research is certainly required but the landscape itself tells a story. Stand at the top of Burton Bank and you can see the spread of the town from its early hill-top setting into the valley of the Dearne. Walk along Keresforth Hall Road towards Genne Lane and look towards Stainborough and, despite the M1, you will see some of the finest countryside in England. The relationship between town and countryside has been central to the development of Barnsley from medieval times. Its people and its communities were not static; they had to be constantly on the move in the hard task of making a living; and in the course of their work and in social relationships came into contact with people from other areas. The dynamic nature of life and trade was also influenced by religious belief and nowhere was this more obvious than in the rise of nonconformity.

Parts of this book appeared as a series of almost sixty articles in the *Barnsley Chronicle* during 1986/87 under the theme of 'Barnsley Folks of Yore'. I am extremely grateful to editor Don Booker for accepting the original idea and for persevering with it for such a long time. Reporter Bill Blow co-ordinated the series and his interest and encouragement, especially when I had frequently to be reminded to produce copy on time, is much appreciated. I also wish to thank Lord Mason of Barnsley for being kind enough to write the Foreword.

The first few articles had already been presented to an interested audience: listeners of *Second Sight*, the magazine of the Barnsley and District Talking Newspaper Association. My thanks are due to its editor, Tony Heywood-Holmes, for the original invitation and to all the presenters and technicians.

Converting newspaper articles into book form has not been easy. The sequence has been changed, some items have been slightly altered, others re-written; and new pieces have been added on the following topics: coal mining, glassmaking, shops and shopping, the Quakers, law and order, attorneys and the Market Place; 'new' characters also appear: Thomas Keresforth, William Elmhirst and Joseph Bramah.

The production of the book has involved the use of many illustrations, diagrams, maps and photographs. Roni Wilkinson and the hard-pressed graphics team at Wharncliffe Books: Wes, Jon and especially Alan Billingham have borne the brunt of my labours with good humour and great professional skill.

Finally, I would like to thank Professor David Hey, my former supervisor at the University of Sheffield for his help and kindness over many years; to the late Arthur Clayton who was a constant inspiration and friend; and also to Alice Rodgers for advice and proof-reading.

Further acknowledgements are shown at the end of the book. Please note that some of the places mentioned in the text are on private land, and permission of the owner is required prior to any visit.

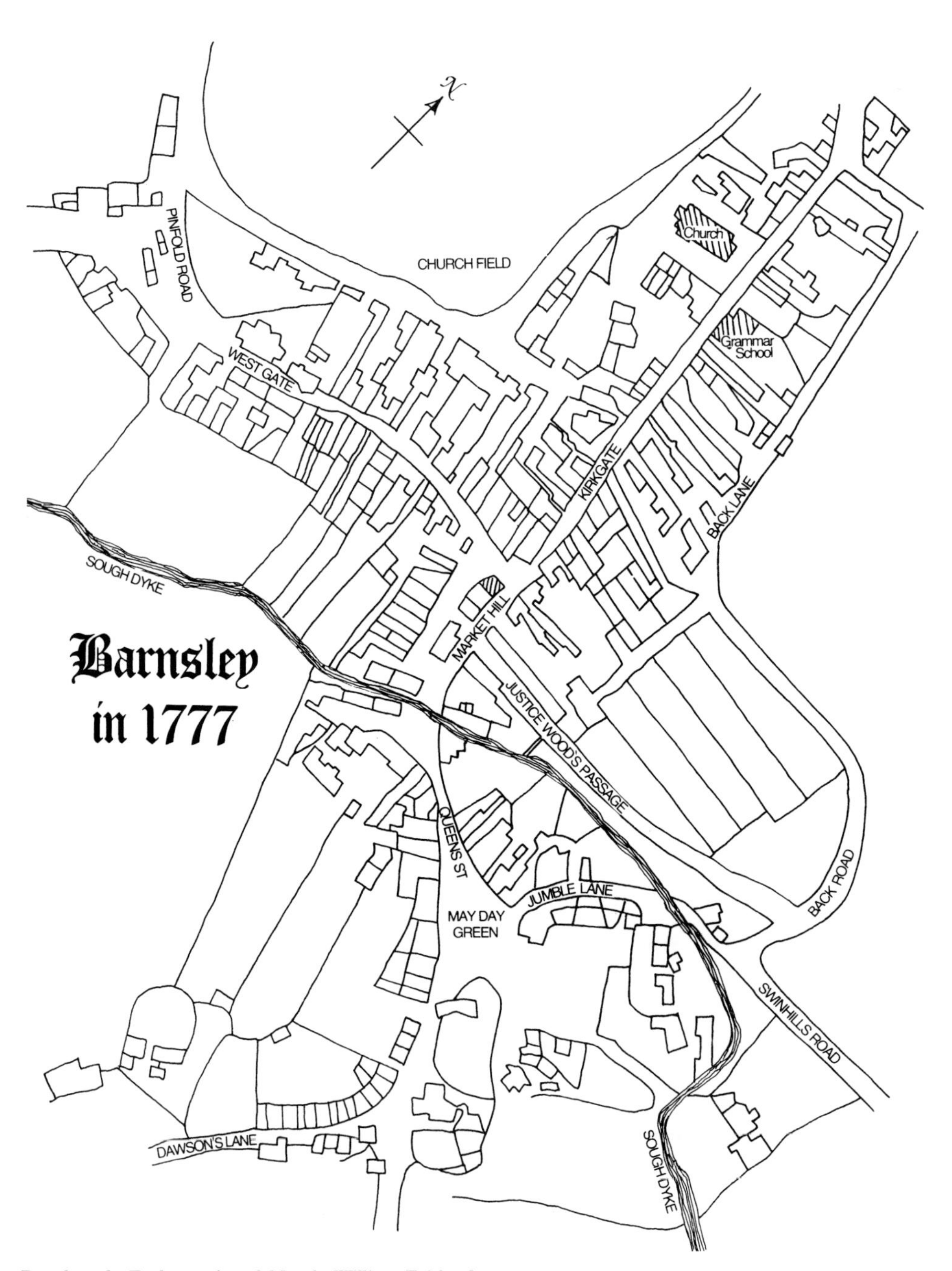

Based on the Enclosure Award Map by William Fairbanks

PART ONE: SETTING THE SCENE

1 PEOPLE & OCCUPATIONS

Very little is known about the lives of the ordinary people of Barnsley before the development of large-scale industry, yet the labourers, farmers, craftsmen, shopkeepers and their families gave the town its identity and character.

Our ancestors of only a few generations ago were not just names in the dusty documents of the gentry; they had hopes and aspirations, certainly a sense of humour and often a Christian outlook at a time when, for most folk, life was very hard and death, especially of infants and children, was commonplace but surely difficult to come to terms with.

By the middle of the seventeenth century, Barnsley was a small but flourishing market town serving farms and villages from a surprisingly wide area. Its geographic position, almost midway between Wakefield and Sheffield, and also by an important trans-Pennine route, meant a steady flow of travellers passing through or staying at inns in the town. Consequently, although the resident population was little more than 150 families, a wide range of goods and services were available.

Adam Eyre, of Hazlehead, in the township of Thurlstone, near Penistone, was a frequent visitor to Barnsley during this period even though it meant a long round trip on horseback. Eyre was a yeoman farmer and though a staunch nonconformist liked the occasional tipple at the inn. Adam recorded his business and social life in a fascinating diary which helps give us an impression of the range of goods and services in the town (the original spelling has been retained):

> *May 11 1647 ... my wife and I came to Barnsley, and lighted at Bower's, but neither master nor dame was at home; so we went to Sara Thrift's* [an innkeeper] *and sent for one Heath, a chirurgion, and willed him to come to Haslehead on Monday next, to blood us, and spent 8d.*

The next day Adam dispatched his servant to Barnsley for the purpose of buying two rye loaves which he accomplished at a cost of fourteen pence. Here are more 'Barnsley' entries:

> *August 11 1647 ... This morne I went with Edw. Mitchell to Barnsley and called at Jo. Shirt's by the way, where I had my heare cutt, and payd for nayles, 12d. To Woodcock for meate, which wee had three weeks agoe, 6s.6d.; for tobacco for my wife, 10d; for threed, 2d; and spent 1s.6d.*
> *December 1 1647 This morne I went to Barnsley, where I spent 1s.8d., and payd for a pair of gloves, 1s.6d.*
>
> *December 6 1647 ... and I went to Barnsley and got my horse burned in the mouth, which cost me 4d. Then I went to Sara's, where I dyned with Mr. Ellize, ye lawyer, and spent 1s.8d., and 4d. for threid and so home, in all 16 myle, and it began to snow and rayne at night, and was very cold. Sara promised I should have 4 hogshead a weeke before Candlemas.*

The south prospect of Barnsley, circa 1719, based on a sketch from Samuel Buck's Yorkshire Sketchbook.

January 21 1648 ... This morne I went to Barnsley to enquire for a copy of the indictment, but the sessions were ended and all gone, so I called on Marsh and spent 2d., and at Sara's 1s. ... and when I came home I was very angry, and caryed myselfe unsivilly. God forgive me this. I paid for oil and aqua vitae 4s. [strong spirit, probably brandy].

It was more than coincidental that some of the most enterprising families of Barnsley were closely connected with the Society of Friends. In the 1650s a tiny Quaker burial ground, one of the earliest in England, was deliberately sited on a bleak spot above Burton Bank, Monk Bretton, and forty years later a small meeting house was added.

Despite widespread persecution, these remarkable people made enormous contributions to the business life of the town over several generations. Robert Leatham, for example, who died in 1707, was one of several members of the Society having grocery and drapery businesses in Barnsley and his son, also named Robert, had stock valued at almost £3,000 and was probably Barnsley's most successful shopkeeper and trader during the first two or three decades of the eighteenth century.

It is interesting, also, that some of the pioneering giants of the developing linen industry, men such as the Wilson brothers and Dearmans, were Quakers who had been brought up in the grocery and drapery trades.

A taxation return, based on the number of hearths per household, provides an interesting view of Barnsley society in 1672. At the very top of the list was 'Mr' Robert Daniel, an attorney, who paid tax on ten hearths.

A further sixteen residents had more than five hearths, a mixture of 'gentlemen' such as Edward Armitage of Keresforth and Thomas Wood, who lived in a substantial house at the bottom of Market Hill, and wealthy mercers (dealers in fine fabric) such as Stephen Ludlam.

A 'middle' group of over fifty people had between three and five hearths; they included 'professionals' such as James Heath (barber-surgeon) and Francis Usher (apothecary), several grocers and drapers as well as a range of craftsmen and farmers. The final group, sixty-two names, were either craftsmen such as weavers, cordwainers (shoemakers), blacksmiths and wiremakers or servants, labourers and widows.

The presence of quarter sessions, and of course the market days, were obvious boosts to trade of all kinds; they were the great social occasions when gossip and news could be exchanged and bargains and sales agreed.

There were also the fairs and feast days which attracted a lot of visitors. Barnsley even had its occasional horse races, held for example, on Barnsley Moor in 1709. On Wednesday 30 July, 1717 a plate of £15 value was run 'by any horse, mare or gelding not exceeding fourteen hands high'. The race dinner was held at the *Old White Bear*, Shambles Street, kept by Henry Bowles, Clerk to the Races. The races were revived in 1851 and 1859.

By the middle of the eighteenth century, the number of families in Barnsley had increased to about 350 and residents began to benefit from improved communications. After 1760 there was a regular coach service, 'if God permits', between London and Leeds on FLYING MACHINES WITH STEEL SPRINGS. Passengers from the south alighted at the *White Bear* (Royal Hotel) where they were served breakfast on the fourth and last morning of the journey.

In the 1780s the Balloon Coach halved the travel time and when it became the mail coach a fast service of thirty-one hours was possible.

Yet just imagine the difficulties, in a bad winter, at the Barnsley end of the Sheffield-Barnsley stage: from Birdwell via Blacker to Worsbrough village, through the Park and Mount Vernon Road, over Bank Top (where the *Three Tuns* coaching inn once stood), then down Mount Vernon, Sheffield Road, Cheapside, Queen Street,

Old White Bear Inn, *Shambles Street.* (Tasker Collection)

ANNO DOMINI 1657

Though superstitious minds do judge amiss this Burial place; yet let them know hereby that the Scripture sais that the Earth is the Lord's and I say so. This, therefore, being so, and by the people also set apart for the Churches use as a Burial place, it is holy or convenient and good for that use and service as any other earth. And it is not without scripture warrant, or examples of the holy men of God, to bury in such a place: for Joshua, a servant of the Lord, and Commander-in-Chief or Leader, or Ruler of the people of God, when he died was neither buried in a Steeple house, now called a Parish church, nor in a steeple house yard; but he was buried in the border of his inheritance, and in the north side of Mount Gaash, as you may read. See Joshua 24 ch. and the 29th and 30th verses. And Eleazar, Aaron's son, who was called of the Lord, when he died they buried him not in the parish church, nor in a Steeple house yard, but they buried him in the Hill of Phinehas, his son, which was given him in Mount Ephraim, as you may read, Joshua the 24th, the 33rd verse. And these were buried. And so were they in Abraham's bought field; Genesis, the 23rd chapter, the 17, 18, 19 and 20th verses. Though superstitious minds now are willing unto the truth to bow, who are offended at such as burie in their inheritance, or bought fields, appointed to that use.

Above: *Inscription on a brass plaque of 1657 once placed at the entrance to the Burton Bank burial ground at a time when persecution was rife.*

Below and right: *Seventeenth century gravestones of the Nicholson and Fletcher families, rescued from the old Burton burial ground by Barnsley Friends.* Alan Billingham

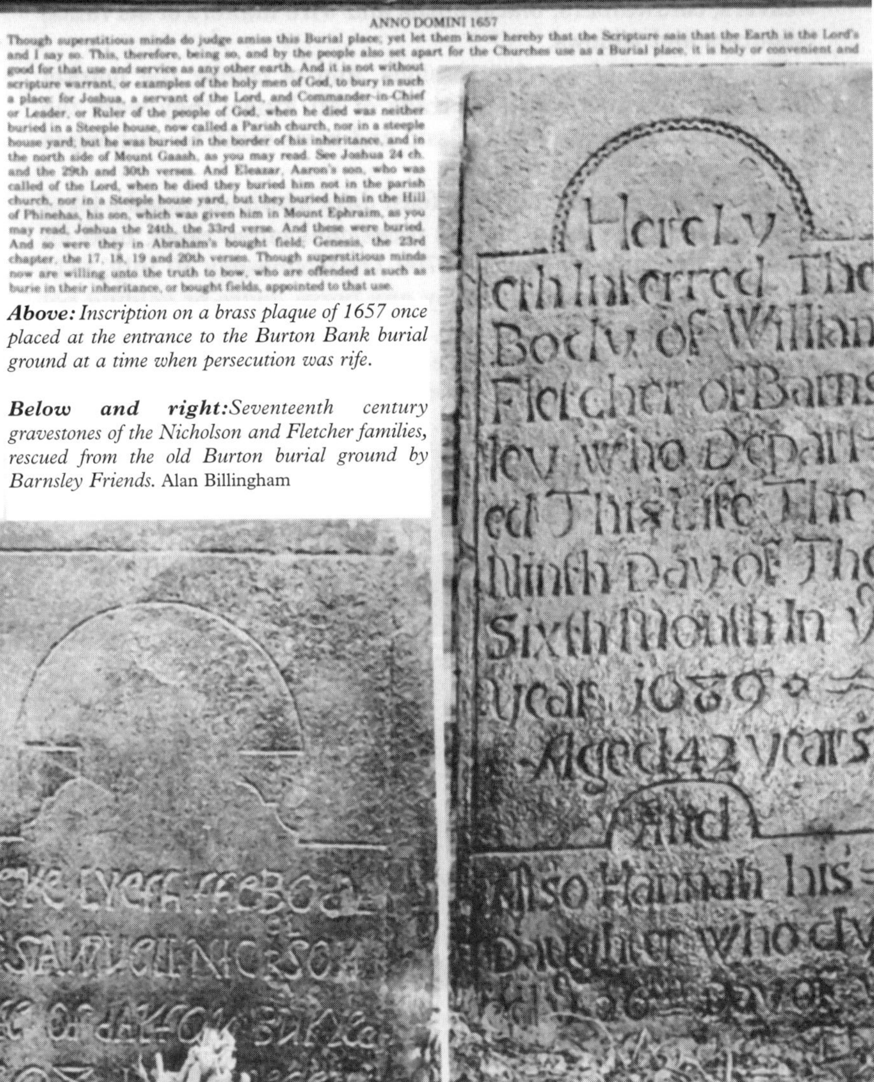

the west side of the Market Place into Kirkgate (Church Street) with a change of horses at the *White Bear* followed by a good run down Old Mill Lane to Wakefield Road and Leeds.

St Mary's church registers for the last quarter of the eighteenth century provide us with the first really detailed picture of how locals earned a living. Occupations of most adult males are recorded and the following summary is based on burial entries:

Labourers	33	Bricklayers	2	Innholders etc.	13
Farmers	4	Builder	1	Butchers	7
Gardeners	3	Plasterers	3	Cheesemonger	1
Millers	3	Plumbers/Glaziers	3	Grocer	1
Maltsters	2	Weavers	4	Mercers/Drapers	4
Gamekeeper	1	Bleachers/Whitsters	4	Hardwareman	1
Bailiff	1	Hatter	1	Fruiterer	1
Cow doctor	1	Breeches-maker	1	Bookseller	1
Cordwainers	19	Tailors	5	Apothecaries	2
Saddlers	4	Flaxdresser	1	Barber	1
Currier	1	Linen worker	1	Midwife	1
Blacksmiths	6	Linen Manufacturer	1	Schoolmasters	2
Whitesmiths	3	Colliers	12	Clerk (curate)	1
Wiredrawers	14	Carriers	2	Gentlemen	2
Nailers	3	Baker	1	Yeomen	2
Carpenter	1			Fiddler	1
Coopers	2			Drummer	1
Clockmakers	7				
Masons	2				

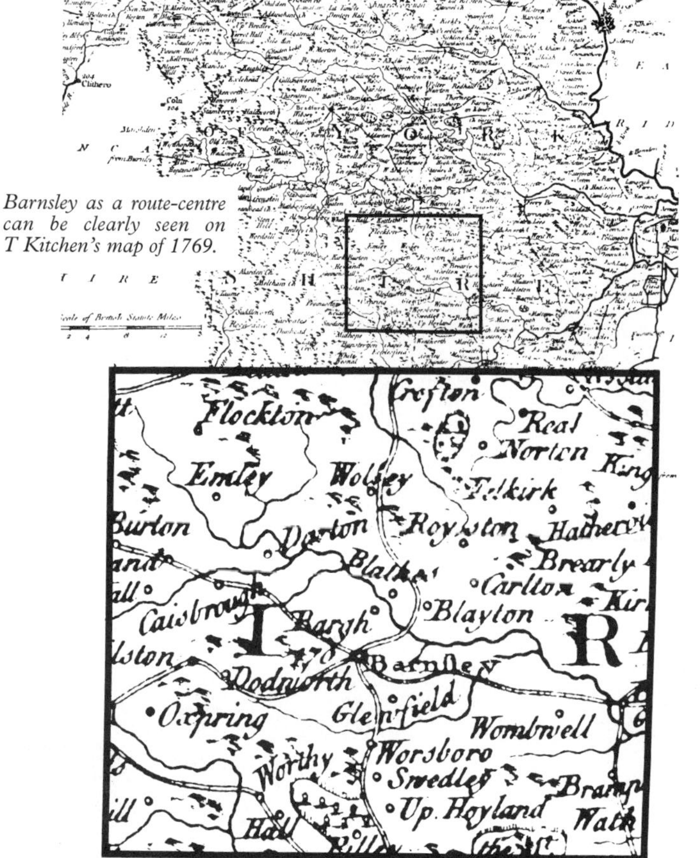

Barnsley as a route-centre can be clearly seen on T Kitchen's map of 1769.

Barnsley's importance as a centre for outlying farms and villages is reflected in a wide range of traditional crafts and trades. Wiremaking was the only notable industry and had given the town something of a reputation since medieval times; but, along with coal-mining and perhaps glass-making, were part of a predominantly rural scene.

For much of the seventeenth and eighteenth centuries it was the retail shops, warehouses, markets and services which gave Barnsley both character and life.

However, one almost forgotten craft deserves mentioning for personal reasons: James Winter, my maternal great, great grand-father, who lived in Silver Street and later New Street, was a cordwainer or shoemaker by trade. Barnsley had a strong association with leather working. A Society of Cordwainers, which still meets, was founded, as a friendly society, in 1748.

John Wesley preached in Barnsley on Friday 30 June 1786 and attracted a large crowd. He recorded in his journal the following account:

> *I turned aside to Barnsley, formerly famous for all manner of wickedness. They were then ready to tear any Methodist preacher in pieces. Now not a dog wagged his tongue. I preached near the Market Place to a very large congregation; and I believe the Word sank into many hearts. They seemed to drink in every word. Surely God will have a people in this place.*

Wesley's prayers were soon answered: informal meetings of a new society were held in a room in Eastgate and by the close of the century Westgate chapel was erected, eventually replaced, in 1846, by the substantial Wesleyan chapel on Pitt Street which was demolished in 1984.

Most interestingly, exactly 200 summers after the great preacher's visit, a new church arises from the rubble.

'Wesley's Steps' now rest at the front of the Emmanuel Methodist church, Huddersfield Road, Barnsley.

John Wesley, 1703–1791.

The yard of the Old White Bear *where 83-year-old Wesley climbed the steps of an outbuilding and preached to the crowd.* Tasker collection

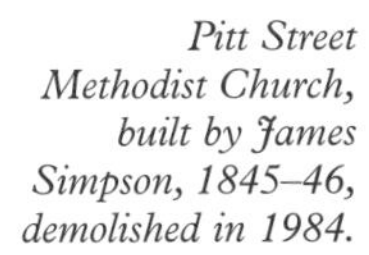

Pitt Street Methodist Church, built by James Simpson, 1845–46, demolished in 1984.

2 MEDICAL CARE

The Apothecary

By the late seventeenth century, many people in Barnsley lived in overcrowded households amidst insanitary conditions. The busy life of the market town provided a sure breeding ground for highly infectious diseases.

The absence of any really effective medical care led to a high demand for the products and services of the apothecary. A good one became a respected and eminent citizen and was well rewarded for his professional skills.

The term apothecary originally meant 'warehouseman' because he was the keeper of the stores of drugs, spices, perfumes and sweetmeats in a large medieval household. By the sixteenth century, although apothecaries continued to work alongside physicians, they had become enterprising shopkeepers as well as storekeepers.

Francis Usher, from a well-known Barnsley family, was a mercer-apothecary who had a shop in the town during the second half of the seventeenth century. The term 'shop' requires some clarification. In those days there was little difference between wholesale and retail trading and skilled craftsmen would make their goods on the premises and some shops were really workshops. In a sense the apothecary was a craftsman, preparing various remedies but he was also someone who offered services and goods for sale.

Usher's probate inventory (a list of personal effects and goods) was drawn up shortly after his death, on 30 August 1703. He was certainly an enterprising character. His 'purse and apparel' (ready money and clothes) amounted to a very substantial £116, about ten times more than contemporaries of a similar status.

Unfortunately, the appraisers did not list his shop contents, simply describing them as 'Shop goods and Hustlements', though some careful accounting had been done since they were precisely itemised at £32 9s. 6d. The total value of the inventory, which also included all his household goods, was £202 but there were important 'extras': old Francis had been in the habit of loaning sums of money ranging from a few pounds to £250, at interest, to Barnsley people, bringing the potential value of his personal estate to well over £900. Before the establishment of a proper banking system, leading shopkeepers such as Usher would frequently loan money and it is not uncommon to find people owing 'desperate debts', probably based on little or no security and very unlikely to be repaid.

William Rooke, whose forebears lived in Barnsley during Tudor times, became a noted local apothecary. The Rookes lived in a timber-framed house on May Day Green called St Annes.

William died in 1729 and although his probate inventory only amounted to £35, it provides us with the first detailed look inside of a Barnsley apothecary's shop. The property was similar in size to Ushers, consisting of kitchen, buttery, back chamber, chamber over the kitchen, shop, cellar and stable. The shop contents are particularly interesting:

An apothecary's shop, from a seventeenth century print by Fairthorne. British Library

	£	s.	d.
One limbeck, three mettle mortars and shop chest	1	0	0
Forty nine loose boxes	0	5	0
Two chests of drawers	0	10	0
One ovall with potts glasses and medicines	2	0	0
Two double quarts painted	0	5	0
Three dozen of plain quarts with some flint viols	0	5	0
One dozen syrup pots	0	4	0
Two dozen of Oyle and oyntment potts	0	9	0
Six pair of scales and weights	0	7	0
Druggs of sundry kinds to value of	12	10	0
Gallypotts and other hustlements	0	7	6
Six bottles with cordial waters	0	18	0

The shop, perhaps dimly lit, was thus furnished with what was probably a great shop chest and the walls lined from floor to ceiling with shelves for labelled boxes and painted glass jars, pots and phials. Herbs and medicines would be displayed and some stored, perhaps in the chests of drawers. It must have been a very aromatic place, especially since most medicines would be manufactured on the premises.

A 'limbeck' or alembic was a kind of still, usually of copper, used to extract oils and essences for perfumes and medicines. In a sense it was a small portable laboratory. The use of mortars and pestles would enable a huge variety of herbs to be ground. Various 'unguents' would be in great demand for applying to sores, wounds, teeth etc. Syrups and conserves, usually based on wild flowers and honey were the popular health foods of the day. Plant roots would also be stocked, as well as home-made preparations either sold direct to customers or to other shops for re-sale.

Apothecaries were originally members of the Company of Grocers and, despite legislation, continued to stock food and drink. A 'cordial' was literally a cardiac stimulant, strong liquor of the type Adam Eyre purchased in Barnsley, containing herbs and probably sweetened. It was the apothecary's skill which made the liquid so much different from anything to be obtained from a grocer's shop. There may have been a little competition from small shopkeepers such as Elizabeth Moss who stocked 'Daffy's Elixir', a well-known patent medicine.

Many eighteenth century folk would go to the town apothecary because they could expect help from someone whose training and experience was essentially practical: it was the best community medicine available. The number of weigh-scales in William Rooke's establishment probably indicates that he had several assistants, and perhaps an apprentice to help with the business.

Many of the preparations sold were meant to 'clear the system' and included powerful laxatives and inhalations. Tobacco was occasionally used, via very sinister looking syringes, as an

Right: *An apothecary's shop in the late seventeenth century.* Batsford

Below: *An alembic or copper still.* Science Museum, London

One way of healing a cut in the seventeenth century, and an operation for a broken back (1634). Batsford

enema, maybe as a last resort! The unfortunate sufferers of venereal disease were treated with 'Venus' or turpentine. Some of the so-called medicines were desperately futile attempts at combating the most horrible diseases of the day such as smallpox and typhoid.

Yet in small provincial towns such as Barnsley there is no doubt that their services were in great demand for many miles around. A versatile apothecary would not be adverse to stitching wounds, setting bones and pulling teeth. In other words it was a mixture of advice, applied psychology and practical dexterity.

John Armitage (1692–1748), a specialist appraiser of William Rooke's inventory was also an apothecary, lived at Keresforth, and was from one of the leading families of Barnsley. In his will he included a small bequest to his sister 'out of my real estate in Barnsley' which may have included a shop. His administration bond, a rough indication of his status, was signed by two fellow tradesmen: William Roper, grocer (this family also kept the *White Bear*, later the *Royal Hotel*), Richard Chappell, woollen draper (and a churchwarden at St Mary's). John Hallifax, a noted Barnsley clockmaker, was a witness to the will.

Some Barnsley apothecaries traded over several generations and gradually improved their professional status. Richard Pickering, who made his will in 1754, had real estate in Ackworth as well as an apothecary's shop in Barnsley. He left his son, also named Richard, his business and he soon became known as 'apothecary and surgeon'. The site of St George's Church was purchased from Richard Pickering MD, the building being consecrated in 1822.

Daniel Beckett, the third son of Gervase Beckett of Barnsley, was also a well-known apothecary and medical practitioner. He became known as 'Dr. Beckett' and the 'Town's Doctor'. Daniel did not limit his services to the wealthy but made a point of treating and supplying medicine to many poor people. By 1748 he had entered into a partnership with Mr John Hall, perhaps a sign of a growing practice but moved to live in Shafton, with his new wife, dying there in 1751. A monumental inscription paid glowing tribute:

> *His eminent abilities in the practice of physic, joined with a benevolent and humane disposition, rendered him highly valuable in life, and greatly lamented in death.*

Daniel's elder brother, John Beckett (1704–1767) became a wealthy Barnsley grocer and built a fine new town house on Church Street which became known as 'Copper Hall', apparently because of his unusual method of paying the workmen. This interesting building, now gone, later served as a rectory and college annexe. John's second wife, Elizabeth, was the sister of William Wilson, a Quaker who helped to establish the linen trade in Barnsley.

Joseph Beckett (1751–1840) succeeded his father at Copper Hall and extended the family's business interests to manufacturing, becoming so successful as to be regarded as 'the father of the Barnsley linen trade'. Joseph also helped develop a banking service, setting up the Beckett and Clarke and later, the Beckett, Birks and Company partnership.

John Staniforth Beckett, Joseph's only son, was also a very successful merchant and banker but he used some of his fortune to build, and endow with a sum of £5,000, the Beckett

The author

Dispensary (1864). A twenty-bed surgical wing, also financed by Beckett, was added to help deal with the increasing number of victims from colliery accidents.

The old Beckett Hospital was closed down in 1977 and demolished two years later, but certainly not forgotten: part of the archway of the hospital's main gate has been rebuilt as 'a permanent memento' and sited by the entrance of the new Churchfield housing complex community centre on the old land of the hospital, Church Lane.

Apothecaries clearly played a very important part in the history of Barnsley. They were involved in a mixture of community medicine and commercial enterprise. The next time you decide not

Beckett's Hospital which was closed in 1977 and demolished two years later. Author's collection

to trouble your doctor but call at the chemist for advice there may be some distant echo of the town apothecary but please remember: he was very much the general practitioner of the day, the poor and ordinary person's doctor but frequently the last hope during times of crisis.

The Barber-Surgeon

Barnsley had a succession of barber-surgeons during the seventeenth and throughout most of the eighteenth century and the Heath family were especially prominent.

James Heath must have been a well-known local character since the cutting of hair and trimming of beards meant a steady flow of custom to a workplace where news and gossip could be exchanged in convivial surroundings but the little shop was also the setting of more gruesome practices: pulling teeth, blood-letting and even amputations.

In the early 1700s the barber's trade was supplemented by income from the latest fashion of the day: the wearing of wigs, especially periwigs, and James Heath would certainly have been able to curl the hair of wigs, using instruments called pipes and probably made wigs to order. Human hair was consequently in great demand and a valuable stock item. The head had to be closely shaven so as to ensure a snug fit and the barber would also require delousing skills when restoring old wigs.

Let us now take a brief glimpse inside James Heath's shop. The customer would likely see several chairs, some worked by apprentices. Forms, perhaps with cushions, would be available for waiting one's turn. The room may have been furnished with hangings (curtains), a few pictures and of course, with a looking or 'seeing' glass as they were often known. Water would be heated in a 'chafin dish' which contained hot coals or charcoal. Razors would be briskly sharpened on hones (whetstones). Shelves would house objects similar to those found in an apothecary's shop: gallypots, glasses, ointment boxes and rows of everyday instruments and appliances of the trade. Scissors and combs would be found next to surgical knives and blood porringers or dishes.

The art of blood-letting was a popular treatment for all manner of ailments and some folk would swear by the value of having a regular session irrespective of their state of health! Arthur Jessop, a much-travelled Holmfirth apothecary, describes the process very well in a diary entry taken from the year 1745:

I bled myself this afternoon in the left foot and took a great quantity of blood. On Sunday in the evening of the 16th of December I caused John Haigh to bleed me in the left arm in Bed and to take a large quantity of blood. On Monday 17 December I caused him to bleed me again in the left arm, and to take as much blood as before. On Wednesday the 19th December I caused him to bleed me in the right arm … when Dr. Thompson came to see me on the 21st December and I told him that I had been bled three times, he shook his head, and said I had been bled too much, and it would weaken me. I told him it was by my own order, and it had done me good.

James Heath probably belonged to a local guild, served an apprenticeship under his own father but was unlikely to have had any academic training. However, he could certainly read and write since he was called upon to witness wills of Barnsley people as well as acting as an appraiser for probate inventories.

Despite contrary legislation, the barber-surgeons of provincial towns were relatively free to do as they pleased though their 'craftsman' status placed them well below the physician.

The Physician & Surgeon

By the end of the eighteenth century the barber-surgeon link in Barnsley was gradually being replaced by apothecary-surgeons and professional men such as Henry Rock, surgeon and physician (1743–1815). Even so, the specialist surgeon continued to demand a practical training.

In the *Wakefield and Halifax Journal* of 11 June 1813, is the following advert:

B. ROWLEY
Surgeon, Barnsley,
is in want of an apprentice.

At the fringe of the medical scene were a multitude of pedlars of medicines, quack doctors, untrained midwives and 'wise women'. We don't know a great deal about these colourful

A *quack selling patent medicines.* Weidenfeld & Nicolson

characters and information often comes from contemporaries who had their own interests threatened. Arthur Jessop referred to some in no uncertain terms:

> *She had been such a fool as to meddle with a running doctor who deserved whipping out of town.*

John Hobson, of Dodworth, in his diary for 1730, had a similar opinion:

> *He* [Thomas Crabtree] *had a good estate but is now reduced and gets his living by going about and selling patent medicine to kill worms.*

Henry VIII showed considerable foresight when establishing what could be regarded as the first medical act, in 1512:

> *Physic and Surgery is daily within this Realm exercised by a great multitude of ignorant persons as common artificers, smiths, weavers and women who boldly and customably take upon them great cures and things of great difficulty in which they use sorcery and witchcraft to the great hurt, damage and destruction of many of the King's people.*

In reality, very little could be done to curtail the flow of so many unorthodox practitioners and some, such as bone-setters, were far from being charlatans.

Most physicians had to undergo a classical university education. Indeed, it was possible to obtain a medical degree without even examining a patient.

Yet several Barnsley doctors deserve attention. William Elmhirst of Houndhill, Worsbrough, described himself as 'Batchelor of Physick' in his will of 1702 and was clearly concerned that his sons should continue the family profession, leaving 'my study of books with the chest that they are in to the three sons that shall turn student in either of the universities or be an apothecary or surgeon, otherwise I give them to my nephew, John Lamb, surgeon, as fitteth for his use'.

William was a student at Clare Hall, Cambridge, and had been awarded a MB (*Medicinae Baccalaureus*) in 1670. He built Genne House but died unmarried at Newark in 1715, aged 71.

William was succeeded by his nephew, another William and it was his son, a third William Elmhirst who carried on the family medical tradition becoming a very popular Barnsley area doctor until his death, from falling from his horse near Hangman-stone toll-bar, Birdwell, in 1773.

Surgical instruments used at the time. Batsford

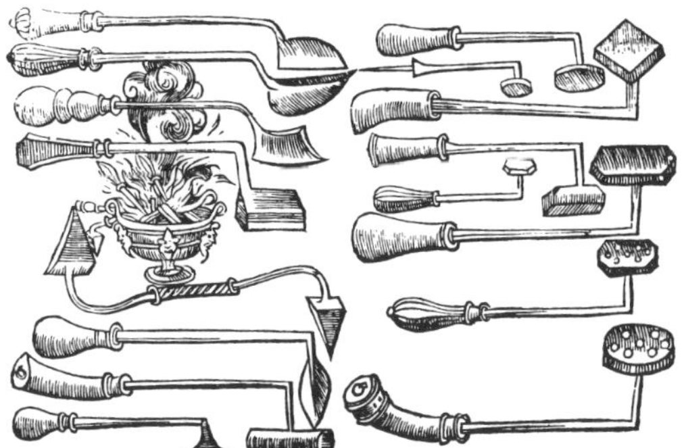

There is also an interesting memorial to another early Barnsley physician still extant in St Mary's church:

> *Sacred to the memory of John Ellison, M.D., Fellow of the Royal College of Physicians of Edinburgh. He was studious in his profession, of which he had a universal knowledge. A kind and affectionate husband, a faithful friend, and a truly honest man. Died 13 April, 1791 aged 57 years.*

William Elmhirst's residence, at Houndhill, Worsbrough. KL Graham

Another memorial pays glowing tribute to a later local physician, James Dow MD who

> *... during thirty years as a medical practitioner in this town, to the inhabitants of which, rich and poor alike, he was endeared by his virtues, worth and usefulness. As a man, he was an exalted and independent spirit, and of a nature social, beneficient, gentle and just. As a physician he possessed a profound knowledge of the science of his profession, and applied it with senstitive anxiety to justify the confidence and realfise the hopes of his patients .. etc*

Dow died, aged 57 years, in 1832. He practiced at 29, Church Street and his name is commemorated in the passageway between Church Street and Eastgate, opposite the old Technical College building.

The state of early medical care may seem somewhat confused even by the standards of the day but in rising industrial towns such as Barnsley there was an increasing demand for a wide range of orthodox and unorthodox medicine.

Traditional remedies and patent medicines were still the main recourse for help for most Barnsley families. The old apothecary may have disappeared but the druggist and chemist continued some of the traditions of community medicine, as of course many still do today.

3 Life & Death

The Plague

Man's mortality was no more evident than in the communities of Tudor and Stuart England. Death was commonplace. It was an everyday topic of conversation. The ephemeral life was parodied by macabre effigies of the dead on their tombs.

Go into St Mary's Church, Worsbrough and you can see a remarkable two-tier oak monument of Roger Rockley who died in 1533 in his mid-thirties. You couldn't have more stark reminder of the transitory nature of life. On the upper bunk lies a young knight, in full armour, his face in the direction of heaven, his feet resting on a cushion and his hands at prayer. Below is his shrouded skeleton resting on a richly carved base of heraldry.

Plague had become endemic in Northern Europe, erupting into terrifying epidemics at frequent intervals. It was the most feared of all diseases. The death cart rumbled along the dirt and cobbled streets of Barnsley during 1585 when 72 interments, almost three times above the norm, were duly laid to rest by an overworked sexton. Pepys recorded in his diary for 12 August 1665:

> *The people die so, that now it seems they are fain to carry the dead to be buried by daylight, the nights not sufficing to do it in. And my Lord Mayor commands people to be within at 9 at night…*

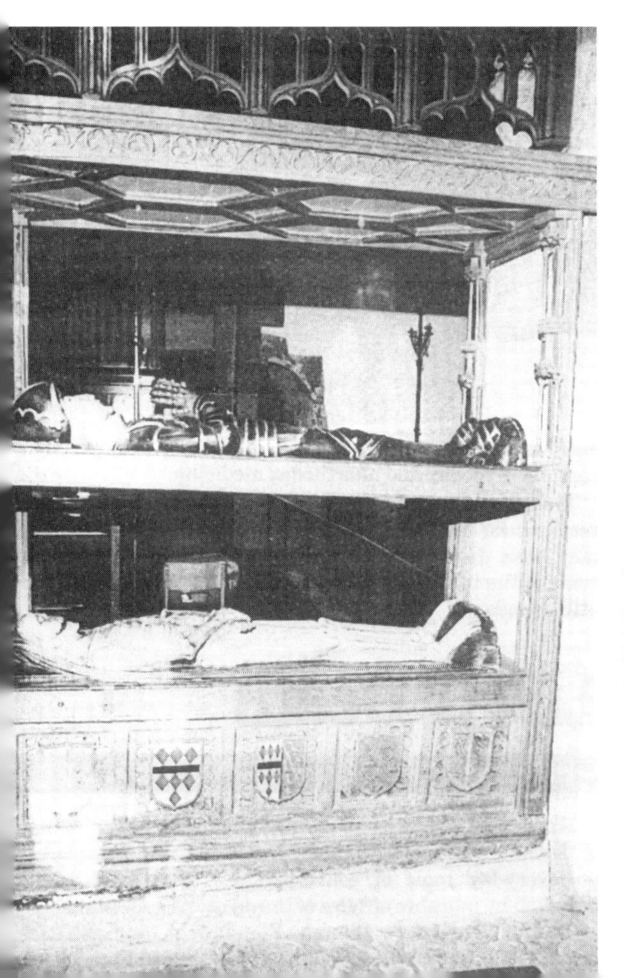

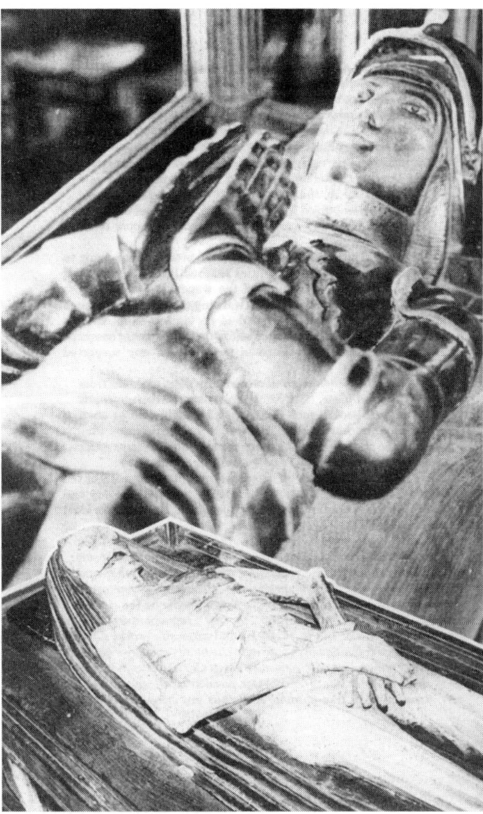

Rockley monument in St Mary's Church, Worsbrough. Alan Billingham

The great pestilence of 1664/5 must have brought near panic to the town. News of huge mortalities reached Barnsley via pulpit and print. The High Constable of the wapentake of Staincross issued an order to local constables warning them of the continued presence of the plague. They had to be vigilant, and careless householders were to be brought before the next Quarter Sessions. There were strict instructions in the event of any suspected infection:

> *... if any householder shall receive any p'son yt comes from any infected place, ... then the constable of each towne is not only to secure such p'son, but also such p'son as shall receive him, her or them, and cause ye house where they are to be shut up until such time as they shall receive order from the next justice of ye peace for their releife.*

The subject of death was by no means morbid. Many wills of the period give us an insight into the 'mental world' of the day and show a sincere belief in a far better life ahead. Here are two local examples from the Tudor period:

> *In the Name of the father and of the sone and hole goste so be yut ye second daye of June (1571) ... I, John Jenkinson of Over Cudworth ... yeoman, of whole and pfect minde and memorye laude and praise be therefore gyven unto almyghtie god nevertheless diseased in bodie by the wishes of almightie god calling to my remembrance the uncertaintie of life in this frail and anserable world ... I gyve and commend my soule unto the hands and governance of my savior and only redeemer Jesus Christ through whose most precious death and bytter passion of all my sinnes I trust to have free pardone And thus any hoope as laid in my behove. And my bodie to be buryed in the church yeard of the pishe church of Roystone...*
>
> *In the Name of God Amen The xxtie of ffebruarie Anni.dm. 1558 I Alys Storie of Burton grainge in the countie of yorke ... wedowe seke in body but laude and praise be unto almightye god of good and pfect remembrance ordayne constitute & make this my last willl and testament in maner and forme following ffirst and principallye I geve my soull unto the hande of almyghtie god my creator and redemer trusting and also belevyng to be saved throwe the meryte and passyon of hys sonne Jesus Christ and to be inherytor of the Kingdome of heaven and my body to be buryed in the church yearde of Roiston as nye to the bodye of John Storie my laite husbande as possible mayebe...*

John Jenkinson's bequests included the sum of ten shillings 'to the mending of the Kyrk [church] bridges' and also for the repair of a 'causey' or causeway (a raised stone pathway) in Barugh. The Darton connection was understandable: an important branch of the family resided at Gawber Hall, an interesting timber-framed house, now sadly demolished. They also owned land in Pogmoor.

Gawber Hall, demolished in the mid 1930s. Tasker collection

Alice Storie left small items of money and furniture to relatives and friends, including six shillings and eight pence to her sister-in-law's children in London 'if my goode will extende so farr.' Elinor Banke received 'my best frocke but one,' her favourite going to John Tylmesley (but perhaps not for his own use!) along with a cupboard, silk hat and white cap.

The widow also gave a bee hive to Royston church, the 'wax to fynde lighte before the sacrement ... remayning as yt was at Christenmas last past,' and the honey was to be distributed to the poor and needy each year.

Smallpox

After the plague disappeared in the mid-seventeenth century, smallpox took its place as the most dreaded of all diseases. There were three types of smallpox, but it was the 'variola major' which caused widespread suffering and death.

Very few families escaped the virus though the very young and the poor were most vulnerable. By the eighteenth century smallpox was the most common and most lethal disease of young children and crowded towns such as Barnsley were highly susceptible to epidemics.

John Hobson of Dodworth recorded the presence of the disease in a diary entry of October, 1733:

The smallpox have been very mortall in Barnsly; a great many children have died lately.

Two years later, Arthur Jessop, a Holmfirth apothecary, also mentioned smallpox as well as another virus which could also cause many infant deaths:

The small Pox were very mortal at Halifax, Honley and many other places this summer ... The measles had been prevalent before then.

The cause of death of most Barnsley people are shown in the church registers for the year 1777 giving a unique picture of the state of local health. During the period June to December more than half of the 41 burials (where a cause was given) were smallpox victims. Almost all who died from smallpox were under the age of five years, typical of the country as a whole, and there was a marked increase in casualties during the summer months.

Interments usually took place the day following death. Other causes of death were as follows:

Dropsy..*2*
Consumption..*5*
'Decline'..*7*
'Waste'..*1*
Childbirth...*1*
Distemper..*1*
'Teeth'...*1*

Apart from 'Teeth' (teething), all the above were of adults.

The effects of smallpox was devastating on particular families. Tobias Fletcher, a noted Barnsley clockmaker who lived from 1750 to 1813, had been married only four years when his infant daughter and son were buried within a few days of each other. In his will Tobias was able to pass on his tools of the trade and stock to three sons, who carried on the clockmaking tradition.

John Mallinson, flaxdresser, lost two sons and a daughter in a horrible period from July to August. Ironically, provided one could survive the hazards of infancy, there was a reasonable chance of living to a grand old age. Quite a few burials were of people in the 70 to 90 age range.

Many adults recovered from smallpox but the disease left its mark: at its mildest hundreds of pitted depressions in the skin but survivors could also be permanently disfigured, lame, deaf or blind and likely to be thrown on the mercy of the parish. To have escaped the disease was almost a sign of beauty and of course powder and 'beauty patches' were fashionable

Sick bed scene, from a woodcut of 1689.

attempts to hide the evidence. The use of make-up, especially by men, was largely a consequence of the ravaging disease.

A relatively mild attack of smallpox was even encouraged by some people in the belief that it would ensure future immunity. In 1717, Lady Mary Wortley-Montagu, wife of the British Ambassador in Constantinople, returned to England after having her infant son inoculated with the virus.

A few years later, following a terrible outbreak of smallpox in London, she had her five-year-old daughter inoculated in the presence of physicians who were impressed by the mildness of the subsequent attack. Such aristocratic approval no doubt helped to popularise inoculation and Lady Mary is usually given much credit for her efforts.

An obelisk in Wentworth Castle gardens, near to the mock castle, has the following inscription:

TO THE MEMORY OF THE
RT. HON. LADY MARY
WORTLEY MONTAGU
who in the year 1720
introduced inoculation
of the smallpox
into England from Turkey

Dr John Woodward's paper to the Royal Society, given some six years earlier, had greater influence. Inoculation was far from successful. It could cause death, resultant attacks were not always mild and it even spread the disease. The idea soon lapsed, only to be revived in 'an improved' form during the second half of the century. The following advertisement appeared in the *Sheffield Public Advertiser* of 22 January 1774:

The uncommon deviation lately made in this town and neighbourhood of the smallpox, has induced Mr. Hawklsley, Surgeon, to inoculate all poor persons who apply to him, without fee or reward.

The discovery of the cowpox vaccine by Edward Jenner in 1796, followed by years of careful experiments eventually led to the near eradication of the disease by the end of the nineteenth century. Vaccination was one of the most remarkable achievements in the history of medicine.

The discovery of a one hundred and forty year old corpse bearing the hallmarks of smallpox recently halted an archaeological dig at the site of Christ Church, Spitalfields, near London. Three students were actually vaccinated after they had unearthed the body in the church crypt. The survival of the virus may have been very unlikely but the incident does show understandable respect for one of the most horrid and feared diseases of our ancestors.

A Gentleman's Funeral

The surname 'Oxley' is frequently recorded in the church registers of Barnsley during the second half of the seventeenth century. Some were farm workers or craftsmen but others aspired to far greater status.

John Oxley was certainly of the latter category. When he died, in 1690, he was probably quite young and unmarried, in his will describing himself as 'gentleman' and his condition as 'being sicke of body but of perfect memory'.

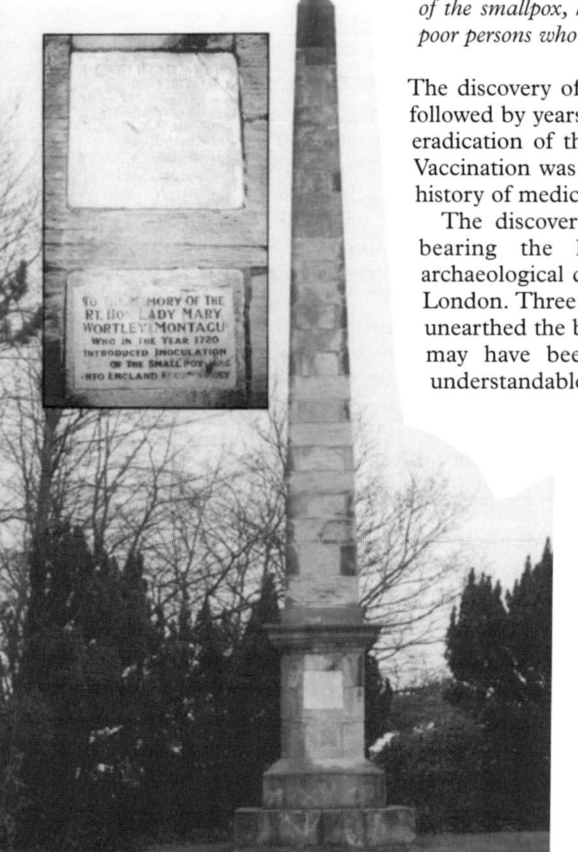

Obelisk in Wentworth Castle grounds to the memory of Rt Hon Lady Mary Wortley Montagu. Alan Billingham

Two sisters, Mary and Margaret, were to inherit land in Barnsley and a brother, Francis, was to receive his 'capital messuage' – probably a substantial town house. A small estate in Hooton Pagnell would enable an uncle, also named John, to receive about £7 per annum and brother Francis a further £5 'to buy clothes'.

Perhaps aware of his impending illness, John Oxley had recently disposed of a farm and half an acre of land in the Far Field of Barnsley for £400, to Mr John Rooke of Greenfoot. There was apparently very little left of John Oxley's goods and chattels when, on 21 May 1690, four friends and neighbours visited his home and completed the following inventory:

	£ s. d.
Imprimis. His purse, apparrell & ready monys	*45-12-00*
Item. Two mears	*8-00-00*
Item. Two Guns	*1-00-00*
Item. Feather bed a Rug 2 pillows & a bolster	*1-06-08*
	Totall 55-18-08.

However, what followed was a remarkable list of 'disbursements', drawn up by the executors, Jonathan Whitlitch and Joshua Andrews' which provide us with a very rare insight of 'the cost of dying' of a relatively well-to do Barnsley inhabitant of three hundred years ago.

The list starts by itemising some of the expenses for the funeral meal which would appear to have been quite a lavish affair:

	£ s. d.
To Mrs. Usher for Gloves and biscuits	*9-18-09*
To Mr. Littlewood for the same	*7-16-00*
To Mr. Legat for spices	*14-00*
To Mr. Smith for the same	*10-00*
To Mr. Collier for wine	*3-00-00*
For meate and drinke	*4-10-00*

Local shopkeepers clearly benefited from a considerable amount of trade and the funeral must have had a large number of guests. The custom of buying gloves, gowns and rings for relatives and friends of the deceased was fairly common during the seventeenth century and was occasionally mentioned in wills:

> *To Hannah Wood and Mary Hollingworth five marks to buy them a mourning gown with* [1670, Will of John Elmsall, Royston]
>
> *...and ten shillings to buy each of them a pair of gloves...* [1675, Will of Mary Broadhead, Monk Bretton]
>
> *I give to my nephew Copley and his son and daughter...a guinny to buy a ring with...* [1702, William Elmhirst, Houndhill, Worsbrough]

Returning to the disbursements incurred by the executors of John Oxley, they also listed various other items of expenditure:

	£ s. d.
To the ministers	*1-16-00*
For the Coffin	*13-00*
To the poore clarke and saxon [sexton]	*5-00-00*
To the Appothicary	*4-04-06*
For his table & care of him during his sickness	*2-10-00*
Paid 5 guinnes left by his will	*5-07-06*
For proving the will & ingrossing	*1-07-06*

Finally, there were one or two additional items:

	£ s. d.
For a Quart assesmt. [ie. rates] *& small debts*	*1-05-06*
For two loads of wheat & a halfe	*1-11-00*
A years rent for the West Roids [a field]	*07-00*
To William Conway for a mare wintering	*1-00-00*

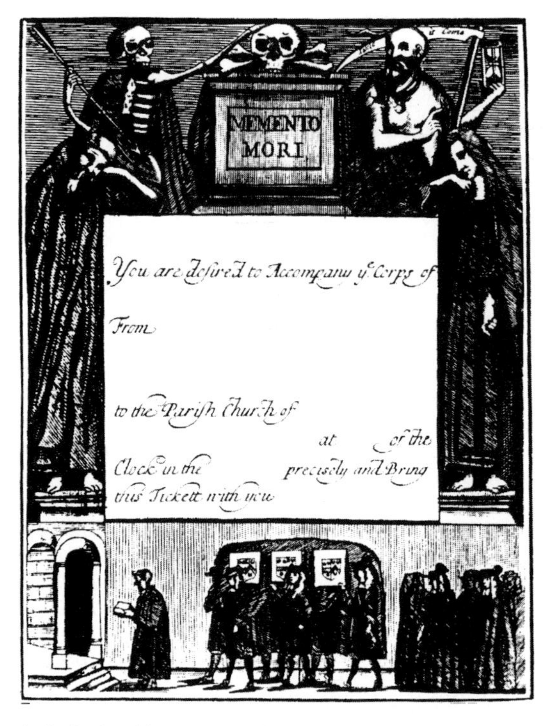

An invitation ticket to a funeral. Pepys Library, Cambridge

The document was witnessed by his two sisters, Mary and Margaret but it was also noted that, 'There is a Chiefe rent of 14s. 6d. due out of other lands that we find is 10 years in arrear which will surmount the remainder of the inventory'. In other words the deceased's expenses exceeded the valuation of his goods and chattels!

Burial fees at St Mary's Chapel mirrored the accepted social divisions of the day. At the bottom of the scale 'if the corpse be interred only in a winding sheet,' the minister received 10d., and the clerk and sexton just 4d. each. 'Coffin'd bodies' increased the dues to the respective parties to 1s. 4d., 8d. and 8d. These were the rates for burial in the churchyard or, strictly speaking, the chapelyard.

Fees increased considerably for anyone buried in 'the body of the chapel,' some parts were more sacred than others and there were additional expenses to consider. There was a general payment to the minister of 2s. 6d. who also, since about 1720, received 3s. 6d. as payment 'for breaking-up the ground.' The clerk's dues amounted to 2s. 6d. and the sexton's 1s.

The chancel was limited to those who could afford to pay as much as 8s. 6d. but the most exclusive places for interment were to be found 'within the rails, near or about the Communion Table' which could cost as much as eleven shillings. However, it was wealth as well as social standing in the community that determined burial in a favoured part of the church. The memorial to John Oxley, gentleman, who died in 1690, has long disappeared from Barnsley chapel but an appreciation of his affection by family and friends has been preserved by the survival of a most unusual document.

A plague broadsheet of 1665. Museum of London

4 Manorial Lords

Manorial Lords

The ownership of land in Barnsley can be traced back to the old manorial system, back to dukes and earls, royal agents and merchants and beyond them to monastic rule. It is a story of enterprise and influence, of planning and patronage which affected the lives of ordinary people and resulted in the making of modern Barnsley.

The Monks of Pontefract, c. 1150–1536

After the Norman Conquest, Barnsley eventually passed into the hands of the Cluniac priory of St John at Pontefract. Almost four centuries of ecclesiastical rule began. The monks had tremendous influence on the future importance of Barnsley. An unimportant village at the eastern edge of Silkstone parish was to become a well-known town of the West Riding of Yorkshire.

The key to this transformation was the establishment of a weekly market and annual fair on a new site about half a mile downhill from the original settlement which became known as 'Old Town' or Old Barnsley.

The nucleus of the hill-top site continued to be occupied but the new site, nearer to the Dearne valley, an important medieval routeway, was also well placed for traffic between Wakefield, Sheffield and London.

A new street pattern was laid out: Westgate (Shambles Street), Eastgate, Southgate, Kirk or Church Street, with the market, (once held at Fair Field, an open space to the east of the church) being established down the broad street of Market Hill.

The granting of a royal charter, by Henry III, in 1249, set the seal for Barnsley's future importance as a small but flourishing provincial town.

May Day Green was to become a traditional place of entertainment as well as business. It was later surrounded by huts and wire smithies, almost certainly had a May-pole and when the fair was held must have presented a very lively scene: horses and cattle sold on the Common, pigs sold from the old Swinhills road and the crowds entertained with a multitude of pedlars, quacks and street sellers, each no doubt with their own distinctive cries set amid the spectacle of bull and bear baiting.

A quack or 'mountebank', a familiar scene at markets and fairs. Batsford

On May morning wreaths and flowers were suspended from the May-pole on May Day Green and folk danced around it for much of the day. The Puritans put an end to the custom but it was revived after 1660.

The monks must have been proud of their re-building and dedication of the Norman chapel of St Mary which was to serve many generations of Barnsley people as a 'chapel of ease' of Silkstone parish. The chaplain was given a small amount of land and an annual pension of 102 shillings, paid by the prior out of tithes of corn, hay, wool, lamb and tolls of two fairs in Barnsley.

By Tudor times the monks enjoyed the ownership of the manor and its court, market, fairs, demesne and waste land and the tithes of the whole township. The market charter excluded competition for miles around and, not surprisingly, Barnsley outshone its neighbours, developing its own character and identity.

The Crown, 1539–1695

At the dissolution of the monastries, their land and rights passed to the crown. The twelve brethren left at St Johns surrendered the house in 1539. Two distinguished stewards were appointed at a nominal salary of twenty shillings per annum to supervise affairs. Sir George Darcy and Thomas Beaumont were assisted by William Thwaites, the official receiver, who was paid £5 and a bailiff, Thomas Hagley who only received £1.6s.8d. The crown lands of Barnsley were managed sometimes by a collector or by a 'farmer' who held the whole on lease.

Being a collector could be a very lucrative office. During the reign of Charles I (1625–49) a character called Edmund Rogers grew rich in office. Rogers must have been a shadowy figure, living at Midhope, in Bradfield parish but wielding enormous influence on Barnsley folk.

His will included a long list of legacies ranging from £10 to £1,000 but he had a genuine affection for the town. He left £10 for the erection of a clock in the town-hall of Barnsley, £50 for a new school-house and a further £50 for a house for the preaching minister.

A Herald (a crown official) announcing the King's decision to dissolve religious houses. Barracuda Books

Seal of Godfrey, Prior of St John's, 1268–83. Barracuda Books

Flamboyant Coat of Arms of the Osborne family.
(from Joseph Hunter's, *South Yorkshire* 1828, vol. 2)

Thomas Osborne, first Duke of Leeds (1632–1712), great-grandfather of the fourth Duke, Thomas, who bought the Manor of Barnsley. (after a portrait by Van der Vaart).

Roger's funeral expenses amounted to a substantial £50, paid by Ellen Rooke of Greenfoot out of money she owed him by bond. Rogers also left to the poor of Barnsley his tithe of corn and grain from Thorpe Audlin and Wentbridge. He was buried in the chancel of St Mary's. The handling of money and dispensation of favours made Rogers into a kind of early 'banker', a profession which was a feature of Barnsley's later commercial development.

Isaac Waterhouse, a wealthy merchant of Halifax, held the lease of the crown lands in 1609 and his sons, Daniel and Isaac, appear to have inherited the tithes. The younger Isaac, who died in 1672, had a mercer's shop in Barnsley, a type of business which was also to become a noteable local enterprise.

At the close of the seventeenth century the Crown quitted its lands in Barnsley in favour of the Dutchman William Bentinck, Earl of Portland. Barnsley passed on to his son and heir who was created Duke of Portland by George I. Barnsley was in the hands of this absent friend only a few years but the family of his successor had interests in the town over several generations and family connections to the present day.

In 1735 the manor of Barnsley cum Dodworth was purchased by the illustrious Thomas Osborne, 4th Duke of Leeds who was then only twenty-one-years-old. The Osborne family mansion and estate was based at Kiveton in the ancient parish of Harthill, almost twenty miles away.

The young Duke added to his influence, and affluence, by the acquisition of the castle and manor of Conisbrough in 1737. Thomas kept careful records of his Barnsley estate with the help of his attorney, William Marsden.

An excellent series of rentals provide us with detailed information about Barnsley and its people during the middle years of the eighteenth century. The Duke's possessions in Barnsley included the tolls from the market and fairs, the Manor House (occupied by William Marsden) and its land, the Market House and public Bakehouse (soon to be rebuilt by the Duke), rents from a dozen or so cottages, and various other rights and interests such as the 'coney' [rabbit] warren, the Court Leet which dealt with petty offences and elected officers such as the constable, pinder etc., the 'Scavenger Fee' which related to clearing street refuse and numerous rents from stallholders and other occupiers of the manorial lands.

The Duke even had the rights to a water corn mill and a coal mine on Barnsley Moor which had been leased by the Queen and her trustees to Sir Sydney Wortley and his two sons. At the time of the purchase of the manor, the mill was said to be 'down' and the mine 'not at present

Rose Cottage, home of the Howard Brothers whose land was once owned by the Duke of Leeds. It was demolished in 1986 for redevelopment. Stan Bulmer, Barnsley Chronicle photographer

wrought' though it was said to have a potential value of forty pounds-worth of coal per annum and was valued at two hundred pounds.

Apart from odd patches of former Crown land such as the Shaw Lands the Osborne family could certainly claim to 'own Barnsley'.

The fourth Duke died in 1789, when his son, Francis Godolphin, enjoyed the Barnsley Estate for a further ten years. The manor passed to Francis's son, George William Frederick, who died in 1855.

The possession of a deed which conveyed Rose Cottage and its land from the Duke of Leeds to the father of the Howard brothers provides a very interesting throwback to the time when Barnsley acres were held by invisible yet recognisable landlords.

Part Two: Setting the Scene

Private Jottings

Poor Curates

Barnsley had seven curates during the second half of the seventeenth century. These brief incumbencies must have resulted in considerable uncertainty to both chapelry and worshippers at a time when new religious movements such as the Quakers were fast gaining in popularity.

The status of Barnsley's fleeting parsons was not assisted by a very modest living. Anthony Preston, 'clerke' and 'curatus de Barnsley' died in 1691. He had been minister for about two years. Although he died intestate (i.e. without making a will, or at least the will was not proven) his brief probate inventory survives:

	£	s	d
Imprimis his Apparell	*00*	*10*	*00*
In the parlour			
Item. A Hall Bed & Bedding	*00*	*10*	*00*
Two Chairs	*00*	*01*	*08*
Two Buffett Stoolles	*00*	*01*	*00*
A Little Table	*00*	*01*	*00*
A Box of drawers	*00*	*01*	*00*
A Close Stoole	*00*	*01*	*00*
In ye Chamber			
A Box with Books in	*02*	*00*	*00*
A Bedstead	*00*	*04*	*00*
A rad Coloured Rug	*00*	*02*	*00*
A Warming Pan	*00*	*02*	*00*
Two Iron Potts	*00*	*02*	*06*
Other household Stuffe & houslement	*00*	*03*	*00*
	03	*19*	*02*

Clearly a very frugal list of goods and chattels and limited to just two rooms. It is interesting that the most valuable item was his 'Box with Books in'.

Preston's successor, William Denton, was twenty-four-years-old and many parishioners hoped that he would have brought more permanency to St Mary's. Unfortunately, he died in 1696 leaving four of his friends, John Oxley, Thomas Fayram, Josia Coldwell and John Smith, the task of drawing up an inventory:

	£	s	d
Imprs. his purse and Apparrell	*06*	*00*	*00*
Goods in his Roome and in his Studdy as follows			
It. his Bookes both great and Smale	*25*	*00*	*00*
It. one horse and Saddle	*04*	*00*	*00*
It. one lookeing Glass	*02*	*00*	*00*
It. one Watch	*00*	*10*	*00*
It. one Little table and a deske	*00*	*10*	*00*
It. one Standard and Mappes	*00*	*05*	*00*
	38	*05*	*00*

Once again there were only two rooms mentioned, and the possessions, apart from what appears to have been a formidable library of books, were few and of little value. However, poor William also had debts amounting to £100 and the expense of his funeral added a further £20. Denton died intestate, and if he was not supported by any surviving relatives the chances of local folk being repaid for goods and services was nil.

The ministry of Thomas Peighen (1696–1726) at last resulted in some stability and coincided with a period when the endowment was increased, though at a very modest level. By 1714 the incumbent still only received £22 per annum but several freeholders and inhabitants, recognising an urgent need for help, enclosed thirty-three acres of land from the common, and, with other dues, Peighen received a few pounds more each year. However, when he died, in August 1726, his goods and chattels were considerably more comfortable than his immediate forebears:

	£	s	d
Purse and Apparrell	*01*	*10*	*00*
Goods in ye Study Chambr. bookes of Severall Sorts	*05*	*00*	*00*
a round table	*00*	*03*	*00*
a table with drawers in	*00*	*03*	*00*
a booke stand	*00*	*01*	*00*
2 Chaires and a buffitt Stoole	*00*	*01*	*04*
a little rainge	*00*	*02*	*00*
the foreside of a close press	*00*	*01*	*06*
Goods in ye Chambr. to ye Street a bed wth. Blew hangings fethr. bed fethr. bolster & 2 fethr pillows a blew rugg & 2 blankitts	*02*	*10*	*00*
a pr. Deele Chest of Drawers	*00*	*15*	*00*
Seaven Chaires	*00*	*08*	*02*
a little table wth. a drawer in	*00*	*02*	*06*
one rainge wth. brass bosses a fire Shovel & tongs.	*00*	*06*	*00*
two doz. Diber Napkins and little table cloths	*00*	*10*	*00*
2 doz. hugaback Napkins and little table cloth	*00*	*06*	*00*
4 pr. sheets 4 pr. pillow drawers	*00*	*10*	*00*
Goods in ye Parlor one bedstead wth. hangings a fethr. bed and Chaff bed a fethr. bolster 2 fethr pillows 2 blankitts	*01*	*05*	*00*
one rainge wth. brass bosses	*00*	*05*	*00*
An Ovill table	*00*	*02*	*06*
6 old chaires	*00*	*04*	*00*
a Close Stoole Case	*00*	*01*	*00*
Goods in ye house one rainge fire Shovell and tongs and grate	*00*	*08*	*00*
a little Square table	*00*	*00*	*08*
A Couch Chair	*00*	*01*	*06*
an old line (linen) wheell	*00*	*00*	*06*
Dresser and Pewter Case	*00*	*05*	*00*
ii Pewter dishes	*01*	*02*	*09*
a doz. old plaites wth. 4 little ones	*00*	*06*	*00*
a warming pann	*00*	*02*	*00*
two old brass candlesticks a Copper Cann	*00*	*01*	*00*
a Gridiron	*00*	*00*	*06*
Goods in the Back Kitching a brass pann two iron potts	*00*	*03*	*00*
two Stands a flaskitt & watr. Kitt	*00*	*01*	*06*
A Seeing Glass	*00*	*01*	*00*
three Rouletts	*00*	*01*	*06*
othr. houslamts	*00*	*02*	*00*
	17	*11*	*11*

The appraisers, Thomas Hutchinson, Francis and William Dilch and Thomas Ellison had obviously taken a great deal of trouble with the inventory, itemising anything of value in each room. The layout of the dwelling was typical of many small houses of the period:

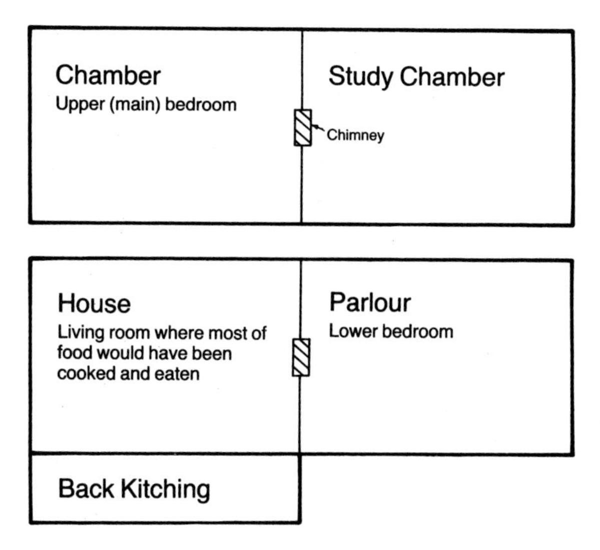

Thomas Peighen left a widow, Mary, and at least one son, John, who was a saddler by trade.

A young graduate parson from a well-known Worcester family took over the living at Barnsley and began an association which was to last more than three generations and provide us with detailed information about life in Barnsley during the reign of George III.

The Incumbency of John Mence the Elder, 1726–1761

John Mence was born in St Helen's parish, Worcester in 1696. He was the eldest son of George and Abigail Mence who had four more sons and three daughters. The Mences were a respected and well-to-do family. John's uncle Benjamin, for example, served as Mayor of the City of Worcester in 1715.

Mence married Sarah, a cousin, daughter of Richard and Elizabeth Mence of Powick. Elizabeth was the daughter of Edward Cookes. The Cookes founded Worcester College, Oxford, to which several generations of the Mences were to go as founder's kin. Sir Thomas Cookes, in his will of 1701, left £10,000 'for the erecting of an ornamental pile of building in Oxford and thereto adding, raising, creating or endowing, such and so many scholarships and fellowships as they should think …' An endowment was made for Gloucester Hall which was converted into Worcester College with provision for a provost, six fellows and eight scholars.

John Mence graduated from Oxford with a BA degree in 1720, aged twenty-three. Six years later he accepted the living at Barnsley. The minister then lived in a small residence in Old Town. By 1737 a new parsonage house had been built, partly at his own expense and partly by voluntary contribution. He certainly needed the accommodation. John now had a growing family: two girls born in 1731–2 and three sons, John (born 1734), George, who died in infancy (1736) and a second George, born in 1737. Four more daughters were born in the new parsonage which now stood near to the church.

A plaque on the wall of the chancel of St Mary's church refers to the Reverend John Mence as 'a most upright man and of this flock for 35 years, the faithful pastor who departed this life, October 19, A.D. 1761, in the 75th year of his age'. The monument was erected many years after his death, resulting in an error relating to his age. His son, John, recorded the words that he wanted for his father's memorial, clearly stating the age of sixty-five, adding 'It would be placed best on ye south side a little above ye spring of ye Arch facing ye Pulpit: this expence is not to be undertaken by any of my children but such as them as are prosperous. A plain white Marble Tablet abt. three foot by two is all that is required.'

Worcester College Hall, Oxford. JHA Sparrow Esq.

St Mary's Rectory in about 1900, but formerly the private residence of Joseph Beckett and known as Copper Hall. Author's collection

The Incumbency of John Mence the Younger

John, the minister's eldest son, was thus born at Old Town but brought up from the age of three in the new parsonage. With seven brothers and sisters it must have been a very busy household and especially hard for Mrs Mence who was held in great affection by her husband and children. Sarah Mence died on 10 January 1756, aged 51.

John had been baptised by his father on 11 February 1733. He entered Worcester College as a scholar, matriculating on 4 July 1751, aged seventeen. Like his father he was awarded a B.A. The Buttery Books of the college show his expenditure as an undergraduate: £25.5s.3d. in year one, £23.1s.1d. in year two and £18.7s.1d. in his final year. Unfortunately there is no information about his life in Oxford from 1751 to 1755.

After graduating it is likely that young John returned to Barnsley and helped with his father's ministry, perhaps doing some local preaching. Between 1757 and 1760 he received £150, described as 'Presents made me at Harrogate by the Gentry of England, Scotland and Ireland for preaching to the Company', which does suggest discourses which were well rewarded by the wealthy members of congregations. John probably took over the ministry at Barnsley in 1761 when he was just twenty-seven-years-old.

The discovery by the author of a memo book kept by John Mence during most of his ministry provides new information about the parson's family and his Barnsley parishioners of two-hundred years ago. The parchment-bound volume, measuring eight inches by six inches and containing 142 pages, was found in Hereford and Worcester Record Office. A photostat copy has now been lodged in Barnsley Local Studies Library. The book contains various jottings and accounts, probably begun in about 1770, but with notes relating to the Mence family

A splendid view of St Mary's, photographed by Warner Gothard in about 1890. Author's collection

This photograph of St Mary's 'new' interior would have been unrecognisable to Mence. Author's collection

from 1762. The notebook's great charm is its almost total lack of order. One can imagine the parson carrying the pocket book with him on his daily rounds, pausing now and then to record a local saying, song or riddle. Items of a spiritual nature are fairly sparse, though he does give practical advice on how to make a sermon. His main concern was to keep a record of family and parish income and expenditure.

Mence's private jottings inevitably refer to his neighbours, friends and flock. He was very aware of his own family background, taking the trouble to record his ancestors and fostering family links with his relatives in Worcester.

The notebook opens with a verse from a favourite Psalm, 103:

1781. Presents sent to my Couz. at Worcester

		£	s	d
Octr 27th	A Box wth 4 Potts of Bullas Cheese & Jam			
1782	cost about the sum of	0	16	0
Feb: 3d	Six Tongues – 22 lb.	0	10	0
June 30th	Two fine Hams – 34 lb value	0	15	0
1783.	*Seven Pair at 3/6 & three Pair at 4/6.			
Feb: 10th	Ten Pair of fine Thread Stockings*	1	18	0
Apl 28	Two fine Hams 34 lb Wt. worth	1	1	0
June 10	Two Potts of Troutts value	0	5	0
Sept 15th	A potted Hare [£16 : 12 : 0]	0	3	4
Nov: 27th	A prodigious fine pine-Apple	0	7	6
1784 Jan: 26	A potted Hare [£17 : 3 : 0]	0	3	6
Sep: 28	Four Quarts of Cramberries	0	2	0
1785 May 16	Two fine Hams worth alt 13:13:8 [£6:6:4] In all £20	0	15	0
1786	July 1st Six fine Neats Tongues 18 lb ½	0	18	0

'Presents sent to my couzn, at Worcester': a sample page from Mence's notebook.

Bless Lord O my Soul, and forget not all his benefits;

then, perhaps because he was writing from memory, he changes the next verse slightly to:

Who forgiveth all my sins: and he healeth all thine Infirmities.

The next two verses are transposed.

At the bottom of the page he writes in a later and more frail hand:

N.B.1800
A choise Aple got against ye House Side,
followed with
Rec'd of Mr. Skelton £2.10s.0d. due the twenty seventh of August last.

There are other jottings which are very clearly written. In one example he gives, again almost certainly from memory, verses one to six of Psalm 103 but with the word 'Wrong' ending the entry. Such random thoughts help give us some insight into the mental world of an eighteenth century parson.

Sermons – and a Riddle

Mence made an interesting note headed 'A Receipt how to make a Sermon.' Here is the recipe:

Read first of all ye collect, Epistle and Gospel carefully over, and ponder them over in your Mind. Have a Bible open before you, and seek the Lessons. If there be a Narrative in them, expatiate thereupon. An Historical Remarck or two will add Grace to ye literary Production; and ye congregation will declare ye Praise. If you wd. shine in this way; you must frequently try your Skill: for there is nothing like Practice to perfect yr. work. The Guidance of God's H Spirit sh'd be earnestly importuned; and His Blessing upon yr pious Endeavours. I have been pretty successful ye way, having ye Knack how to make a sermon, by Experience, and observation.

Scattered through the notebook are a few other ideas for sermons and favourite passages he wished to remember. He noted the following from Second Corinthians, Chap. XIII (latter part of vs.5):

Know ye not your own selves how that Jesus Christ is in you, except ye be Reprobates?,

and the second part of verse 19 from 'Haggai' II:

From this day will I bless you.

Against the verses from John,

Hereafter I will not talk much with you

Mence has written the note,

Proper for a Farewell Sermon.

John Mence obviously thought much of these little verses which were perhaps used as ideas for his sermons but he does not tell us how he intended to develop his texts.

However, we are given an insight into one of his private prayers:

A private Prayer for Sunday Morn: O Ld., I beseech thee to prepare my soul to worship thee with Reverence and godly Fear; purify my Heart from all vain, wordly, and sinful Thoughts fix my Affections on Things above; give me Grace to receive thy Word in an honest and good Heart, and to bring forth Fruit with Patience, And grant yt ye ascending of my Prayers and Praises unto Thee. and ye descending of thy Graces and Mercies unto me, may so fit and prepare me for thy pub: Worship yt all thy Ordinances maybe profitable to me, in and thro' my Bd. Ld. and Saviour.

In one of his random entries Mence appears to be studying Proverbs and copies out verses 15–16 from Chapter XXX as follows:

The Horse-Leach hath two Daughters, Crying, Give, Give. There are three Things that are never satisfied, yea, 4 Things wch. say not, It is Enough. The Grave. and ye barren Womb: the Earth yt is not filled wth water, and the Fire yt sayeth not, It is Enough.

Verse 17 ('The eye that mocketh at his father, and despiseth to obey his mother, the ravens of the valley shall pick it out, and the young eagles shall eat it') is omitted through either accident or design. He goes on to write out verses 18–31:

There are three Things wch are too wonderful for me, yea 4 wch I know not; The Way of an Eagle in ye Air, ye Way of a Serpent upon a Rock: ye Way of a Ship in ye midst of the Sea; and the Way of a Man with a Maid. For three Things the Earth is disquited; and for 4 Things wch it cannot bear. For a Servant wn he is filled wth Meat for an odious Woman wn she is married, and an Hand Maid that is Heir to her Mistress. There are 4 things wch are little upon the Earth, But they exceeding wise:

The Ants are a People not strong.
Yet they prepare their Meat in the Summer
The conies are but a feeble Folk;
yet make they their Houses in the Rocks;
The Locusts have no King, yet go they forth by bands
The Spider taketh hold wth her Hands, and is (in) King's Palace
There be three Things that go well yea 4 are comely in going. A Lion wch is strongest amongs Beasts, and turneth not away for any.
A Grey-Hound, an he Goat also,
and a King agst wm there is no rising.

Verse 22 should read, 'For a servant when he reigneth; and a fool when he is filled with meat.'

The above are but brief insights into Mence's spiritual life but give us an indication of the thoughts and prayers of an eighteenth century parson.

The notebook includes numerous humourous entries, no doubt inserted to enliven the yearly financial statements. Here is an example of a Barnsley riddle:

A Riddle

It is a round Whickett
Hemm'd in by a Thickett
And w't ever passes
Is strained through glasses
It is reported to dwell
Like a Monk in a cell
You say it is quiet
I flatly deny it
It wanders about
without stirring out
Another great Fault
It cannot bear Salt
And an hair can disarm
It of every charm

Barnsley Chronicle readers Mr and Mrs Brian Jepson of Monk Bretton suggested a likely answer: the tongue.

Life on a Frugal Scale

John Mence probably married during the early 1760s, shortly after succeeding his father at Barnsley. His first child, Benjamin, was born in 1765. Mence was then in his late twenties and his wife, Jane, daughter of John Ryall, of Wakefield, was four years younger. The young minister gives a delightfully frank 'word picture' of Jane, written when she was sixty:

Strictures of ye form and comeliness of Mrs. Mence Her Person is rather above ye midle Size; rather portly & inclinable to feed: of a Majestick Appearance and expessive countenance: of a dark complexion, and darting Look: her Eyes dark brown: her Shape comely & graceful: her Gait & Tread firm & intrepid. Her Hair black & glossy; and upon the whole, a fine Figure. And for Strength of Body and Steadiness of Mind had scarce her Equal.

Then comes a note on 'Her other Qualifications':

The Wife of one Husband: and One that hath brought up a Family of children: yt hath not departed from the church of England: is Sober, chast & temperate in all Things, and hath liv'd Sixty Years with her Husband from her Virginity.

The family which Jane brought up consisted of five boys and six girls, born during their first twenty years of marriage. Two of them, George and Lucinda, died in infancy. Benjamin and the second eldest son (John) followed in their father's footsteps. Both were admitted as scholars at Worcester College, Oxford, on 23 June 1781 when they were aged sixteen and fourteen, and graduated in April 1785. The two youngsters continued to reside in college for several years and appear to have been elected fellows in 1790.

A younger Mrs. Mence?

Benjamin and George followed their father in the Barnsley living, making the third generation of Mences to enjoy it. Benjamin was incumbent in 1804 and John curate in 1806 until his death in 1816. Benjamin who appears to have suffered from ill-health, let out the living and returned to Worcester where he died in 1847.

John Mence did not find the Barnsley living a very generous one, in fact he found it very difficult to support his growing family. In 1784, when he was fifty years old, he found himself having to appeal to the Stewards of the Feast of the Sons of Clergy for financial assistance in order to apprentice his eldest daughter. He carefully copied out the petition in his notebook:

The humble Petition of John Mence of Barnsley, in the County of York, Clerk
Showeth
That your Petitioner has a curacy of ninety Pounds a Year only, and hath nine children, and is desirous of puttin out his eldest Daughter Sarah Apprentice.

That year Petitioners Dau. is now of the Age of fifteen years, and was never put out Apprentice, but is now willing & desirous of being put out Apprentice to Mrs. Hanh. Witham, Milliner of Sheffield, who is willing to take your Petitioners said daughter Apprentice for ye Term of five years, for the sum of Twenty Pounds which sum your Petitioner most humbly prays the Corporation to grant for that Purpose.

And yr Petitioner (as in Duty bound) shall ever pray

A brief note from the minister's wife, Sarah, follows:

The Petition is to be signed by a neighbouring clergyman, and the Church Wardens where the Party dwells.

Sarah was obviously keen that everything was above board and legally binding. A couple of 'reminders' followed, written in Mence's own hand:

Indentures printed for the Stewards, with the Arms of the Corporation Office, No 13 in Paper Buildings, in the inner Temple, London, as also Petitions

No Child can be apprenticed for a less Term than Five years, nor under the age of Fourteen…

Mence was most careful to show the exact nature of all his expenditure and provides a very detailed analysis of costs incurred in 1787 (when in his early fifties) for a family of nine.

It is certainly a frugal list, with no mention of any luxuries:

1787 An Estimate of House-keeping & Clothing, being nine in Family, taken upon a frugal scale.

	£	s	d
Apparrel	*20*	*0*	*0*
Meal and fine flour	*16*	*0*	*0*
Meat	*14*	*0*	*0*
Groceries	*12*	*0*	*0*
Milk & Butter	*10*	*0*	*0*
Malt	*9*	*0*	*0*
Various other things	*8*	*0*	*0*
Shoes	*6*	*0*	*0*
Coals and leading	*3*	*0*	*0*
Physick	*2*	*0*	*0*
	£100	*0*	*0*

In 1785 he compiled a list of his 'Housekeeping & Wearing Apparrel & other Expences', estimated from the first twenty-four years of his incumbency. The list makes very interesting reading, and illustrates once again Mences concern to make ends meet:

	£	s	d
Apparrel £600; Bed & Table Linen £25	*625*	*0*	*0*
Bread Meal & fine Flour	*200*	*0*	*0*
Shambles Meat about*	*200*	*0*	*0*
Malt about the same sum of	*200*	*0*	*0*
Butter & Milk for my Family	*200*	*0*	*0*
Groceries, Soap Starch & candles	*200*	*0*	*0*
Shoes for my Family & Self	*155*	*0*	*0*
Furniture & Repairs of it	*100*	*0*	*0*
Coals & Leading about	*80*	*0*	*0*
Servants wages about	*70*	*0*	*0*
Nurses Physick Advice & Deliveries	*46*	*0*	*0*
School Wages	*30*	*0*	*0*
Books, W. Paper, Pens, Ink	*30*	*0*	*0*
Journeying £24; Pocket Money £10	*34*	*0*	*0*
Postage £10; Wine & Rum £10; Leases £5	*25*	*0*	*0*
Building £36; Pump £14 & ye well	*50*	*0*	*0*
Presents to my Couzen at Worcester	*20*	*0*	*0*
	£2265	*0*	*0*

*i.e. Butchers' stall meat

This Account began Jan. 1st 1762. Ended December ult 1785.

It was not unusual at this time for even modest families to have a servant and certainly Sarah and John must have needed all the help they could afford because of the size and nature of their household. John was obviously keen to cater for all the basic needs of his family, including medical care and schooling. There was virtually no 'disposable income'; £10 pocket money over twenty-four years would not have gone very far via two adults and nine children!

In 1791 Mence drew up a revised list of household expenses now covering a thirty-year period. The grand total had increased to £3,000 and therefore gave a convenient average of £100 per year. His income from almost all sources varied between about £80 and £95 during the years when his family was still young, so it must have been a great struggle to survive with dignity. After 1780 his income rarely dropped below £100 and when coal was exploited on his land it increased to £200, ironically at a time when the family was grown up and when he needed money less. The way in which Mence, and indeed many other ordinary parsons, strove to maintain large households and keep up appearances is one of the most fascinating aspects of the notebook.

Relatively little is known about the remainder of Mence's children. His youngest, William Cookes (born in 1781) became a noted lawyer and, according to his tombstone 'for more than thirty years an attorney in this town (Barnsley), respected by all, beloved and regretted by the poor, who departed this life February 2, 1843 in the 61st year of his age'. WC Mence had six children, the eldest attending Worcester College in 1834, taking a BA (1839) and MA (1844). He became rector of Prestwould, Leicestershire, for twelve years, continuing the family clerical tradition.

Benjamin Mence held the living at St Marys until 1850 when the family association finally came to an end after four generations. Charles Turner Mence was a solicitor in Barnsley but the death of George Cookes Mence (1859) may have marked the end of the direct link of the family with the town.

However, a marriage notice in the *Barnsley Chronicle* of 8 September 1906, contains interesting details 'of an old Barnsley family':

> *A picturesque and interesting ceremony took place a few weeks ago in a small village in North Wales, when Miss Dorothy Mytton, elder daughter of Captain Devereux Herbert Mytton, J.P.,D.L., was led to the alter by Mr. William Charles Mence, who is a member of one of the oldest and most respected Barnsley families.*

The report concluded,

> *At the present time no member of the family resides in Barnsley, although they still hold a considerable amount of property in the town, and always take a great interest in its welfare.*

More Financial Concerns

Patronage was a fact of eighteenth century life. A living was like a seat in parliament or a college fellowship, something awarded as a favour and enjoyed as a privilege. Yet there was a huge gulf between rich and poor clergy and John Mence certainly experienced difficulty in bringing up his large family and attending to the increasing duties of a resident parson in Barnsley. Despite a distinguished family background he was one of thousands of impoverished 'blackcoats' occupying livings of £50 to £100 a year.

It is understandable as to why financial jottings dominate the notebook. Mence devotes many pages to itemising his yearly income. In common with many other prelates his income started to improve. The rise in the value of tithes and the glebe land, as a result of improved agriculture, helped this development. The exploitation of coal resulted in a further boost to his standard of living. The jottings give us a very detailed insight into the sources of income of a parson in the reign of George III.

The 'Glebe' was land assigned to the incumbent as part of his benefice and the endowment of the church. This was John Mence's most important source of income. Rents from farmers who worked the glebe (about 60 acres) varied from £54, the lowest return (1779), to £137 (1799); the average income was about £80. The yearly rent returns show that a steady consolidation of tenancies was taking place. For example, in the early years the glebe was let to ten tenants but in 1797 the number had decreased to six and the rents had risen. Thirteen acres of common land was let for just £13 in 1762 but for £21 in 1794. Mr Horsfall, an ironmonger, rented one plot of land for as much as £52 in 1797. As a prosperous shopkeeper Horsfall could indulge himself with landed interests and had even acquired Manor Farm, adjacent to his glebe holdings. Mr Horsfall had his wedding out of town, on 26 June 1789 and paid Mence one guinea as recompense.

Mence kept a very careful account of each tenant's rent, usually paid quarterly or half-yearly. It is therefore possible to trace in some detail payments of Barnsley people such as:

Thomas Bowser (over 5 years)
Thomas Teale (11 years)
Thomas Bullas (1 year)
John Dickinson (2 years)
Messers Oxley and Birkinshaw (15 years)
Martha Ellis (9 years)
Samuel Johnson (11 years)
Abraham Rock (11 years)
John Shillitoe (5 years)
William Thompson (9 years)

In addition to rents and the annual tithe charge of £1.17s.10d. which was paid by Messers Hammond, Ounsworth, Liddall, Leadman, and Taylor, Mence received £4 a year from the Queen Anne's Bounty. This was sometimes paid to him by Miss Sarah Radcliffe, milliner, who along with her sister, were interested in parish affairs.

There was also a curious sum of £100 which was used for investment. This was first lent to Mr Edmunds (of Worsbrough Hall) at five per cent interest. In 1768 the money was invested in the Doncaster Turnpike Trust which also brought in £5 per year. The Doncaster and Saltersbrook had only recently been formed so this was quite a modern and opportunistic investment.

James Woodforde, a better-off parson whose eighteenth century diary became a classic of English literature.

Towards the end of his life Mence's income increased considerably due to the location of extractable coal on the glebe land. In 1794, for the first time, Mence's yearly figures include £50 for coal. The coal income was regularly paid by Mr. Samuel Thorp whose father had come to Gawber in the 1730s, living at Gawber Hall and working the glassworks. John Goodchild in his book *Coals from Barnsley* (Wakefield Historical Publications, 1986) provides interesting details of this family who were 'the first major developers' of the Barnsley coal industry. The Thorps' worked several pits in Barnsley and at Cawthorne, Samuel Thorp living at Banks Hall.

Each year Mence also noted his surplice, or as he calls them 'surplus' fees, even writing the word in Greek letters. There were fees for marriages, funerals etc. ranging from £9 to £26, the yearly average being £14. Easter dues brought him a further £4 to £12. Occasionally he gives a little more detail, as in 1796 when he writes:

	£	*s*	*d*
21 town burials (my fees only)	*1*	*8*	*0*
The administering of the Sacrement	*0*	*14*	*0*
The register keeping (sadly too little)	*0*	*10*	*6*
Six churchings of paupers paid for	*0*	*5*	*0*

On another occasion he got 18s.8d. for fourteen town burials and 8s. for keeping the register.

A steady source of income came from catechizing charity boys and girls. Fourteen shillings was paid each year by Henry Armroyd and later G Armroyd, the local schoolmaster.

There were other occasional sources of income. In the early accounts come such items as 'a guinea for preaching to Richard Lawton's club'. Lawton was a bootmaker and these sermons on thrift were designed to encourage savings. In 1765 and 1771 the sum of 6s. was noted for 'fruit in ye folds'. There are also references to scarves received for one guinea, or scarves charged 10s.6d., and an entry for 'six pair of gloves'. These were probably sold by Mence to mourners at funerals.

In 1790 he received an unexpected five guineas. The church organ which, according to terriers (i.e. surveys of benefices and church lands) was 'made by a person unskilled in the art and is by consequence a very bad discordant instrument incapable of repair or amendment in any degree' was, nevertheless, sold. Joseph Beckett, the grocer, linen manufacturer and noted benefactor of Barnsley had been responsible for organising a collection for a new organ which had been installed in 1787.

There was little pressure from either episcopal authority or popular opinion to compel clergy to exert themselves more than they wished. It is impossible to know if Mence had evangelical interests in the sense of being in touch with the bulk of parishioners. He does, however, come over as a pious man, someone who had more to offer than reading a literate sermon to flatter the elegant and privileged who would be sat in the best pews. In a changing community he would have had to be aware of all classes of society.

St Mary's church. The author

Mence never seemed to have the comfort as vividly portrayed in the 'Diaries' of Reverend James Woodforde which provides us with a marvellous picture of eighteenth century country life. Yet the receipt of tithe and the working of the glebe land must have kept Mence in touch with agricultural life, though it is doubtful whether he could offer the same hospitality as parson Woodforde who described a typical day in September, 1776:

Very busy all day with my barley, did not dine till 5 in the afternoon, my harvest men dined here today, gave them some beef and some plumb Pudding and as much liquor as they would drink. This evening finished my harvest, and all carried into the Barn 8 acres.

And on another day:

3 December. My frolic for my people to pay tithe to me this day. I gave them a good dinner, sirloin of beef roasted, a leg of mutton boiled and plumb puddings in plenty.

Family Presents & Other Gifts

Mence never forgot his Worcester origins. There was a regular exchange of presents between himself and his cousins. He calculated that he had spend £20 over a 24-year period for 'presents to my cousin at Worcester.' This may have been William, son of Benjamin Mence, of the St Helen's branch of the family. William was two years John's senior and had been up at Merton College whilst he was at Worcester. John also sent gifts to 'my cousin at Islington.' Perhaps this was William's elder brother, the Rev. Benjamin Mence, again of St Helen's, who was rector of All Hallows, London Wall, and then vicar of St Pancras.

John had great pride in keeping in touch with the elder branch of the family. The most human and interesting part of his accounts concern lists where he calculates the value of the exchange of family presents. In 1779 he sends off to Worcester:

One ham value half a guinea
6 hams as good £3.3s.0d.
12 neats tongues 2s.6d. each.
A pound of eringo root 6s.
A pound of coffee 6s.

In return 'My cousin at Worcester' sent in the same year two cotton jackets (trimmed) and two potts of lampreys.

In 1780 Sarah, Mence's eldest daughter, produced 'A fine Muzlin Apron and Handkerchief' which was sent to Worcester along with 'Three potts of Bullas cheese and one of Sloes, six Garters and a pair of Scissors.' A pair of Stockings was also included, the total valued at £3.2s.8d. In return came more lampreys, and a mysterious box 'with several valuable things in it.' 'Bullas', probably refers to a fruit cheese made from plums.

In general, food was sent from Barnsley and miscellaneous materials from Worcester. The food items are particularly interesting. In 1781 Mence sent twelve tongues, in two equal batches, worth twenty-four shillings or about nine pence per pound. In the same year four hams were dispatched, weighing 66 pounds, for twenty one shillings. No doubt the Barnsley butchers were pleased with this trade. In the summer and autumn he was forwarding 'A piece of Camblitt Weight both 52lb', valued at £1.14s.0d., 'Seven Pair of Thread Stockings (£1.4s.0d.)' and, quite an extraordinary item: 'Two pine Apples' which went with a brace of partridge (for 2.6d.). Camblet or Camblet was originally a costly oriental

Mence may have enjoyed a smoke and glass of ale in one of the numerous inns of Shambles Street.

fabric but later substituted via various combinations of wool, hair, cotton or linen. It would have been bought from a local mercer's shop. 'A box with four Potts of Bullas Cheese and Jam' (cost six shillings) completed Mence's gifts to his cousin for 1781.

His cousin did not seem to reciprocate with the same frequency or volume of goods. In 1782 Mence received 'Some old Cloths and a Piece of Linen for a gown' (from Benjamin) and the following year 'A parcel containing Sattin, Piece of Cotton, Piece of Huckkaback (a stout woven linen used for towels), Diaper (a patterned linen fabric used for napkins)' and 'thirteen yards of Green Stuff (i.e. probably worsted) all together worth near ten pounds.' Cousin John also sent 'a piece of pink and yellow shalloon.' This was a closely-woven material, used for linings.

Mence continued to supply Barnsley hams and tongues and several other interesting food items. Two 'Potts of Troutts value 5s.' were sent in June followed in September by a 'potted Hare' (3s.4d.) and in November there was 'A prodigious pine-Apple' (7s.6d.). Presents recorded as being sent between 1784 and 1788 included another potted hare, four quarts of cranberries, 'Two fine hams worth about 15s.', six tongues, a brace of partridges and a melon.

There are one or two other entries which enliven the financial statements. He notes, for example a little saying of a Mrs Carwood, one of his parishioners:

Bread a day old
Beer a year old
Roast beef hot or cold
And a good wife that never scolds

Like all parsons Mence received gifts from the leading citizens of the town. These monetary items were not very frequent but he carefully records every one on a page of his notebook:

Presents made by ye neighbouring Gentry and c. in the course of my Ministry at Barnsley in 24 years.

	£	s	d
Lord and Lady Strafford	2	2	0
Thomas Cotton Esquire	2	2	0
Messrs John Dixon Clerk and Wm. Garlick	1	1	0
Mrs. Rebeckah Wood	1	1	0
Sir Francis Wood at sundry times	19	9	0
Francis Wood Esq.	1	1	0
By an unknown hand	5	5	0
Messrs Fisher, Clerk and Pierson Esq.	1	1	0
Gamaliel Milner Esq.	1	1	0
Mrs. Walker or Marriott	1	1	0
John Shepherd and Doctor Wood	1	1	0
Doctor Wells of Willingham	1	1	0
Joseph Becket Esq	1	1	0
Mr. Lodge Clerk 10s.6d. T. Edmonds Esq.	1	1	0
Wm. Fenton Esq. 10.6d. The Rev. M. Bright	1	1	0
From the Marsden's Family	1	1	0
Total	*£42*	*0*	*0*

Songs, Stones & Sewing

Mence may have had some musical interests and was especially fond of *Captain Death,* a 'favorite song':

The Muse and the Hero together hath fired
With the same noble views in their Bosom inspir'd
As freedom the love, and for Glory contend
The Muse, and the Hero yet mourn as a Friend
But still let the Muse her poor Tribute bequeath
To one British Hero, it's brave Captain Death.
Two Hundred and more were our brave compliment,

And sure braver fellows to sea never went
Each man was as valiant, and as bold as Macbeth
They fought for great Britain and brave Captain Death.
Fire Thunder Ball Battle were soon heard and felt
Wth Sighs that the Heart of Bellona woud mill
The shrouds were all torn, and the Deck fill'd wth Blood
And Scores of dead Bodies were thrown in the Flood
The Flood from the Time of Noah and Seth
Ne'er saw such a Fellow as brave Captain Death.
At length came the Bullet that was winged with Fate
Our brave captain dropp'd, and soon after his Mate,
Each officer fell, and a carnage was seen
Wch soon dyed the Waves to a crimson from green
Till Neptune rose up and pull'd off his Wreath
And gave it to Triton to crown Captain Death.

Two transcripts were made of this heroic ballad.

The Barnsley cleric also copies out twice what seems to have been a popular song of the period:

The women all tell me I am false to my Lass
That I forsake my poor Chloe and stick to my Glass
But to you Men of Reason my Reasons I will own
And if you don't like them pray leave them alone.
"Her Roses and Lilies were just in their Prime
Yet Lilies and Roses are Faided by Time
But Wine, mighty Wine such a benefit flows
That we liked it ye better the older it grows.
My Chloe has dimples and charms I must own
But tho' she can smile, yet in Truth she can rome
Then tell me ye lovers of Liquor Divine
Did you ere see a Frown in a Bumper of Wine
She two might have poysoned ye Joys of my life
With Nurses and Babies and squalling and Strife.
But my wine neither Nurses or babies can bring
And a big Belly'd Bottle is a mighty good Thing
Then let my dear Chloe, no longer complain
She's rid of her Lover, and I of my pain
For in Wine, mighty wine many comforts I spy
Sh'd you doubt wht I say take a bumper and try.

Chloe seems to have been running in his mind since another version of the song, with an altered middle section, appears a few pages later.

On another page Mence makes a list of precious stones, but for no apparent reason:

Precious Stones are
the Emmerald, ye Ammithyst;
the Topaz, ye Belellium, ye Ruby
the Birryll, the Amber;
the cornelion; ye Onyxstone;
the coral and ye Sapphire
and Chrystall.

Next to this unusual entry he describes *The Picture of Industry:*

This generally is a female
Character, and must of course

have ye necessary apparatus
to adorn the Nedle-Work, and perfect
it's admirable cunning.
The Flowers that proceed from the
Needlepoints are to be much admir'd
And ye imitation of Nature's self
from well chosen shapes and glowing
colour heighten ye ingenuity of ye Artist.
This is ye Ladies fort; and with patience
and Perseverence in ye Employment
does credit to the industrious sisters.
Their candle goes not; nor can they prevail to eat the bread of idleness.

There is no doubt that Rev. John Mence would have been astonished to learn that his private jottings, eventually to be deposited among family papers in the Worcester archives, would have a wide public airing more than two centuries after his death. The fact is they provide a very personal and therefore unique insight into the life and times of an otherwise obscure Yorkshire parson. Barnsley should be proud of the three generations of the Mence family.

The Mence family memorial tablet in the chancel of St Mary's. The author

6 Hobson's Barnsley

John Hobson was a gentleman tanner who lived at Dodworth Green. His diary or 'Journal' covers the final years of his life, from 1726 to January, 1735. Hobson was buried at Silkstone on May 15th, 1735. His writings remind us of one of the most important functions of market towns such as Barnsley as places of news, gossip and social intercourse.

Hobson recorded many visits to Barnsley when business was mixed with pleasure in the convivial atmosphere of the inn or dining room. Barnsley had many attractions, especially for those with both leisure and means at their disposal.

Hobson certainly did not have a bottomless purse, indeed much of his money would have been tied-up with his tanning trade which required considerable capital investment but his gentleman status enabled him to mix with the upper levels of Barnsley society. He would enjoy visiting the town with clerics, doctors, JPs and gentlemen farmers. Special events would also attract his interest, ranging from fairs and funerals to horse races and Quarter Sessions.

'Hobson's Barnsley' means far more than the experiences of a fairly privileged individual because ordinary families would certainly have recognised the people and events and were often part of the commentary.

The Journal opens in the winter of 1726 when, as now, communications could be disrupted by severe weather:

January 1st, Saturday – The night before, and that day, there fell a great snow. The London post stop'd two days; the Northern post one day; no passage over the moors to Woodhead. The minester, Mr. Baynes, of Dronfield, lost in snow nigh Grindlefirth bridge.

12th. – The frost and snow continues. At Barnsley, in company with Mr. Spencer of Cannon Hall, who was in morning for his wife's brother, Mr. Ashton of Hethersidge,

Hobson, as a tanner, was a shrewd judge of oxen and clearly thought that Hawksworth had paid far too much for them. Oxen were still used as draught animals, as well as horses, and could be brought and sold at fairs.

In June several deaths of well known locals are recorded:

22nd. – At Barnsly. Mr. Hodgson, steward to Sir George Saville, died last Sunday.

23rd. – Thursday night about 10, Mr. Thomas Peigham, minister of Barnsley, died, having been melancoly several years. His father was vicar of Silkstone, before Mr. Wainhouse.

29th. – Mr. Cavendish Neville, of Chevet, buried at Royston. He died of a mortification of the foot,

A tanner: Hobson's 'servant' or workman would have done the physical work. Book of Trades/Author's collection

Cannon Hall, enlarged by famous architect John Carr and local mason, John Marsden, 1765–67 with further major alterations in 1778 (interior) and 1804–5 (wings heightened). The author

> *occasioned by cutting a corn. His foot was cut of before he died.* [It was probably Gervase Neville who died; he was succeeded by Cavendish Neville at Chevet Hall] *John Warrener, a melancholy man, found dead in his bed at Barnsley.*

Hobson was quite busy during the summer and autumn of 1726. He continued to visit Barnsley but also went on business to Settle (N. Yorks) and entertained and accommodated his uncle who had journeyed from London. Work was also in progress at both tanyard and dwelling house.

He also found time to visit 'Woosboroug feast,' Silkstone Feast, and spent a day at Penistone Races. These were not only popular social occasions but also places were business contacts could be made. He was very proud of the home improvements:

> *20th.* [Sept.] – *Tuesday. – Guest put glass into the sash windows in the buttery, being the first that ever was in this town* [Dodworth].

The magnificent Baroque range of Wentworth Castle by Jean de Bodt c. 1710–15. Alan Billingham

News, spread by word of mouth, could travel with remarkable speed, though no doubt questionable accuracy.

On Sunday, 9 October, Hobson recorded an attempted burglary that had taken place earlier in the day:

> *About 11 a clock in the forenoon, two horsemen came to Mr. Goodwin's the minister of Tankersly, and asked for him. There was only in the house a maid and his two children. She told him he was at church. They desire to be let in: she says her master had the key in his pocket: then they begun to give ill language, and told her she lyed, and attempted to break in: she put the 2 children in a closet, got a spit and run it at them: flung hot broth in one of their faces: they discharg'd a pistol at her: then they went to a door, broke it open; she barricaded the indoor with chairs and stools, and made a great noise. They, being afraid the people of the church should hear her, went off, taking only a foul shirt along with them. When service was don Mr. Goodwin's man pursued them as far as Ringston hill* [Felkirk]*: his horse tired, so they got away.*

On 23 October Hobson attended Silkstone church when five 'spurrings' or banns of marriage were published but there was also some bad news:

> *The smallpox has been very mortall at Silkston, few children escaping that had them: some families burying two in a coffin. They are begun in Dodworth, and one dead.*

A most unusual occurrence was described by the diarist in an entry of 23rd December.

> *At Wakefield. That day three week last past, Mr. Hopkins, minister at Kirk-heaton (formerly of Wooley), aged 56, emasculated himself with a razour. He had taken the precaution to make ligaments about his body and thighs, to prevent bleeding, and had a chirugeon ready in the house to assist him, tho' not privy to his design. He managed the cure so well that he read prayers last Sunday, and designed to preach on Christmas day. The reason was not melancoly, he being in his perfect senses, but he did it by way of punishment upon himself for being so foolish to have had criminal conversation with his housekeeper.*

There is only a brief entry for Christmas Day when the congregation at Silkstone received news about the tragic effects of recent bad weather:

> *At Sacrament. Tuesday, the 13th instant, was such an ill day for frost, snow and wind that severall people had perished in comming over the moors from Woodhead, and some lost their lives in going from Sheffeild to Heithersedge.*

The last entry of the old year was on the 28th when Hobson visited the Fentons at Underbank. He was to receive sad news concerning the death, by smallpox, of a child 'for which I stood surety May 19th last.' To make matters even worse Madam Green of Bank Top, Worsbrough, with whom he also had obligations, was buried the previous weekend.

Driveway leading to Underbank Hall, 2.5 miles S.W. of Oxspring. Built by Francis West but came to William Fenton by marriage, in 1715. The author

On the whole it had been a successful year for the Dodworth tanner. He appeared to have prospered, had maintained good social relations and despite some bad news enjoyed himself.

Diary of 1727
In the spring Hobson attended the impressive funeral of a local gentleman:

March 1st, Wednesday. – At the funeral of Mr. Nicolas Burley of Wooley. We had... scarfes and gloves, and Sr John Kay, Sr William Wentworth, Mr. Wentworth of Wooley, Mr. Silvester, of Birthwaite, Mr. William Spenser, of Cannon Hall, Mr. Jarvis Norton, of Kettlethorp, Mr. Thomas Beamont, of Chappelthorp, Mr. Henry Carrington of Views. He was buried on the west side of the churchyard. Mr. Burleigh, tho' he was bred up an attorney, had but a mean opinion of the profession, and never practized, but had a stock in the ironworks. About a fortnight ago he rid out upon a young horse, to take the air, having been in an ill state of health a long time; the horse, being affrightened, leapt from under him, and he could not help himself, but lay some time before he was found ... to the great regret of his friends and acquantance.

30th [March]. *The milner of Stainborough had a little boy drowned in the damn.*

However, much of the spring was taken up with travel. Hobson made his usual visits to Barnsley from his Dodworth Green home but also travelled to Huddersfield, Aldborough, Northallerton, Darlington, Durham, Stockton, Sunderland and York.

Hobson's busy social and business life progressed into the summer and he continued to record local and national events:

10th [June]. – *At home. Last night, about twelve, Simon Heely died of a pleuritick feaver. He was well last Munday, and came to Dodworth feast, to see his mother. 'Tis said he drunk 10s. in brandy that day. He was mightyly swell'd when dead. He was buried on Sunday. This may be a warning how people drinck brandy to excesse.*

18th. – The 'Evening Post' says King George died Sunday last, about 2 in the morning, at Asnaburg.

28th, Wednesday. – At Barnsly, at the proclamation of King George the Second. The gentlemen cockades in their hatts, of red and orange ribbon.

29th. – At Rotherham races.

Beech Farm House ('The Old Courthouse'), where the Burley ['Burleigh'] *family lived in the early 1700s.* The author

'The Dancing Master', 1652, shows that Barnsley's Thomas Frudd was in one of the few frivolous lines that even prospered in Cromwell's Commonwealth. Bell & Hyman

> *13th* [July]. *– At Peniston. Sr Thomas Wentworth and Mr. Turner are making interest against the next election.*
>
> *29th. – Coz. George Walker and his wife Mr. Shepherd and his wife, came down from London.*
>
> *30th. – At church. Silkston feast. Mr. Brook of Richmond preacht. 10th* [Aug.] *– dined at Mr. Fenton's* [Underbank]*; and at Peniston races. Sam Cawthorn, of Burton, won the plate.*
>
> *30th. – At Barnsly. This day came on the election for the knights of the shire of York. There was no opposition, my lord Downs having declined; so Sr Thomas Wentworth and Mr. Chomondly Turner are elected.*

Some interesting local stories were recorded by the diarist during October:

> *7th. – Francis West, of Heigham, shomaker, was buried at Darton, aged about 80. He was well till last Tuesday at noon, then was suddenly taken ill, and died on Thursday. He has often told me that he could remember since that that there were so many large trees grew on Heigham common that he has walked from Dodworth lane to the lane that leads to Barnby furnace on a summer day, and the sun could scarce shine on him; and now there is not so much as a stump to be seen, nor has not been for these many years past.*
>
> *25th. – At Barnsly. Mr. Frudd, the dancing master, buried. I have heard say that his grandmother was executed at Barnsley, for stealing a silver spoon, and it was afterwards proved that she was innocent. There is a place on Barnsly common still called Gallow*[s] *hill.*

Barnsley was not unusual at having a dancing master. It was a popular activity for those who could afford the tuition, though Frudd would not appear to have made much money for his services. In his will of 25 August, 1725 he left his real estate to his wife, Elizabeth 'provided she keeps my name.' His eldest son, who may have carried on the family business, was given the 'Hous Shop'. A third son only received one shilling but his youngest son got £10, the same as his daughter.

Thomas Frudd's probate inventory, a list of his surviving goods and chattels, was drawn up by friends and neighbours on 4 November 1727. It gives us an interesting glimpse of a small Barnsley household of the period:

Thomas Frudd of Barnsley, Silkstone, Dancing Master, 4 November, 1727. Appraized by Francis Hawksworth, Johnathan Silvester, Thomas Day and John Archdale.

	£	s	d
Imprs. his Purse and Apparell	01	01	00
In ye Kitching			
One range ffire Shovel and Tongs Briggs reckons End Irons	00	05	00
2 Spitts and a Pr. of Racks One Beefe fork and Basting Laddle; One Warming Pan; One Smoothing Iron and Heaters and i Slice; 2 Chopping Knives a Toasting Iron Chafing Dish and ffrying pan 2 large Iron Truers	00	06	08
Two Iron Potts One Iron Pan and 2 Brass Pans	00	06	00
Twelve Pewter Dishes and a Doz. Pewter Plates One Limbeck; Two Pewter Quarts and 3 Pints; One Pewter Candlestick; 2 Salts; One Mustard Box; One Jack and half Jack	01	08	00
One Pasty Pan; Two Dripping Pans; One Dish Cover half a Doz. of Petty Pans	00	02	06
2 Brass Candlesticks; One Copper Can	00	01	06
1 Long Settle and a Squabb; 2 Pewter Cases and Dresser 1 large Chair 3 stools	00	12	00
Salt Pye	00	00	04
In the Little Parlour next ye Kitching			
2 Ovel Tables 1 Doz. and 4 Chairs	01	04	00
In ye Lower Parlour			
One Servant Bed One Long Settle One Table One fform	00	13	00
Little Chamber			
One Bed and Beding and hangings Belonging to it One Chist	01	10	00
In the Large Chamber			
2 Little Beds with. Beding 1 Table upon ye. Stairs One Chist	02	00	00
In ye Brewhouse			
One Lead 4 Tubs and 2 Kitts and Grate belonging	02	00	00
In the Cellar			
14 Barrells	01	00	00
2 Temeses with. other Huslemt	00	04	00
In the ffold			
One Pigg	00	06	08
Total	13	00	08

Frudd's reference to a shop suggested a dual-occupation. Being a dancing-master was unlikely to be a full-time job but the inventory offers no real clues and Frudd insists on calling himself 'dancing master' in his will. The chances of finding out his other occupation seemed unlikely, unless he had been involved in land or property transactions.

As part of the old West Riding we are very fortunate at having access to a virtually unique record office: the Wakefield Registry of Deeds, at Wakefield. Most local deeds were registered there from 1704. Thomas Frudd leased a 'messuage, tenement or dwelling house,' with outbuildings, in the 'Peasehillnooke' area of Barnsley (this land stretched from the bottom of Market Hill along modern Peel Street and towards the site of St George's church) from Henry Fozzard who was a wiremaker. Frudd is described as a barber and it is likely that he was involved in cutting hair and trimming beards rather than as a barber-surgeon. It is fairly unusual to find a brewhouse at such a modest property but it may have been useful personal and business asset.

On 21 November Hobson attended the funeral of Cornelius Wood who

had been at Mr. Carrington's Monday ... and as he was coming home, there were netts set upon the Common for the catching of rabbits, and he rid against one of the cords, which occasioned his horse to fall and through him down, and he pitch't upon his head, and was so bruised that he never recovered ... He was buried at Darfield, in the great quire, near to his master Eaton, who was minister there.

Again, deeds can help to throw more light on Hobson's friends. Cornelius Wood was a Barnsley innkeeper, probably of the *Black Bull* which, in 1716, was situated 'in a certain street commonly called Kirkgate (Church Street).' There were two Henry Carringtons but Wood may well have visited the one who was an attorney and who lived at Worsbrough Dale.

The diarist's final entry of the year was on 30 December when he journeyed to Rotherham 'to conduct Joseph Haigh and his bride to Thurlston.'

Diary of 1728

The subject of death must have been an everyday topic of conversation. During 1728, Hobson took care to record the passing of seventeen people who were mainly friends and neighbours.

Sometimes the diary entries are quite brief:

March 6 – John Ellis, of Silkstone, dead.

16th [March] – *Mrs. Scott, of Silkstone, dead.*

April 25th – Old Mr. Mawhood, of Ardsley, buried at Darfield.

Others gave more interesting detail:

30th [May] – *Joseph Parkin, of Ben Bank, died, having been a long time ill of a sore knee, which at last mortified. 3rd (August)–In the morning, at 3, Mr. Wilkinson died. Last Tuesday was sevenight he was seized with a dizziness in the head which ended in fever.*

10th [September] – *That day, Michael Milner, a noted quaker, buried at the burying-place at Burton, in the same grave that his father, Gamaliel Milner, and his mother were buried, who occasioned that place to be inclosed for that use; and she was the first that was interr'd there.*

The burial ground, carefully sited on Burton Bank, Monk Bretton, is one of the earliest in England though in recent years has been sadly neglected.

Hobson received a somewhat surprising visitor on November 26:

John Thornton, son of the late Tempest Thornton, supposed to have been long since dead, was at our house. He has been above 20 years a soldier; was at the battle of Malplaquet; went on an expedition to Canada; has been ever since at Anapolis Royall, in Nova Scotia.

Funerals were solemn but sociable occasions and Hobson's gentleman status ensured that there were frequent invitations. During the year he attended at least five. Two of these were local affairs meaning a relatively short journey from his Dodworth Green home to Silkstone church:

8th [June] – *At the funerall of Mrs. Brooke, of Feildhead, who died the Tuesday before, at noon.*

5th [August] – *At the funerall of Mr. Rich Wilkinson. He was buried within the rails, the 2nd grave from the south wall.*

Others involved journeys to Mexborough, Worsbrough, Hoyland Swaine (for an aunt who was a Quaker) and Sandal Magna. His visit to 'Worsboroug', on 9 June was for the funeral of Jane Fleming of Swaithe. Hobson recorded that

She came well from scool on Wednesday, was taken ill in the night of worm fever, and died on Fryday.

Throughout the year Hobson continued to make regular visits to Barnsley. Business was combined with pleasure. He took great pains to mention the 'company' in which he socialised. In February it was with 'Captain Smith', in June with 'Mr. Tolson, a clergiman, born at Wath,' in July with 'Mr. Short, a Scotchman, practising physick at Sheffield' and also with 'Mr. Thomas Hawksworth of London.' The latter would seem to have been a very interesting character, a poor apprentice to a Dodworth tailor who now had 'a considerable estate,' selling riding-hoods and hoops for petticoats to fashionable London ladies. Hobson records that Hawksworth had '... but £50 to begin the world with, which he had sav'd by his industry ...' September also saw Hobson in the company of 'a young clergyman' Mr. Wroe, who was the son of a Manchester doctor, a 'Mr. Elmsall' and the formidable Justice Henry Wood, Clerk of the Assizes.

Hobson was understandbly on the look out for suitable animals for his farm and tanning business and he also seems to have conducted his affairs very well:

February 21st – At Barnsly. Sold 4 oxen for £29.5s.

22nd – Bought two oxen for £13.3s.

May 1st – Bought a pair of oxen, £11.14s.

St Mary's, Worsbrough.

The diarist also visited Pilley, Wortley, Penistone, Hope (Derbyshire) and Thirsk where, on 18 October he was in company with two tanners 'who, when they were undressed and going to bed, were wrestling: the latter (Samuel Whitehead) got much injured, and wee left him in the surgeon's hand.'

There were also excursions to the races at Penistone (August 1st) when the plate of £3 was won 'by a horse out of Lancashire' and the plate of £5 'won by a mare from Garfurth [nr. Leeds].'

In the afternoon of 11 September, he visited Wakefield races, perhaps a more prestigious meeting since ten horses competed for a plate of twenty guineas. The winner was 'My lord Danby's horse.'

On 1 June, Hobson had the pleasure of attending St Mary's, Worsbrough when he was godfather to Edmund, son of Edmund Greenwood of Swaithe.

On 29 October, Hobson noted, with no further comment, that 'Coz. Jane Mawhood, aged nigh 60, married to Mr. John Micklethwaite, of Ardsly, under thirty.'

In the summer Hobson met Mr Skelton, an octogenarian former gamekeeper to the Wortleys. Skelton would seem to have been quite a character, with a colourful memory going back more than sixty years. He described 'old Sr. Francis Wortley' who was taken prisoner by the parliamentary forces at Walton Hall, near Wakefield, as 'tall, proper man, with grey hair and one of the first who took up arms for the king.' Wortley was put in the Tower of London, where he died and was buried at Westminster.

The Wortleys also had a house at St Helen's Well, near a pagan and later Christian place of pilgrimage. Fine ashlar masonry could still be seen near to St Helen's Farm, now demolished, about twenty-five years ago. An impressive mansion house once stood here, built by Sydney Wortley for one of his mistresses. Unfortunately, a probate inventory relating to the house gives little impression of its former grandeur but it must have been the most dominating domestic building in the area. The site was the scene of a notorious murder and uprising, and the increasingly dilapidated edifice was no doubt the focus of a great deal of gossip and speculation. Skelton informed Hobson that 'there was a room called the yellow chamber, thro' which, if anyone attempted to carry a candle in the night, it would burn blue and go out immediately'. This occurrence was, according to Skelton, a consquence of supernatural forces rather than anything else, especially since he had often seen, as he sat by the fire, 'the apparition of a boy or girl walk along the gallery.' One can just imagine the 86-year-old imparting the tale to an attentive Hobson. Skelton went on to describe his association with Nevison, a former exciseman who became a famous highwayman, eventually executed at York.

St Helen's Farm, near Laithes Lane, Athersley. Remains of an outbuilding of the Wortley mansion can be seen on the right. All the buildings were demolished around 1976. The author

Another successful year for the Dodworth tanner, a year during which he appeard to continue to prosper, and certainly one he enjoyed.

Diary of 1729

John Hobson had spent New Year's Eve enjoying a hearty meal and good company at a neighbour's house. Perhaps he put to the back of his mind any fears and doubts about the future. On past evidence he had every right to look forward to another successful year of business and pleasure. However, no one, even a gentleman, could feel easy about the growing number of mortalities reported from near and more distant places.

Bad weather in January was only to be expected but Hobson's first diary entry of the New Year set the tone for a grim winter and depressing spring:

The beginning of the year is attended with a pretty large snow, which has continued a fortnight.

The diary entries for the first quarter of the year are infrequent and mainly concern news of deaths and burials. Brief comments, perhaps made in haste, do not disguise an increasing worry about the spread of disease:

March 12th.–At Barnsly, in company with Mr. Farrow, minister of Mexborough, where there was 7 burials last week; in some years scarce any at all.

The only light relief has been recorded by Hobson a few days earlier:

Went a-coursing with Mr. Clerkson into Mr. Wortley's liberty; kil'd 3 hares.

Hobson spent Good Friday at home and when completing his diary noted two deaths:

Thomas Cawthorne, of Bank Top, in Wosperdade, dead, aged about 88. He was a descendant of the Cawthorns of Benbank in Dodworth. Abel Rich dead in Sheffield jail.

Abel Rich appears to have made a remarkable recovery since four days later the diarist was to visit Sheffield where Abel was 'alive in the jail'!

By mid-April Hobson was far from happy about his affairs. The health of his parents was causing concern as was the state of his personal finances. Not surprisingly, Hobson's own health began to decline:

15th, Tuesday.–Spent the morning in meditating on the ill posture of my affairs. My father had been lame for several years; my mother old and infirm, wore out with age and care. Several careless servants, not fit to look after business; I so weak and so much out of order that I could not tell when I should be capable myself; payments coming upon me, which … I knew not how to provide against; besides, I had received a letter from London which gave me an account how the parliament was going to lay such a duty upon Geneva and all compound liquors as would certainly ruin the distilling trade, so I supposed my brothers would be incapable of assisting me upon any emergency; all which thoughts depressed my spirits so much, and made me so weak, that at nine a clock, when I got up, I supposed myself dying … [Hobson's brother was a London distiller].

Interestingly, Hobson's first attempt to improve matters was by prayer and, having 'no fearful thoughts', and, not discouraged 'at the apprehensions of death which I felt every minute approaching', he sent for Reverned John Clarkson, MA, the vicar of Silkstone, who arrived at Dodworth Green at about noon. The sacrament was administered to Hobson and his parents. The sudden illness would seem to have had an influence on his philosophy of life:

> *... and I hope the impressions which this day's sudden illness made upon me will never go out of my mind; and when I think how suddenly death may overtake one, it will make me lead a more circumspect life for the future, and allways have regard to my latter end.*

By nightfall there was a visit from Joseph Gregg, one of Barnsley's apothecaries. Hobson was already feeling much better but one wonders if Gregg's treatment made matters worse:

> *... he* [Gregg] *applied large blistering plasters to the wrists of my arms and to my back, which tormented me very much, and occasioned me to have the stranguary all night. He said it was nervous fever.*

A local physician, Doctor Smithson, also visited Hobson and appeared more concerned with the patient's psychological rather than physical condition:

> *At night came Dr. Smithson, who upon talking with me privately, found quickly that it was a mentall as well as corporeall distemper, and told me that I had the hypochonddriock passion upon me, which then I could not believe, as being a meer stranger to that distemper, but found his words very true, for I was afterwards very often so much disordered in my thoughts that I could not rest nor govern them.*

For several days afterwards Hobson suffered from 'a shaking fit for an hour' followed by a 'shaking fit for 5 hours.' A Cambridge physician, Dr Bolderstone, who probably had family connections with the Hobsons, examined him and was of the opinion that 'it was an intermitting feaver,' a diagnosis which was at odds to the opinion of Dr Smithson who apparently had suggested St Vitus' dance.

Hobson gradually recovered from his illness and his diary entries became more regular. On 18 September he reported an interesting example of a relatively new and popular gambling event:

> *A foot-race upon Bakewell course, betwixt a Staffordshire man, nick-named the Beggar Lad, and a Woodland man called Thorp, for 100 guineas a side. The Staffordshire man won the wager.*

News of mortalities from the capital continued to cause concern:

> *November 13th. – Mrs. Sarah Wordsworth brought down from London to be buried at Peniston, where there is a great mortality; the weekly bills being increased from 600 to 900. The week after they were 993.*

The Diseases and Casualties this Week.

Abortive	4	Impostume	8
Aged	45	Infants	22
Bleeding	1	Kingsevil	4
Broken legge	1	Lethargy	1
Broke her skull by a fall in the street at St. Mary Woolchurch	1	Livergrown	1
Childbed	28	Meagrome	1
Chrisomes	9	Palsie	1
Consumption	126	Plague	4237
Convulsion	89	Purples	2
Cough	1	Quinsie	5
Dropsie	53	Rickets	23
Feaver	348	Rising of the Lights	18
Flox and Small-pox	11	Rupture	1
Flux	1	Scurvy	3
Frighted	2	Shingles	1
Gowt	1	Spotted Feaver	166
Grief	3	Stilborn	4
Griping in the Guts	79	Stone	2
Head-mould-shot	1	Stopping of the stomach	17
Jaundies	7	Strangury	3
		Suddenly	2
		Surfeit	74
		Teeth	111
		Thrush	6
		Tissick	9
		Ulcer	1
		Vomiting	10
		Winde	4
		Wormes	20

Christned: Males — 90, Females — 81, In all — 171. Buried: Males — 2777, Females — 2791, In all — 5568. Plague — 4237

Increased in the Burials this Week — 249.

Parishes clear of the Plague — 27 Parishes Infected — 103

The Assize of Bread set forth by Order of the Lord Maior and Court of Aldermen, A penny Wheaten Loaf to contain Nine Ounces and a half, and three half-penny White Loaves the like weight.

A Bill of Mortalily during the Plague. Batsford

The weather was also causing problems:

> *26th* [Nov.] – *The great flood on Wednesday last done great damagg all over the country. At Warrington cawsway 12 people drowned. At the wier miln* [Wortley] *a pore boy taken down. At Wakefeild all the coals and ship plank taken away.*

Here are Hobson's final few entries for 1729, a year he would never forget:

> *December 3. – The roads full of disbanded soldiers; a peace being made with Spain. Mr. Walker, the recorder of Leeds, dead.*
>
> *9th. – At a christening at Mr. Fenton's daughter, call'd Frances.*
>
> *16th. – At home. John Pashley, of Bolton, came to invite us to the funeral of his sister Mary. His mother died about a fortnight ago. They both died of a feaver, with swellings in their head and throat, there being a great mortality there; 15 or 16 having been buried there lately.*
>
> *22nd. – This morning wee hear Mr. Edward Spenser, of Cannon hall, is dead, having been a long time ill of an atrophy. 24th, buried at Cawthorn, in the quire belonging to Barmby hall, and has appointed Mr. Mathew Wilson and Mr. Cockshut his executors.*
>
> *28th. – Mr. Smith, of Heath, dead.*

Diary of 1730

Hobson's first diary entries for the year 1730 concerned the death of his mother:

> *January 13th, Tuesday. – About a quarter before nine in the evening my mother departed this life. 17th, interred at Silkstone, in the great quire within the rails.*

Despite his financial problems the burial reflected the gentry status of his family and indeed the capability of paying for such a privileged place of interment.

Almost all of the entries which immediately followed related to the death or burial of local people. Hobson was quick to record the passing of any well-known person, especially where drinking was involved:

> *18th* [March] – *Yesterday, Mr. Henry Carrinton, of Views, was buried at Worsbrough. This day fortnight at Mr. Hawksworth's, in Barnsley, at the eating of a barrell of oysters, where perhaps he might get too much liquor. He fell into a fit of the stone and strangury, and a feaver, and died on Saturday last, about 7 o'clock at night. He has left an only daughter.*
>
> *21st* [March] – *Mr. John Green, of Banks, buried at Cawthorn. He died the 18th instant, about 8 o clock at night, of a lingering distemper, occasioned by too much drinking. He enjoyed the estate six years; left no issue, and is suceeded by his brother Samuell.'*

Carrington was a gentleman attorney and lived at Glew House in the parish of Darfield. 'Mr. Hawksworth's' could refer to an old Barnsley inn called the *Boot and Shoe* which was mentioned in a deed of 1716 and was situated in Kirkgate. Josia Hawksworth, yeoman, said to be of Burton Grange, leased the property from John Dickinson, a

Banks Hall, fine early Georgian home of the Green family; later occupied by Samuel Thorp, coal owning son of William Thorp, founder of the Gawber glassworks. Alan Billingham

Barnsley butcher, and would appear to have lived at the inn. The name of the inn is not unusual but could well reflect the number of shoemakers or cordwainers working in the town at this time.

John Green, of Banks Hall, Cawthorne, was about thirty-six-years-old when he died. He had succeeded to the estate following the death of his elder brother, William, who also died in his thirties, in 1729. In his will, John left his wife, Mary, £61 per annum, £12 'to buy her a suit of mourning', a gold watch, various items of furniture, a table cloth marked 'JG' and a mare with a grey tail. She also benefited from rents of farms at Oxspring and Nether Eastfield, Silkstone. Brother Samuel only got ten shillings, but he inherited the family house and estate. The very detailed probate inventory of John Green is a fascinating document which shows the considerable wealth of the family.

The impressive mansion of Banks Hall still exists and in 1730 had the accommodation of a gentleman who usually had 'Esquire' after his name:

Hall, Dining Room, Drawing Room, Little Parlour, Back Closet, Pantry, Lower Parlour, Cellar Head, Laundry, Cellar, Kitchen, Brewhouse.

Best Lodging Room, Closet, Dark Closet, Closet in the Gallery, Culgee Chamber, Master's Lodging Room, Chamber joining the Nursery.

Brown Garret, Silk Garret, Men Servant's Room.

Wainhouse, Yokehouse, Chamber over the Common Stable, Middle Stable, Nether Stable, Soap Garret.

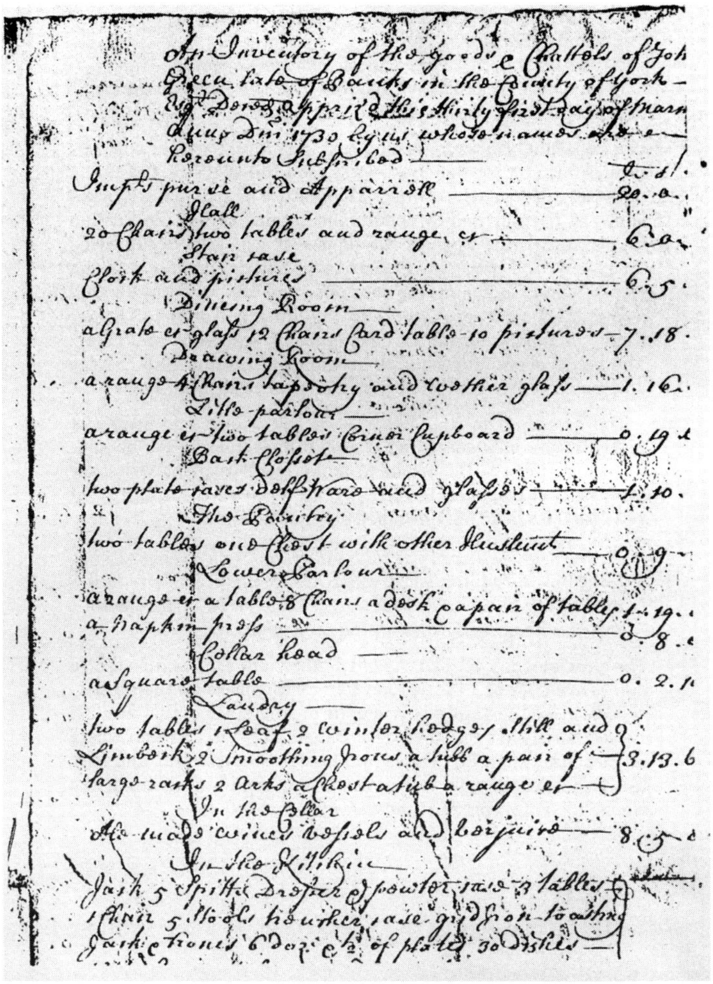
An Inventory of the goods & Chattels of John Green late of Banks in the County of York Esqr. Deceased apprized this thirty first day of March Anno Dom 1730 by us whose names are hereunto Subscribed

Imps purse and Apparrell — 20.0.

Hall

20 Chairs two tables and range etc — 6.0.

Stair case

Clock and pictures — 6.5.

Dining Room

a grate etc glass 12 Chairs Card table 10 pictures — 7.18.

Drawing Room

a range 4 Chairs tapestry and two other glass — 1.16.

Little parlour

a range etc two tables China Cupboard — 0.19

Back Closet

two plate cases delfware and glasses — 1.10.

The Pantry

two tables one Chest with other Utensils — 0.9

Lower Parlour

a range etc a table 8 Chairs a desk & a pair of tables 1.19.

a napkin press — 0.8.

Cellar head

a square table — 0.2.1

Laundry

two tables 1 Leaf 2 [illegible] Lodges Still and Limbeck 2 Smoothing Irons a [illegible] a pair of large racks 2 Arks a Chest a [illegible] a range etc — 3.13.6

In the Cellar

the malt wines vessels and barrels — 8.5.

In the Kitchen

Jack 5 Spitts Dresser of pewter [illegible] 3 tables 1 Chair 5 Stools [illegible] gridiron [illegible] stones 6 doz & ½ of plates 30 dishes

Part of the probate inventory of John Green who died in 1730. Borthwick Institute of Historical Research

The household contents, farm stock and crops, together with the several farm rents came to a very substantial £600.16s.11d.

By the middle of the century, the estate was sold to the Fawkes family of Farnley and by about 1830 became part of the Cannon Hall estate of the Spencer-Stanhopes. It was later occupied by Thomas Wilson of Barnby Furnace, who had mining interests and who probably laid out the gardens, and the well-known coal owner, Richard Thorp, who had collieries at Norcroft. Thomas Ridley, a Northumbrian farmer, probably succeeded Mr. Thorp. The house eventually became an annex of Bretton Hall College and was recently converted into a private residential home.

The rather grim diary entries of the winter and spring of 1729/30 soon changed to what would appear to be far happier times for Hobson. He began

to make more frequent visits, for business and pleasure, to Barnsley, as usual 'in the company' of local gentry. On 20 May he noted an unusual sight:

> *At Barnsly. Saw a cow from Swtizerland with 6 leggs. Two hung down from the back, above her shoulder. She also had along with her a calf about a year old, calved by her, with two legs hanging down after the same mannerr.*

The previous day he had visited Rotherham Fair and bought a pair of oxen (for £12.17s.6d.), no doubt with an eye for their hides.

Hobson was certainly very mobile during much of the year. He visited north-east England, describing a night in Durham where he had 'sup't with Mr Oates and his ten shoemakers', and met Mr Lanes on the way to Newcastle; lay with him there, at the sign of the Fountain, in Pipehall Lane'.

The gentleman tanner also had a trip into Derbyshire and on 25 June was at Thirsk where he 'saw 2 outlandish men, habited like Turks, said to come from Morocco; they were travelling about the country. The noblemen were very civill to them, and conducted them sometimes in their coaches'.

'All Saints', Silkstone. KL Graham

There were also visits to Leeds 'where they are widening the bridge and making additions to the arches. One of them ... fell down, and killed three men, about a week ago', and 'A boatman buried in the midst of Rodwell Haigh (Rothwell), and a stake driven thro' him. He was going to be apprehended for stealing some hens, so he leap't into the river and drowned himself'.

Hobson attended the fair at Sheffield when he lodged 'at Mr. Fell's, at Attercliffe', the ironmaster.

Horse-racing continued to be a popular interest through he does not mention any wagers when he attended Barnsley Races on 10 September. There was certainly gambling taking place three days later 'at a foot race on Barnsley Moor' when 'Thorp of Woodland won the wager'.

After an uneasy start, the year turned out to be a great success and one can detect a growing confidence in Hobson's writing; he was once more called upon to be a godfather (to the son of Abraham Haigh of Hill Top), had paid his Easter dues consisting of 'a dozen and a half of eggs, and 4d. in money' to Francis Goddard, the Silkstone parson who also received one pound for the burial of his mother and an uncle, had entertained friends and relatives at his Dodworth Green home and had generally enjoyed himself.

Diary of 1731

Journeys on horseback were an essential part of everyday life for most Barnsley people. Those with business and professional interests such as Hobson travelled considerable distances and many ordinary folk would make visits to relatives in neighbouring villages and towns. Accidents were common and occasionally fatal. Hobson's diary entries for the year 1731 include several references to riding accidents:

> *April 14th – Mr. Micael Womble got a fall from his horse as he was comming from Mr. Bright's, of Badsworth; received such a concussion in his head that it is thought he will never be right sensible again.*

Michael Womble was the younger son of William Wombwell, of Wombwell, esquire and practised as an attorney at Wakefield.

One unfortunate minister lost his life on the relatively short though difficult journey from Wakefield to Emley:

> *25th* [June] – *Mr. Pen, minister of Emley, returning from the visitation at Wakefield, fell from his horse and died soon after.*

Another man, who had family connections in Barnsley, met his death on a well-used highway:

> *October 1st – Last week Bosville Midleton, of Burrowbridge, tanner, as he was coming from York, was kil'd dead with a fall from his horse.*

An unusual and dangerous habit was described by Hobson in the very next entry:

> *6th – Mr. Exton Sayer, of Durham, got a fall from his horse, of which he died. The horse was frightened by a paper which he took out of his pocket to read.*

Excessive drinking and riding was also not to be recommended:

> *17th* [April] – *David Cawthorn, of Bank top, in Wosperdale, dies. On Wednesday last he was at Barnsley, and being very much concern'd in drink, got a fall from his horse on Barnsly common, and was never sensible after.*

David Cawthorne was a yeoman farmer of some substance and lived at a place called 'Bank End' in an area probably near to Darley Hall. The new turnpike road was soon to pass by with the *Rose and Crown* serving as a noted posting-house, a welcome resting place for weary travellers.

On 30 April, four neighbours, led by Rev Francis Hall, rector of Tankersley, who lived at Swaithe and later at Bank Top, visited Cawthorne's farm to carry out the legal process of drawing up an inventory of the deceased's goods and chattells. The document was proven at York in May 1731 but Cawthorne died intestate (no will). His house consisted of kitchen, 'house' or living room, together with a parlour or ground floor bedroom and buttery.

Upstairs were three 'chambers', used as bedrooms, and one used mainly as a store for small farm tools. Outside was a barn, granary and stable. There was little or no corn in store but the buildings housed larger agricultural implements such as harrows, ploughs, yokes etc. There were two wains (carts) and a cart kept in the granary though a separate wainhouse stored timber. In the fold was a large pile of manure and a quantity of lime. Cawthorne had corn in store 'in

Darley Hall. Alan Billingham

chambers at Barnsley' (fifty loads of wheat valued at £17 and ten loads of 'blendcorn' at £3) and more than fifty loads of corn stored at a place called 'Yiews' (Yews) in Worsbrough Dale, locally pronounced and often spelt 'Views'.

A list of recently sown crops provides us with an interesting record of local land-use:

'Corn on the Ground'	£	s	d
Nine acres & a half of Barley	*23*	*15*	*00*
Ten acres & a half of wheat	*15*	*15*	*00*
Ten acres of Pease and three acres of Oates	*13*	*00*	*00*
Corn upon the ground at Yiews			
Seven acres of wheat plow'd & sown	*1*	*8*	*00*
Seven loads of wheat sown	*3*	*6*	*06*
Seven acres of barly 4 times plow'd & harrowed	*5*	*12*	*00*
Five Sacks & a mett of Barly sown	*2*	*7*	*03*
Eight acres of Ley Barly plow'd & sown	*1*	*12*	*00*
Three quarters of Barly sown	*2*	*4*	*00*
Eight acres of Oates plow'd & sown	*1*	*12*	*00*
Nine sacks of Oates sown	*1*	*16*	*00*
Three acres & a half of Pease plow'd & Sown	*0*	*14*	*00*
Four loads of Pease sown	*1*	*8*	*00*
18 pd. of clover Seed was sown in Grimewell Ing	*0*	*6*	*00*

A 'mett' was sack containing about two bushels.

Throughout the year Hobson recorded more than thirty deaths in his diary. He continued to delight in commenting on bad habits:

> *7th* [April] – *Mr. Robert Hall, curate at Stainborough, buried at Worsborough: he had contracted a habit of drinking, which kil'd him at last.*
>
> *12th* [Sept.] – *Old Edward Garner found dead in bed this morning. He was very well the night before. He had a rupture, and lead an intemperate life for many years. On Wednesday last he was at Wakefield races where his horse got out of pasture and came home, so he was oblieged to walk afoot to Mapplewell where he lay all night, and came home a-foot next day; which fatigue might perhaps hasten his death.*
>
> *1st – Seas'd suddenly with a violent fit of the stone. Sent for Dr. Smithson and Mr. Armitage.*

Again, we see how he was quickly able to acquire the services of a physician and an apothecary, and could even afford to be treated in his own home. He recovered sufficiently to make a journey into Derbyshire where, with distinguished company, he drank the waters at St Anne's Well, Buxton. Earlier he had travelled once more to north-east England, calling at Newcastle where he stayed 'at the Sign of the Three Indian Kings' and Sunderland.

On 18 March Hobson described the arrival of a monument to commemorate his mother:

> *My mother's marble monument came from Wakefield.*

It was placed inside Silkstone church on 3 May by Josia Hawkesworth, probably a local mason.

Two earlier generations of Hobsons are displayed on this memorial in Silkstone Church: John Hobson I (1620–1705) who married Elizabeth Princess of Woolley and John Hobson II (1654–1732) who married Helen Fretwell of Herringthorpe. Alan Billingham

Hobson described an unusual wager in an entry of 28th April:

> *Another jumping match upon Brotherton march, for £500 a side, betwixt Richard, the son of Mr. Joseph Oates, of Derby, and the same Staffordshire man, call'd Creswell; they weer to jump 60 jumps alltogether. Creswell won the wager.*

Creswell must have been delighted at his win since £500 was a large sum by the standards of the day but he no doubt had expenses to dish out to his friends and helpers.

On the whole it had been a fairly quiet year for the Dodworth tanner but 'reading between the lines' he was becoming increasingly anxious about his own health and certainly that of his father.

Diary of 1732

Hobson opened his journal for 1732 with news of several local deaths:

> *January 29th – Old Lady Wentworth, of Hickleton, dead. She was wife of Sir Michael Wentworth, and grandmother to the present Mr. Wentworth of Wooley.*

> *February 10th – On Saturday last an apprentice of Robert Leatham's died suddenly as he was walking by himself in Barnsley field. This morning Mrs. Burdet, of Fall head, died of a feaver.*

The Leathams were an important family of linen-drapers.

Towards the end of the month Hobson was in Barnsley but it was 'a slow fair for oxen' when presumably little buying or selling was taking place. However, he did take the opportunity to dine with 'Mr. Selwood, formerly steward to the Dutches of Bedford.'

On the 26th Hobson noted the marriage of two Barnsley shopkeepers:

> *Mr. Gregg, the apothecary, married, on Monday last, to Margaret, the daughter of the late Mr. George Shilletoe; as allso Mr. Beckett, the grocer, was married, the Thursday before, to Mary, the sister of Mr. Crookes, of Burton* [Monk Bretton].

Beckett had a shop in Market Hill. He was the second son of Gervase Beckett, of Barnsley, wiremaker. The marriage only lasted a few months; Mary died in July. His second marriage was to Elizabeth, daughter of Joseph Wilson of Monk Bretton. Their eldest son, John, moved to Leeds where he became a very successful merchant and banker, becoming Lord Mayor in 1775 and 1797.

Hobson witnessed a formidable event when visiting Barnsley on the 3rd April:

> *Saw Mr. Spencer's* [of Cannon Hall] *great ox killed there. He had been feeding 3 year. His quarters weighed 108 stone; tallow 181bs; his hide 11st. 4lbs. he was sold at 4d. per pound.*

On 5th May there is an interesting reference to the old woodland craft of charcoal burning. The exponents were usually called 'wood colliers':

> *Will Lindly, of this town* [Dodworth], *now basket-maker, aged near 90, says that he was bound apprentice to a banister maker, which was a large sort of hamper, then in use, for the carrying charcoal to the furnaces on horse-back, one on each side of the horse. They were made with a bottom to pull out, for the convenience of emptying. They were wide at the top, narrow at the bottom, which gave the colliers an opportunity of cheating, by filling them hollow, so they were left of, and sacks used in their stead: this was the year 1660.*

The charcoal was in demand as fuel for the local iron industry.

Hobson would frequently visit 'old Lindley' who would delight in recounting stories about local families and events.

On the 18th May a further case of intemperance was recorded:

> *This day Mr. George Crooks was buried at Royston. He died Munday last, at night, of a consumption, occasioned, as he thought, by too much liquor, which he got when he went to see Mrs. Spencer, of*

Cannon hall, which overpowered him so much that he was oblieged to lie in a close [field], *under a hedge, all night.*

Another example on 2nd June:

Jonathan Godier, the joyner, died, about a fortnight ago, at Doncaster; he kill'd himself with drinking. He did most of the joyner work at Stainborough hall [Wentworth Castle], *being servant to Mr. Thornton; and also the best staircase at Banks* [Banks Hall, Cawthorne].

Our local communities were often extremely generous and helpful to neighbouring – even distant places – where people had suffered misfortune. Hobson describes an interesting example on 3rd July:

John Bradsbury, of Sadleworth, having lately had his house and barn burnt, came to ask relief. He his an old man, aged 87, and has sold havercake backstones [oat-cake bakestones] *in this country upwards of 60 years. He says he is a relation of Mr. Bradbury, the noted dissenting teacher of London, whose ancestors came out of that country. His father was a taylor; lived in a little house near Woolley, behind Darton, where Mr. Bradbury was born.*

July was quite a busy month and no doubt an enjoyable one. There were visits to Ardsley and Birchhouse feasts and Hobson was pleased to take delivery of a new clock from London.

Early August saw Hobson visiting Keighley where 'Jacob, the ostler' was found dead in bed 'occasioned by drinking, and a surfeit of cold by going out in a rainy morning.'

Two unfortunate events took place by the middle of the month:

14th – This morning died Hannah, the wife of Henry Guest, glazier, sister of Joshua Pashley, of this town, on a bruse she received by a horse on Wednesday last, in the afternoon, on her eye, head, shoulder, and back, being rid over by one of Mr. Womble's [Wombwell] *servants;Shillitoe, the steward, whipping the horse and making him run away with the rider.*

20th – A young man, who had listed himself yeasterday, hang'd himself this morning at Barnsly, in Mr.Roper's back kitchin. [Probably the kitchen of the White Bear, Church Street]

Towards the end of September Hobson's health took a turn for the worse:

27th.- My indisposition increased;I could eat nothing; became weaker and weaker. I was reduced so very weak that I could not raise myself up in bed; and so very lean that I had nothing but skin and bone left; so that there was but small hopes for my recovery. So I had the Sacrement administered to me by Mr. Clarkson, who prayed with me allmost every day.

Hobson continued to be very ill for several days and he suffered further personal loss on October 13th.

My father, having been ten years lame with the gout, three of which he went on crutches, and seven years sate in a chair, which had four little wheels to move him up and down, begun to be worse, the gout getting into his stomack, and died on the 19th day, being Thursday, about eight a clock in the morning.

John Hobson, senior, was buried at Silkstone on 22 October 'within the communion rails, close by my mother, in the 78 year of his age, being born Jan. 6, 1654.'

Hobson was unlikely to have attended his father's funeral for on 29 October (Sunday) he was able to get out of bed and go downstairs 'having been confin'd ten weeks in a room, and lay most of that time in bed …' However, recovery was 'very fast' afterwards. 'Deo gloria.'

Diary of 1733

Hobson's diary entries for the beginning of the year reflected his own personal illness and a further concern about news of yet more mortalities:

January 16th – Walk out to the tan-yard, the first time since last August. Great numbers of people have been ill of a cold at London, which, if not prevented by bleeding, ends in a feaver. And now, at Edinburgh, they are above 8,000 persons ill of the present cold.

7th [February] *– A great mortality in London, there diing the last week in January, males 729, females 859, in all 1,558. Increased, in the burials this week, 805.*

14th – Deaths at London. Males 597, females 629, in all 1,166.

Hobson would have read these figures in a provincial newspaper; they were taken from the so-called 'Bills of Mortality' which have been shown to be unreliable, but population studies do show that this was a period of high mortality in many communities.

At a local level the diarist records more deaths:

A Sugar-loaf (left) and mould. Museum of London

20th [Feb.] *– Mr. Green's son, of Banks, aged about 1½ years, dead of a feaver. Yesterday Elizabeth, the daughter of Mr. Cockshut, of Cawthorn, died at Retford, of the small pox.*

27th – This morning Mrs. Gill, of Sandall, died of the distemper.

The next day Hobson presented a mourning ring to Reverend Clarkson, vicar of Silkstone, in memory of the recently deceased John Hobson senior. There was also a gift of a sugar loaf which was an expensive luxury and probably obtained from one of the town's confectioners or grocers. It was top quality sugar made by allowing the water to drip slowly through clarified sugar syrup in order to displace the molasses; the refined sugar then hardened to form a cone. Only the rich could afford to buy the sugar in a loaf form. For the poor a few ounces would be scraped off into a twist of paper or they could purchase poor quality 'bastard' grades. Shopkeepers obtained supplies from the new refineries in London and the major ports.

An unusual death was recorded on 21st March:

John Woodhead of Pillah [Pilley]*, found dead at Skoles* [Scholes]*, nigh Peniston. He was an ignorant man, and wandered from place to place. The night before some bad boys set doggs upon him, which bit him very much, which is thought occasioned his death.*

On 29 April Hobson attended church at Silkstone, apparently his first visit for eight months, again perhaps a reflection of his illness. The very next day he dismissed one of his servants:

Discharg'd Ann Turton, for malitiously putting butter in the ale when it was working, and several other faults.

Yet more local deaths were noted during the summer months but then, in August, came news of an attempted murder:

5th – Mr. Wombwell's son, of Barnsley, stabb'd Mr. Richard Oates, the noted leaper, with a penknife into the breast, as they were quarrelling in an alehouse at Horbury. Mr. William Wentworth happened to be by who prevented Mr. Wombwell from doing any more harm. It was thought the stabb had been mortall, and Mr. Wombwell was secured; but there being hopes of Mr. Oates' recovery, he is admitted to bail.

Hobson continued to have problems with his household staff:

31st [September] – *Sometime this month Humphrey Feilding, our man, misst £2.12s, which was gone out of a box in the chamber over the kitching; and, a little time after, sister misst five guineas and 11 shillings out of the scrittoire in the hall, which she found yeasterday, dropt into the chest of drawers in the new chamber, thro' a reft* [i.e. rift, cleft or breach] *on the top of the drawers.*

It was not until October that the tanner did any travelling when, on the 8th he went to Saddleworth to view an estate which was offered for sale at £1,800. Hobson offered £1,400, a considerable sum at a time when the goods and chattels of a 'husbandman' farmer or craftsmen could be valued at less than £50. The offer was refused.

Hobson was clearly interested in extending his landed interests since a few days later he offered £1,500 for the Saddleworth estate but the bid was once more turned down. Another visit to Saddleworth in November resulted in agreement and £1,580 changed hands.

The close of the year was noted for very mild weather:

31st [December] – *There has been very fair open weather ths month; no frost or snow; some wind as warm as April; primroses sprung in the hedges; flowers in the garden; such a season has not been known in the memory of man.*

The old year ended on 24 March, the day following remained as the civil and legal New Year's Day until the introduction of the style of measuring time devised by Pope Gregory XIII, but not introduced into the United Kingdom until 1752. In that year 3 September was reckoned to be 14 September and dating carried on from that date, New Year's Day becoming 1 January. Hobson's health and well-being continued to cause concern, curtailing both business and social contacts. The purchase of an estate may have been one way of ensuring some regular income in the future at a time when running the tanyard was clearly becoming more difficult.

Last entries ... 1734/35

Hobson spent three days in late January serving on the jury of the West Riding Quarter Sessions held at Doncaster. He gives no details of cases, in fact the diary entries continue to concentrate on reporting local deaths:

January 13th – John Downing of Silkston, the mason, dead of pleurisie.

February 17th – Mr. Gamaliel Milner of Burton grange, died on Fryday night last of 4 days sickness. He had a man died the same night, and a maid the night before; several of the family ill besides. Mr. Wombwell, the atturney of Barnsly dead.

March 15th – Mr. Norris, formerly minister of Denby chappell, dead. On Tuesday last Mrs. Ann Brooke, sister to Mr. Brooke, of Richmond, buried at Leeds old church.

April 15th – R[obert] *Leatham, of Barnsly, a quaker and linnen-draper, died this day of a pleuritick feaver. He had intended to go to London with Mr. Oates, but began to be ill a day or two before he should have set out.*

The spring of 1734 was a very pleasant one:

May 1st – Here is the forwardest spring that ever was known in the memory of man: the trees in full leave, the hedges green: a month ago a vast of blossom upon all sorts of trees; the sloe trees out of blossom; the haythorn [hawthorn] *in full blossom; the tulips almost over; everything grand and flourishing.*

Hobson's landed interests and 'gentleman' status meant that he could vote at an election. On 16 May he visited Wharncliffe Lodge, perhaps being entertained there by the Wortley family. Mr. Wortley having 'put up for candidate unexpectedly'. On the 23rd Hobson journeyed to York where he voted for Sir Miles Stapleton and Mr. Edward Wortley. However, Wortley does not appear to have been successful, Stapleton and Cholmley Turner were returned as knights for the county. Ingenious methods could be used to solicit votes. The Silkstone parish clerk, Francis Goddard, who was obviously ill at the time, was according to Hobson, 'over-perswaded by MC, Dr B, and col. Foley, to go thither (to York) to vote for Mr. Turner and Sr. Rowland Winn. He rid in a chair to Tadcaster, where col. Foley had prommised to send his chaise to carry him forward, but, being disappointed, he went no further'. Goddard died a few days later.

During the summer months Hobson records several other deaths and attends the funeral, at Bolton upon Dearne, of Dr Smithson, who had treated him on several occasions. The event must have been a very grand affair, despite the doctor's testamentary request 'to be privately and decently interred near my late wife Jane Smithson, accompanied by none but my nearest relations, ye parish minister, and eight bearers'. The Barnsley physician had family connections at Bolton and Doncaster.

Hobson continued to show interest in land and property:

> *14th* [Sept.] – *Went along with Mr. Fenton to view an estate in Bradfield parish called Sugworth, that belongs to Mr. Fernihaugh, of Chedle, in Staffordshire, which is to be sold. It is rented at £27 per annum the landlord paying the taxes, which sometimes amounts to £8 a year.*

References to tanning, Hobson's trade, are gone but he does note the killing of a beast of huge proportions:

> *November 2nd – A boar kil'd at Wakefield last week, weighed 47 stone.*

A few days later the diarist 'quotes' from a tombstone, 'newly set up in the churchyard at Heydon, in Holderness'.

> *Here lyeth the body of William Strutton, of Padrington, buried the 18th of May, 1734, aged 97, who had by his first wife 28 children, and by a second wife 17. Own father to 45; grandfather to 86; great grandfather to 97; and great great grandfather to 23; in all 251.*

Smallpox, the most dreaded of diseases, was mentioned on 20 November:

> *This day Mr. James Smith's wife died of the smallpox. His son died of the same distemper, not a year old. Both she and the child both buried in the same coffin, in Leeds old church.*

Here are the final few entries made by Hobson at a time when his health was probably worsening:

> *24th* [Dec., 1734] – *Sister came from Wooly, with Mr. Telford's daughter.*
>
> *January 1st* [1734/5] *James Lindly, aged 7 years, came to our house as parish apprentice.*
>
> *8th – At home. A very snowy, windy day. A great hurrycane at London and other parts.*
>
> *It is interesting how quickly London news could reach Dodworth.*
>
> *11th – Young David Ellison's wife dead in childbed. Buried at Darton.*
>
> *14th – Old David Ellison's wife of Higham, dead.*
>
> *22nd – At Barnsly. Sent 3 turkeys to London; and Mr. Wilkinson sent a hare.*

Perhaps they were sent as gifts but it is also possible that even small items were forwarded for sale, underlining the pulling power of the capital as a market centre.

> *23rd, 24th, 25th, 26th, 27th – At home.*

John Hobson was buried at Silkstone on 15 May 1735. The survival of his interesing diary provides us with a rare personal insight of the life and times of a local gentleman.

PART THREE: EARLY INDUSTRY

7 IRON

Daniel Defoe's impression of early eighteenth century Barnsley was of a town famed for industry:

Thence over vast moors ... we entered the most populous part of ... the West Riding, only passing a town call'd Black Barnsley, eminent still for the working of iron and steel; and indeed the very town looks as black and smoaky as if they were all smiths that lived in it.

The monks of Burton or Monk Bretton mined ironstone at Dodworth and had water-powered iron mills on the Dearne. In 1589 the works consisted of 'a pair of smithies of Iron Mills' driven by 'ould smithie wheels'. The site was leased from the Crown to George Wood who lived at the Manor House in Monk Bretton. Towards the end of the Woods' tenancy the 'iron mills' were the subject of litigation when Wood and his son were accused of interfering with water supply of corn mills on the Dearne. A few years earlier the mills had been in dispute when Elizabeth Vallyance brought an action against Gilbert Talbot, Earl of Shrewsbury, to enforce a contract in their purchase by the Earl who was a large purchaser of monastic property. The Smithies mills were occupied by Sir Francis Wortley from about 1625 to 1636. The place-name 'Smithies' is an interesting reminder of early industrial activity in the Barnsley stretch of the Dearne valley.

A wooded glade less than three miles south of Barnsley was also an important source of iron for local craftsmen. A charcoal blast furnace appears to have been erected next to old smithies at Rockley in Worsbrough township. Excavations carried out by Denis Ashurst and David Crossley in the 1970s have shown that the original site was of considerable importance, consisting of dam, three water wheels for bellows, a bloom hearth, a string hearth, a reheating hearth, and another hearth. The furnace, with a new dam and water-powered bellows was probably producing 400 tons of pig iron per annum and operated until about 1750. It was reactivated during the Napoleonic Wars.

The Spencers of Cannon Hall, in partnership with other West Riding landowners dominated the local iron industry but at least one resident of Barnsley had ironmaking interests. Henry Wood, from a wealthy family of attorneys, bequeathed 'all my Estate and Stock in the Ironworks or trade in Yorkshire, Derbyshire and Nottinghamshire or Elsewhere' in his will of 1720. The industry could not survive without large amounts of capital but it was also dependent on many highly skilled craftsmen.

Smiths & Nailers

Barnsley's tradition of metalworking goes back at least to the thirteenth century when ironstone was mined in the locality.

Four 'smyths' are recorded in the poll tax of 1379: Richard de Keresforth, John Daynell (Daniel?), Thomas de Manethorp and the aptly named John Smyth. These were probably some of the better-off craftsmen, able to pay four or six pence each in tax.

Early wills contain numerous references to household and farm objects made of iron and often craftsmen passed on their tools to sons. John Fernley of Monk Bretton bequeathed ten shillings 'as in nayles or oder harde ware stuffe' to his son-in-law in 1536. Twenty-one years later John Cusworth, the elder, of Royston parish, insisted that his 'great brasse pottes, myne yron chimney' should remain at his house during the residency of his children, but also left another 'yron chimney' to John Gill 'that his father hath of mine'. The iron chimney was a fashionable innovation, replacing the old open hearths of earlier times.

Robert Warren, of Notton and probably a blacksmith by trade, left his son 'two paire of irens one paire of bellows' in 1561. Richard Solteryne, a neighbour, in 1576 left to his daughter 'one newe brede panne' and to his son, 'one other brede panne that was given unto him by his

From *Forge and Foundry* by SE Ellacott, Methuen, 1964.

grandfather … and all my toyles and Iron geare that I work withall savinge my best haitt two axes and a wimble which I give to Agnes' (his wife). Solteryne also had a lease for a windmill at Royston.

By the time of the hearth tax of 1672 Barnsley had at least seven smithies or forges at work. Some smiths – the Trueloves are good examples – continued to practice their craft over three or more generations:

Thomas Truelove c 1667 [blacksmith/nailer]
George Truelove c 1672
William Truelove 1721–1780
Samuel Truelove 1721–1789
John Truelove 1732–1792

Most smiths were not men of great wealth. They had few possessions and relied upon farming in order to support their families. Yet they were skilled workers, providing an essential service and products for both home and farm.

Barnsley also had a number of 'whitesmiths' who specialised in finishing and polishing wrought iron or steel goods. No probate inventories survive for these workers but men such as Samuel and Nathanial Harley, John and Adam Lindley, Joseph Hall, Joseph Wade and Samuel Haigh were all active in the trade during the eighteenth century.

Many of the blacksmiths would have been able to turn their hand to producing nails but there were also a number of specialist nail-makers in Barnsley practising their trade from at least the seventeenth century. Some of them only came to light as it were 'by accident'. Thomas Truelove, for example, was described as 'nailor' when he was examined at Worsbrough in 1667 concerning the possible theft of a horse. In 1698 Thomas Truelove was summoned to appear before the next Quarter Sessions and in the meantime had to keep the peace, especially towards the wife of George Truelove.

Thomas Fletcher, another Barnsley nailer, was earlier (1690) faced with a similar request, objected against by Ann Jepson. Another of the Trueloves, Samuel, was put before the Barnsley Sessions, along with five other 'labourers' to face an indictment from Samuel Smith. In 1696 George Sherwood, nailer, of Barnsley, along with his wife Elizabeth were indicted to appear before the next Quarter Sessions 'and in the meantime keep the peace, especially towards Joshua Anderton.'

Nailmaking was carried out in small workshops, and improvised lean-to structures. Behind a stone hearth would be a set of bellows worked by a wooden pole. The craftsman pulled one or two irons from the fire, hammering them into shape on a little anvil set on a large iron block. The block or 'stiddy' also held the 'hardy' on which nails were cut from the iron rod after being shaped. A unique surviving example of a nailmakers' workshop can still be seen near a private residence at Hoyland Swaine.

Frank Atkinson, who was born in Mapplewell, wrote about Yorkshire nailmaking in 1958. As a boy he was able to talk to many old men who spent all their lives at the trade. He recalled the 'hundreds of little workshops' when the village was one of Yorkshire's most important

Furnace at Low Mill Farm, near Silkstone. The author

nailmaking centres. Frank also described the unusual way in which they 'got paid'. At the end of the week the nailer would take his produce to the 'factor' who paid in kind, with groceries, together with the iron rods from which the following week's nails would be made. Apparently some men worked for years without any money passing hands!

Mapplewell and other local shopkeepers sold their nails to blacksmiths, cloggers and shoemakers but some would, in the words of Frank, 'put a couple of panniers on the back of a mule and jog off on a week's journey into the East Riding and Lincolnshire selling to farmers on the way.'

Nailmaking was generally a man's job, especially when making large nails. However, women and children made smaller nails, and 'many widows kept their families alive by working at the anvil, rocking a cradle with one foot as they hammered. A lovely old photograph appeared in the *Barnsley Chronicle* of 19 June 1987, showing women nailmakers, of Peckett's Nail Shops. Children made tupenny and threepenny nails and women made up to sixpenny and eightpenny; anything above that was a man's job.' The 'pennyworth' of nails referred to pounds and not price. Thus a thousand nails of a particular size weighed two pounds, three pounds and so on. If a man was to make 'tenpenny' nails then they would be 'big uns' i.e. a thousand weighed ten pounds.

Some families specialised in certain kinds of nails, such as horseshoe nails, 'chaplets' or 'stappels'. Whatever the situation, the workers received a very small return for many hours of labour.

The Mapplewell and Darton nailers formed a close-knit community; many of the early families were Quakers and ignored the threats and severe persecution which abounded during the third quarter of the seventeenth century.

John Denton, yeoman, Robert Slater, nailer, both of Darton along with a Mapplewell nailer, John Webster, were summoned to appear at the quarter sessions of October, 1665, 'to make answer unto all such matters and things as on his majesties behalfe shall be objected against him for being at an unlawful meeting of the Quakers … and not depart the Cort without lycence, but there to be delt withall according to the Law …' The nailers were also brought before the church courts on several occasions, but to little effect. They continued to worship in their chosen way, in their own humble cottages, in the open at Burton Bank (Monk Bretton) and at the close of the century at the small meeting house newly erected there.

Hand-made bricks line Low Mill Furnace interior, it was probably last worked in 1840 by Henry Hartop. The author

The Old Nail Forge, Hoyland Swaine. The finest surviving local example of a nailmaker's forge. The Sheffield firm of Absalom Harrop (established in 1850) supplied its final pair of bellows. A local man, 'Nipper' Chappell, is believed to have used the forge on a part-time basis about sixty years ago. Alan Billingham

Nailmaking was a very poorly rewarded trade and the rare probate inventory which has survived tends to confirm this. Thomas Ledger 'of Darton parish' died in 1746. His tiny dwelling and workshop comprised simply of 'house', 'Shop' and 'Little Room'. The latter only contained '7 bunches of Iron', valued at £3.2s.0d. and a couple of pans. In the workshop the following items were listed:

Bellows & Anvils	*£1.5s.0d.*
Steddys & Hammers & 14 Nail tools	*£0.7s.6d.*
2 Arks [chests] *Some Nails Some old Iron and all other Hustlements* [odds & ends].	
Implements & Lumber	*£0.10s.0d.*
The total value of Thomas Ledger's worldly goods amounted to just	£9.5s.0d.

James Taylor of Pilley was a little better off. His inventory of 1740 was valued at £33. In the smithy he had 'One pair of Bellows (10 shillings), three Naile Stocks (4 shillings) and Eight Boors 3 Hammers with other Hustlements (3 shillings).' The tools were generally of very low value, showing the limited amount of capital required to set up in business and it was a trade which combined well with running a smallholding. Taylor had two heifers, a cow, a pig and a mare and grew a little hay and corn. However, the modest status of the nailers should not be under-rated. David Hey in his book *Yorkshire From AD 1000* (Longman, 1986), makes this important point: 'The humble nailing craft not only

A woodcut showing the operation of a traditional nail forge, probably from the English Midlands.

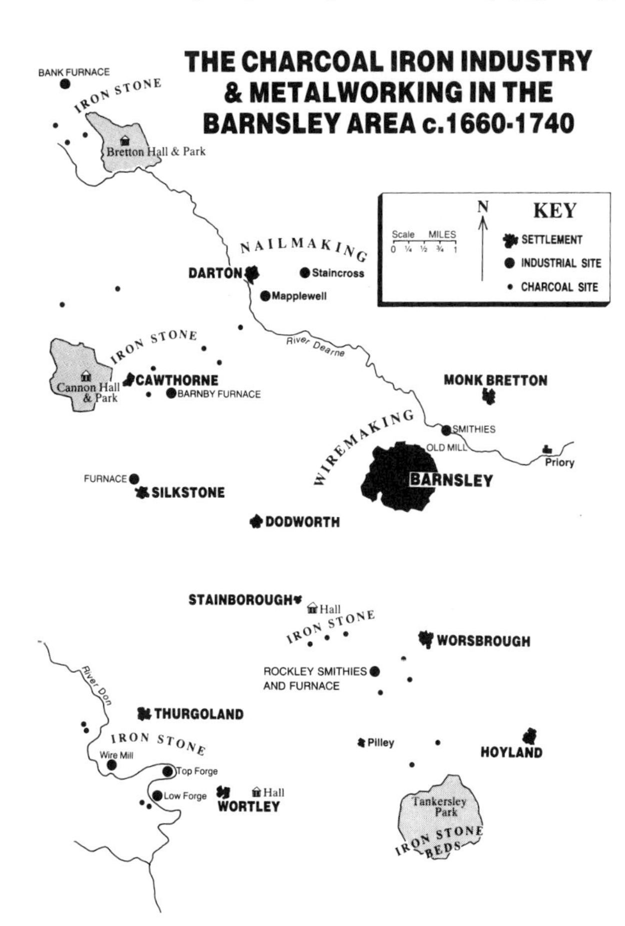

helped to sustain population growth by offering employment, it provided much of the capital needed to launch an industrial revolution'. Professor Hey goes on to give the example of Samuel and Aaran Walker, former nailer-farmers who became leading ironmasters of the north of England.

Frank Atkinson's recollections about the 'payment in kind' practice may well have evolved from earlier times when nailers would obtain supplies from chapmen who obtained the raw materials from slitting mills such as the one at Wortley. Again Professor Hey has shown how the chapmen, perhaps characters such as Joseph Crofts of Barnsley, sold the nails at distant fairs and markets, although from about 1730 the Spencer family of Cawthorne 'became directly involved in exporting nails down the rivers and along the coast to Deptford, where London merchants collected them for redistribution in southern England and America'.

A final note about a Barnsley nailer, Samuel Dilch, who died in 1748 with goods and chattels worth £30. In a chamber he had '700 of Long Iron' and 200 short iron in store, valued at £8.10s.0d. His smithy tools were valued at £1 but he had 'Book Debts' i.e. people owing him money for nails, of £4 and a further £6 was put on one side 'for the Apprentice'. Samuel Dilch was without question a well-known local citizen of Barnsley, his inventory supported and probably written by Thomas Turner, the schoolmaster and several fellow craftsmen.

Spark Lane probably derived from a Staincross family of that name who lived in the area from the early seventeenth century. At least one of the family, John, who died in 1726, was a nailmaker, a very appropriate name for a hamlet which rivalled parts of the Black Country as the nailmaking centre of England.

Wiredrawers

Of all the trades associated with Barnsley, the craft of wiremaking is the most difficult to appreciate and least understood. The fact that it existed as long ago as Tudor times but rapidly declined towards the end of the eighteenth century makes information difficult to come by. Successive writers have no doubts about its importance. Richard Blone, in his description of the British Isles, published in 1669 and quoted in a local almanac gives the following thumbnail sketch:

> *Barnsley, commonly called black Barnsley, from the colour of the soil, and from a colliery near unto it. It is situate on a hillside and near a brook. It is a reasonable well built town with stone houses, and hath a good market on a Wednesday, provisions, mault, all sorts of grain, and wyre here made, which is the only manufacture of this place.*

Historian Joseph Hunter, in his monumental *South Yorkshire* (1822) made a brief reference to the wire trade:

> *The drawing of wire was formerly the most considerable manufacture of Barnsley.*

Barnsley historian Rowland Jackson, writing in the 1850s, supported the view that our ancestors used to turn out the best wire made in England:

> *The Wire Trade is said to be of great antiquity here. We have been informed that upwards of two centuries ago Barnsley excelled every other place in the kingdom for the manufacture of this article...*

Unfortunately there has been a perplexing lack of research in order to try and test or enlighten the above statements. Certainly by the early nineteenth century the trade only employed a small number of hands since only 15 males between 18 and 45 years of age were shown as wiredrawers in a Militia List for 1806. However, this was at a time when the industry had contracted to a handful of firms and by 1814 only George Coward and William Bradley were in business.

The locational factors affecting earlier wiremaking are not easy to identify. Some possible advantages might include the availability of raw material – rod iron produced at local sources such as 'Barnsley Smithies' (Monk Bretton). Silkstone, Barnby and perhaps Rockley was readily available and the only average quality of the ore would not have been too much of a handicap to use. Interestingly, a very early integrated site was in operation on the River Don at Wortley, eventually comprising two forges, a wire mill (1624), a slitting mill and tin plate mill. This site is one of the earliest and most important in the country with a tradition of craftsmanship going back to the Elizabethan era.

Although only a small market centre Barnsley offered a commercial heart from which products could be marketed. Land and premises may also have been relatively easy to obtain though the early activity may have been very small scale, not requiring the use of water power.

An element of chance cannot be ruled out. One enterprising gentleman may have seen a gap in the developing iron industry and in so doing increased both in wealth and status. Gervase Beckett serves as an interesting example. The son of a Barnsley tradesman, by the time of his death, in 1719, this wiredrawer had become a minor public figure, had land in the town and even a windmill at Finningley.

In his will he refers to his 'wire shop' in which he probably employed several hands. Probate records of 'wiredrawers' need interpreting with care since some, such as Beckett, may have been employers rather than craftsmen.

Beckett's eldest son, also named Gervase, carried on the family wiremaking business and appears to have done well for himself. By the 1740s he refers to himself as 'gentleman' rather than wiredrawer, holding public office as a trustee of the Shaw Lands and churchwarden at St Mary's. John, the second son, became one of Barnsley's most prosperous grocers and a third son, Daniel, became a noted medical practitioner. Future generations of the family were leading citizens and benefactors of Barnsley.

When wills do survive they can be frustratingly lacking in information about the trade or business of the testator. Jesper Wright of Barnsley made his will in 1664, describing himself as 'wyremaker' and requesting to be 'buried att the discretion of my ffriends'. He may have been a Quaker. His wife Rebecca got all his goods and chattels and during her 'liffe Naturall' was to have the benefit of a close or field called 'Over Peasyill'. There is little of interest in the remainder of the will.

Curiously, the Peasehill area of the town, from the bottom of Market Hill towards old St George's church, occurs in a freehold deed now lodged in Sheffield City Archives (WM 1253). James Lockwood of Barnsley, yeoman, sold the land to Robert Bower of Barnsley, yeoman for £19.10s. in 1635, but the property was occupied by William Wright, possibly Jesper's father. The Bowers were one of the leading wiremaking families and had family links with the Keresforths.

Wiredrawers, unlike most cordwainers, were occasionally involved in property and land transactions. In 1710 for example, James Abbot of Barnsley, wiredrawer, mortgaged his freehold property to William Fenton, gentleman, for £20. It was described as 'messuage (house) with a workhouse or shop adjoining'.

Henry Fostard or Fozard was another wiremaker who frequently appears in deeds. In 1725 he obtained freehold property in Peasehill Nook from William Ellis, a Barnsley mason. Three years later Henry was involved in raising cash from his property from Thomas Frudd, the town barber-dancing master and an even more complex transaction occurred in 1738.

At least one Barnsley wiremaker lived in Jumble Lane, near May Day Green. Robert Firth, son of Samuel Firth, yeoman, leased his dwelling house 'with Barns, Shops, Folds, Orchards…' to a local joiner, Thomas Holden.

Many of the above were likely to have been the more prosperous wiremakers. There were probably many poor craftsmen who had set themselves up in little 'shops' and like many ordinary folk, strived to make a living with the help of a smallholding. These largely unknown people deserve much more recognition because they were highly skilled craftsmen.

What follows is a list of known wiredrawers who were working in Barnsley mainly during the second half of the eighteenth century. The list is by no means complete and perhaps lends some support to the claims of previous historians:

Thomas Addy, James Addy, Thomas Abbot, Jonathan Birkinshaw, Samuel Blackman, William Beachill, Matthew Birkinshaw, Robert Coward, John Coward, Thomas Denton, William Denton, William Rushforth, Samuel Rushforth, Joseph Rushforth, John Ellis, Thomas Foulweather, John Frudd, Thomas Frudd, Thos. Fostard, Robert Fostard, Thomas Gray, William Hamerton, Thomas Hill, John Hill, George Hobson, William Jackson, John Jackson, Samuel Senior, John Siswick, Richard Stafford, George Storrs, Thomas Liddall, George Laughton, Ben Mason, John Mason, Thomas Mason, William Mason, Joshua Oxley, William Oxley, John Ray, John Rollin, Ben Rooke, John Thompson, Thos. Tomlinson, William White, John Walker, George Walker, William Walker.

Wiredrawing was a process which demanded great judgement; and combined sensitive manipulation with muscle power and required the solving of a series of technical problems. An eighteenth century writer described the preparation of wire (for needlemaking) as follows:

> *Heat it under a pit of charcoal. Lay it red hot under the hammer to take away its angles, to lengthen it out and round it. Have ready a wire drawing iron with different holes; draw your steel wire through one of the larger holes to make it finer; then having re-heated it, through a smaller hole… Continue in this manner till your wire is reduced by those successive drawings to the degree of fineness which is required for the needles you intend to make.*
>
> *Universal Magazine,* September, 1764.

Fine wire was also made for making fish hooks and for use in the watchmaking trade. There has always been a close link with the textile industry. Hard wire was produced for the teeth of cotton

Traditional wiredrawing, from a German manual.

and woolcards and there may well have been some demand for this type of wire on the farm. Riddles and sieves were frequently mentioned in probate inventories.

We are still in the dark about many aspects of the old hand methods of early wiremaking but oral evidence collected from traditional craftsmen and the survival of their basic tools helps to give a fuller but by no means complete picture of the wiremaker's art.

The basic aim of the wiredrawer was to reduce, in cross-sectional area, a metal rod, usually iron, later steel though even precious metals such as gold or silver could be used for use in fine clothing.

A vital piece of equipment was a wortle, an iron or steel plate, about 1-1½ inches in thickness. It contained a series of tapering holes graduating from about ½ inch diameter. The wire was pulled through successive holes, beginning with the largest, gradually reducing in diameter. The wire may have been drawn cold but every so often it had to be annealed. This caused considerable problems since the heating of the metal in order to temper and strengthen it resulted in 'scaling' which had to be removed eventually by the use of acid and lime.

The punching or 'pricking' of the holes in the wortle was a highly skilled affair and in later times resulted in a specialised trade with the unusual name of the wortle plate pricker. The art was in making holes in the drawing plate by means of a hand made taper punch, skilfully made on the blacksmith's fire and gradually tapered down via grinding on sandstones and finishing on the craftsman's leather overall. A hole could be punched from a few thousandths to one quarter of an inch.

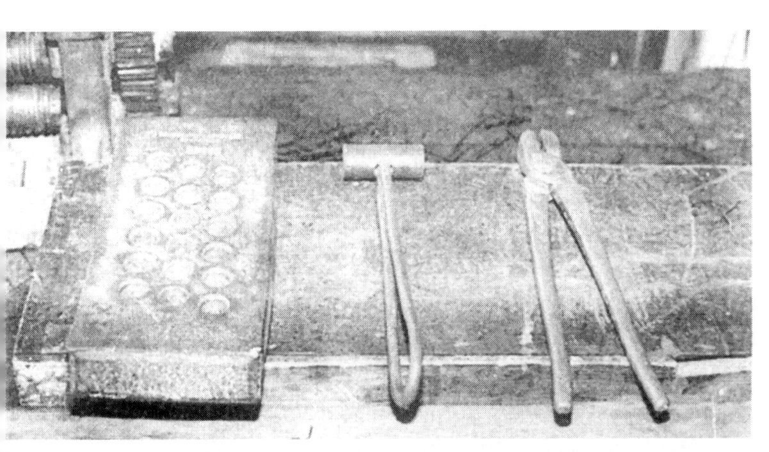

Wortle (left) and wiredrawing tools, Calderdale Industrial useum, Halifax. The author

Another problem to overcome was that the holes in the wortle slightly increased in diameter, dependant on the type of metal being drawn during the pulling through process. The wiredrawer had to allow for this difference when producing wire of a specific diameter. For example, for wire of one eighth of an inch diameter the drawing hole would need to be perhaps two to three thousandths of an inch smaller. The

Wortley Wire Mill, from an old photograph.

speed of the pull was also crucial to the thickness of the wire, another interesting facet of the wiredrawers art.

The wiredrawer's remark of getting paid 'for meking oyles' thus makes more sense when the process is explained.

Early wiredrawing in Barnsley probably took place in small workshops and the entire process would have been carried out by hand, wortles held by tongs and the wire drawn by a heavy tool called a 'dog' via wheels and cranks, pulling through a few feet at a time. However, the Old Wire Mill at Thurgoland, near to the village of Wortley, was one of the earliest industrial sites of its kind using water-power. Believed to have been built in 1624, it formed part of the 'Wortley group' on the River Don using locally produced rod iron. Interestingly, the Old Mill continued in use up to the 1920s producing needle wire, with the Jagger family running the business over three or four generations. Longmuir and Kenworthy, in an article which appeared in the journal *Engineering* in 1913 state that the mill was originally a single storey structure, rebuilt on its foundations in about 1850.

Jonathan Swinden was one of the first masters at the Wortley Wire Mill. He died in January 1728/9 and an inventory of his goods and chattels was taken by his friends and neighbours William Wordsworth, Matthew Butterworth, Robert Askew and James Hirst. Swinden's dwelling house consisted of kitchen, kitchen closet, middle room, dining room, dining room closet, little parlour, best chamber, middle chamber, meal chamber, chamber and cellar. He also had a brewhouse, a 'new building' used mainly for farm gear, a barn and a stable. He lived in some comfort and his possessions included a considerable amount of silver plate. He also had tea and coffee making facilities (luxury items of the time), soft furnishings, a 'clock and case', china

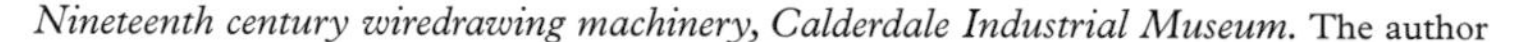

Nineteenth century wiredrawing machinery, Calderdale Industrial Museum. The author

The Wire Trellis Inn. (Tasker Collection)

ware, 'delph ware' – including a punch bowl, and a variety of desirable items of furniture. References to his industrial interests are listed under the heading 'Stable' where he had the following items in store:

		£ s. d.
Old Iron	*2.7.12 (cwts, stones and pounds)*	*1.7.10*
New Iron	3.4.0	2.2.6
Raw Iron	5.4.9	*1.7.6*
Steel		*0.2.0*
Lead		*0.1.6*

Also of interest is evidence that Swinden was overseeing the exploitation of coal in the locality since the inventory included 'Coals on Pitt Hill' (£15) and 'Tools Coal pitt turns Ropes & bucketts' £2.10s.0d. Early industrial activity of some scale was taking place on a little site on the Don, activity which would appear to have contributed to the lifestyle of Mr Jonathan Swinden, gentleman.

By the middle of the eighteenth century the local wire trade began to recognise the implications of falling demand and increased competition. Letters exchanged between our area and London included comments such as 'the wire trade dwindles much' and even advice on the sale of wire stock and newly erected works.

According to the *Universal British Directory* of 1790 there were only nine wire manufacturies in Barnsley and in a few years there were only two: George Coward and William Bradley. From 1829 to 1840 the Barnsley wire trade was represented by the firms George Coward and William Horsfall. After Coward's death, Horsfall, who started business as an ironmonger on Market Hill in the 1780s, became the sole proprietor. Horsfall's works was located to the rear of shops on Market Hill and the steel wire produced there was apparently held in high esteem by watchmaking countries such as Switzerland and America. The old wiremaking premises were eventually bought in about 1905 by another famous Barnsley firm of ironmongers – Messrs. Reynolds and Wadsworth and when a new warehouse was built traces of the old works disappeared.

The Old Wire Trellis, an inn situated near the Gas Nook on May Day Green once served as a permanent reminder of one of Barnsley's most interesting trades.

Postscript

Barnsley wiredrawers were obtaining substantial quantities of iron from Wadsley and Attercliffe forges. In 1690, for example, iron valued at £251.15s.10d. was 'sent to Barnsley.'

S.I.R. 12, Sheffield Archives, courtesy of Professor D Hey.

8 COAL

Early Mining

Coal has been mined in and around the Barnsley area from the early Middle Ages. In 1293 a man was killed in a pit near to his home at Bull Haw, Silkstone. Freeholders from Woolley were accused of getting coal too near to the highway in a court case of 1302. A deed of 1397 shows that Silkstone coal was being worked. In about 1423 locals were summoned to appear at a court in Darton for digging coal from under the lord's wastes.

Monastic houses were also involved in early mining ventures. In 1491 the Cluniac monks of Pontefract obtained a Barnsley coal pit for £8, said to have a life of about sixteen years. The Monk Bretton monks had mineral interests in the Dearne valley and after the Dissolution their coal-bearing land passed into lay hands for further development. A Crown inquiry of 1597, found in The National Archives, records a coal mine in the manor of Monk Bretton which lay in or under a quarry and therefore could not be recovered 'without great labour and expense', though mines were said to be present in 'almost all' adjacent manors.

A late eighteenth century pit-top scene in the Midlands. Wayland

Such scattered references need interpreting with considerable caution. Early mining was on a very small scale and it is not surprising to find proof of coal extraction from an exposed coalfield.

Black Barnsley

For a few days in February 1985, towards the end of the long miners' strike, scores of people flocked to a Barnsley council allotment site, behind Shaw Lane cricket ground, and helped themselves to an exposed five-foot seam of coal. The coal-pickers were in fact encroaching on land from which coal had been won from at least the sixteenth century.

Some of the earliest Barnsley pits were concentrated on the rising ground to the south and west of the town where outcrops could be identified and reached with relative ease. Here the land was a mixture of commons, wastes and moors which Daniel Defoe described as 'having a black hue or colour' and being the reason for the popular description of 'Black Barnsley'. This bleak landscape also included islands of cultivated land around the hamlets of Gawber and Pogmoor, part of the Shaw Lands which had been sub-let through a charitable trust since Tudor times, and in the south lay the ancient Keresforth estate, occupied by the Armitage family in the seventeenth century.

Before 1688 much of the coal bearing land was owned by the crown but mining rights were frequently granted. In 1578, for example, the Queen, by letters patent, demised to John

Coal-pickers exploit the shallow seams, near Broadway. Barnsley Chronicle

Ramsden of Longley, gentleman and Richard Norfolk of Barnsley, yeoman, 'all that her majesty's mine of coal situate on Barnsley Moor, at a certain yearly rent'. Water soon flooded the workings and it was found necessary to drain the water through Thomas Keresforth's lands. The landowner's compliance was achieved in lieu of an annual payment of £5 and ten wain loads of coal during the life of the mine. Even so, Keresforth was a reluctant party to the agreement according to a bill of complaint issued in 1598.

Despite legal disputes, coal continued to be mined in or near to the Keresforth estate throughout the 1690s. Leases and agreements involved the Beaumonts of Darton who granted mining rights to Thomas Rhodes of Keresforth Hill, yeoman and Abraham Rock of Worsbrough, yeoman. In 1693 Rock agreed to pay Rhodes £5 'for such coales as I gott in coale pitt close' along with a further sum to cover recent coal sales and 'such sume or sumes of money as any two indifferent men shall say his Coale Pitt Tooles, Ropes and Sledges and Turnes and Roulers are worth'.

Although drainage was the main problem there are occasional early references to underground gases. In July, the unfortunate James Townend met his death from an explosion of firedamp. Abraham de la Pryme noted in his diary for 28 July 1697 that 'Near Gauber Hall, a mile beyond Barnsley, there is a great coal-pitt which is on fire, and has burned many years'.

Coal under the moor continued to be exploited during the early Stuart period. John Blythman, a well-to-do gentleman who lived at New Laithes (Athersley) gave 'any lease title, interest and term of years which I have of the coal mine within the commons and wastes of Barnsley … unto Robert Burdet' in his will of 1620. Coal mines were also recorded on Barnsley Moor and Skiers Moor (Gawber) in a parliamentary survey taken in 1649.

A Yorkshire Collier. From Walker's *Costumes of Yorkshire*

Local historian Arthur Clayton and the old Silkstone coal wagonway. The author

Late-seventeenth Century Developments

By the late – seventeenth century coal mining was an integral part of the rural scene but only a handful of seasonal workers would appear to have been employed at each pit. Coal was in local demand as a domestic fuel, for use in smithies and furnaces, in brewing and for a variety of crafts and trades. The success or failure of a mining enterprise was highly dependant on keeping the workings free of flooding. The price of the coal at the pit-head was cheap but transport costs, even over very short distances were considerable. A load of coal delivered to poor residents of Worsbrough cost the parish four shillings in July 1703 but Nathanial Shaw was paid eleven shillings 'for leading'. Similarly, a stock of coal from a Kendal Green pit cost two shillings but a delivery distance of about half a mile more than doubled the bill.

After the Restoration, the coal under Barnsley Moor attracted the interest of two ironmasters: William Simpson, a wealthy Sheffield attorney who sub-let to local man, Gamaliel Milner. Milner, who lived at Burton Grange, was a prominent Quaker. In 1675 he was able to bestow legacies in excess of £1,000, including £100 'to be raised out of the coales now upon the hill' and, significantly, 'the growing profits of the lease of the coalepittes yet to expire'.

In 1676 Simpson went into partnership with the Hon. Sydney Wortley, Esquire, the head of one of the leading and least popular gentry families of the region. The Wortleys had been controlling Barnsley's coal bearing land since at least 1663 when Sir Francis paid £3 in tax, the highest amount recorded for local landowners for 'mills and coal pittes'. By 1688 Wortley had entered into an agreement with Richard Firth of Masborough, gentleman, concerning 'All those coal mynes ... upon the waste or moor called Barnsley Moor ... late the possession of Gamalial Milner, deceased' but he preferred to sub-let to Valentine Hurt, an Ecclesfield man.

During the next few years Wortley's interest in Barnsley coal became far more direct. In 1696 he acquired another crown lease, bought out the other royalty owners and leased the mines to

Ann Ambler and Will Dyson (crosslapped) being drawn up the pit-shaft. From the 1842 Report on Children in Coal Mines.

two well-known local families: the Rookes (William and John) and the Shippens (Peter and John). More than twenty years of active mining began.

The Rookes and the Ellisons

The Rookes were a minor gentry family with apothecary and drapery interests in Barnsley. They had family links in Leeds where William Rooke, merchant, rose to become alderman and, in 1683, mayor. The Barnsley Rookes still had coal mining interests in 1720 when a William Rooke entered into an agreement with John Rooke and William Wood of Monk Bretton concerning land and property in Barnsley, including 'one Collyery or Coal Mine... in hilly close and the Ginns or Machines thereto and other utensils belonging to the said collyery or Coal Mine'. Hilly Close is marked on William Fairbank's enclosure map of 1777, locating the mine in the Pogmoor area, near to Slack Hills Farm, in meadowland which had the upper part of the Sough Dyke as its southern boundary.

The Rookes had marriage connections with the Ellisons of Pogmoor who also mined coal on the moor. When farmer Richard Ellison died in 1699 he had a 'Debt Booke and Coales oth' Hill' worth £77 as part of an inventory valuation of £310. In 1727 another Richard Ellison was described as 'collier' when witnessing a deed in which his father, William, was one of the principal parties. A year later, William Ellison paid Joseph Crofts of Barnsley £80 for the right to mine, over thirty years, 'all and every myne and mynes of coales in two closes of land called Pogmoor closes ... with fuel and free liberty to dig drain sink for and make pitts soughs and trenches and to get stack and carry away the coales from therein'.

The combination of farming with business and land speculation worked well for the Ellisons. In his will of 1734 William Ellison was able to give legacies of over £700 to his family with the remainder of his mining lease passed on to sons Richard and Jonathan. The latter was described as 'collier' in a deed of the same year, a term which was then not necessarily a labouring one. Perhaps, more appropriately, a Thomas Ellison was described as 'coalmaster' in 1745.

The Barnsley Moor Collieries

Business papers relating to Sydney Wortley's Barnsley Moor collieries are held in Sheffield Archives (Wharncliffe Muniments/114). The family also had considerable mining interests in North East England and Wortley took advantage of this when administrating the Barnsley mines. There were frequent consulations with his Newcastle staff. In 1713, for example, John Wake and Adam Ogall, both Newcastle men, were employed in Barnsley over a five month period investigating potential new sites by sinking test bores. The job of pit sinking, however, was undertaken by local men, George Earnshaw and William Fletcher who sank two pits at a cost of £5.11s.8d. The shafts of Barnsley pits varied in depth from 22 yards at Townend to over 80 yards on the moor.

The local situation was complicated because of the relatively fast rate of advancement of mining and the subsequent need to gain the co-operation of small landowners. A map drawn by John Carr, one of Wortley's Newcastle viewers (mining engineer) shows a wave of workings advancing towards inclosures owned by local families such as Archdale, Copley and Elmhirst.

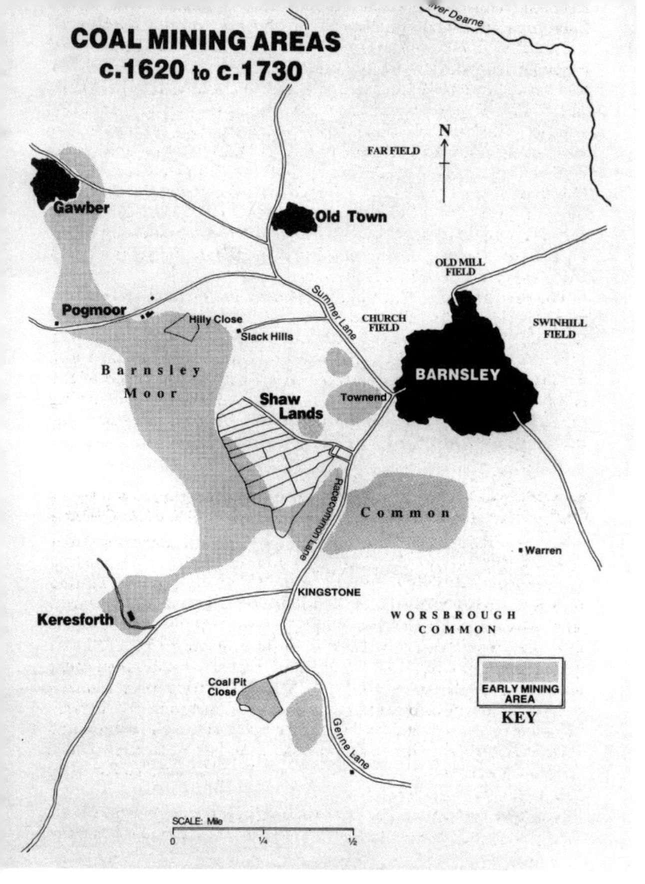

Technical aspects of mining caused the greatest concern to Wortley and his advisers, especially the problem of flooding. In 1712, for example, John Carr, writing from Durham, expressed serious doubts about the frequent flooding of the Barnsley colliery but offered a possible remedy:

> *Your Tennants have absolutely lost the Water Levell which Occation all the Dipp side and best of your Colliery to Lye a new Sough soe that the tenant can get such a quantity of Coales as he ought to have to enable him to pay his rent.*

The mine appears to have been limited to working during dry spells, probably in great haste and in a random and unsafe manner:

> *And for want of the water course being open and free they struggle and get Coales any way they can; whereby they work the Colliery irregularly and out of power and leave the walls or pillars of Coale too thinn and slender to Support the Roof.*

Barnsley Colliery October the 24th 1719

old workings

John Carr's sketch map of Barnsley Colliery. (Courtesy of the Earl of Wharncliffe and the Director of Sheffield City Libraries and Information Services)

The driving of soughs or levels involved considerable expense but there were long term benefits. In 1713 Wortley was given encouraging advice concerning the sinking of a pit and drainage level 'in the highway leadin in from Doctor Elmhurst to Barnsley Moore', probably from Genne Lane towards Racecommon, and 'if soe Coles may be got there for twenty or thirty years att the least'.

Generally speaking, however, men native to the coalfield had the best knowledge of local conditions. Richard Fisher, who described himself as 'Colyar' in his will of 1729 was employed by Shippen as 'his man' at the coal pits which meant supervision of the work at pits in the Townend area and on the moor. Fisher was far removed from being a hewer or labourer at

Half-naked girl with belt and chain dragging coal tubs underground: a picture that shocked early Victorian England. British Museum

Coal engine at Norcroft (Cawthorne),' from a sketch by John C Nattes c. 1810. Barnsley M.B.C. Dept. of Amenities and Leisure

the pits. The colliery correspondence shows him to be a man of considerable skill and authority, his views being frequently relayed to Wortley via Shippen. Here is an example, from 1716, interestingly involving the suggestion of installing a pumping engine:

> *Richard Fisher saith that a Drift of Coles might be got by bringing up a Sugh from the Upor End or Northwest End of the Towne of Barnsley and by seting an Ingan att ye Head of ye Sugh to draw up water 20 yards, this might be Don without going through any land but ye common…*

In 1716 a scheme was devised whereby Wortley might secure the right to mine coal on land owned by Elmhirst, Copley and Archdale, men who already had coal mining interests. A series of careful negotiations ensued, with Carr advising Wortley to offer no more than £25 per acre, an investment which could result in '£300 a year Profitt at Least'.

By 1724 coalmaster John Shippen was paying £24 per annum to Wortley, less an 'allowance' of about £9 in lieu of land tax, the provision of a horse gin and coal provided for Wortley's own use. The 'Barnsley Moor Colliery' consisted of some fourteen pits, two described as 'old' and two as 'water pits'. The coal stocks amounted to 597 dozen, perhaps 1,200 tons, valued at £75, a relatively small output compared with mines on Woolley moor. Drainage of the pits continued to be a major problem. Technical solutions were possible but the expense outweighed the value of the venture.

RECITAL

Of Part of the Truſt Deed,

Whereby the Truſtees of the Shaw Lands, in the Townſhip of Barnſley hold the ſame Lands.

THAT the Truſtees ſhall pay forth and beſtow all the yearly Rents and Profits by them, or any of them, to be in anywiſe lawfully made, had, received and taken of in and upon the ſaid mentioned Premiſes only, in and about the Common Wealth and Profit of the whole Inhabitants recent, now and ever hereafter being within the ſaid Town and Townſhip of Barnſley, towards the making and amending of their common Panniers and Carts there, for the true Service of their Prince or Princes in their Wars, paying their common Tax or Taxes, repareling of their Church or Highways, making or mending of their common Butts, Stocks, Pindfolds, or Wells therein and about, or belonging to Things appertaining to the whole Common Wealth of the ſaid Townſhip of Barnſley; and if it fortune at any Time, that there be any Remainder of the yearly Rents and Profits aforeſaid, over and above theſe Articles aforeſaid performed, fulfilled and done, that then the ſame be put forth in a Stock by the aforeſaid Feofees and their Heirs, partly by the Advice of the greateſt Part of the moſt honeſt and diſcreet Men, being Inhabitants of the ſaid Town and Townſhip of Barnſley, to the Intent to make ſome Increaſe thereof, for the Profit of all the Inhabitants aforeſaid; and that the ſaid Feofees, their Heirs and Aſſigns, or ſome of them, ſhall, from Time to Time make new Feofees, for a continual Performance of theſe Articles.

Barnſley, May 16*th*, 1798.

In the Name of God Amen I
Joseph Barrowclough of Carlton in the parish of Royston and
County of York Collier being of sound mind and memory but
considering the Uncertainty of life do make and ordain this
my last Will and Testament in manner following First I give
and bequeath unto my Daughter Grace Guest the Wife of George
Guest of Royston aforesaid Cordwainer, to my Daughter Hannah
Barrowclough of the City of London Spinster, to my Daughter
Ann Wainwright wife of Robert Wainwright of Smithies
in the Parish of Royston aforesaid Weaver and to my Son
Joseph Barrowclough of Hoyle in the said County of
York Fellmonger one shilling apiece to be paid by my
Executrix herein after named, then I give and bequeath
To Elizabeth my dear and loving Wife all the Tennant
Right of all the farm and lands with their and every of
their Appurtenances also the Cottage I now live on with
its Appurtenances To hold to her during her natural
life at the Will and pleasure of the Right Honourable
Edward Wortley Esquire his heirs and Assigns, and all
my Personal Estate whatsoever I give and bequeath
to my said Dear Wife her Executors and Administrators
for Ever and do make her sole Executrix of this my
last Will and Testament hereby revoking all other
Wills heretofore by me made In Witness whereof I have
hereunto set my hand and Seal this ninth day of March
in the Year of our Lord One thousand Seven hundred
and fifty Six

Signed Sealed published and declared by the said Testator Joseph Barrowclough as his last Will and Testament, and we the persons underwritten have hereunto at the said Testators request in his presence and in the presence of Each other have set our names hereto as Witnesses.

Joseph his + mark Barrowclough

Rebekah her mark Goldthorpe

Ann her mark Naylor

Thomas Turner

Will of Joseph Barrowclough of Carlton, collier, 9 March 1756. Borthwick Institute of Historical Research

On his death in 1727, Sydney Wortley's extensive coal mining interests in Northumberland and Durham and 'all my coalmines and collieries opened and unopened which are situate in and being in the manner of Barnsley …' were passed on to his son and heir, Edward. Within two years the Barnsley Moor mines were abandoned. In 1739 the Duke of Leeds' steward for the manor of Barnsley, attorney William Marsden, wrote to Edward Wortley requesting arrears of rent 'Though the Coalmine is not wrought, nor has been for many years'.

Mining certainly continued in the Worsbrough area, for in 1755, John Tasker, Thomas Mosforth and George Burdet were 'slain by the damp' in Mr Boden's coal pit, off Genne Lane.

The Colliery papers do not give any information about the workmen. It is likely that their numbers were small, perhaps no more than ten, including surface workers. Only a handful of colliers are recorded in the Barnsley church registers, mainly during the 1650s and 1660s but occupations are not generally given at this time, making any conclusion difficult. From 1777 to 1790 when occupations are fairly well recorded some 24 colliers are listed with families such as Scorah and Wyke prominent.

Coal mining remained a small-scale activity in Barnsley so long as the area remained landlocked; the opening of the Barnsley Canal at the close of the eighteenth century was an obvious incentive for the location of new mines but it was not really until the coming of the railways, in the middle decades of the nineteenth century, that Barnsley emerged as a 'mining town' and the age of terrible pit disasters began.

9 GLASS

Barnsley's long tradition of making quality glass products is currently maintained at Stairfoot where the famous Rotherham firm of Beatson Clark has operated since purchasing the old premises of Rylands Glass in 1929; and at Monk Bretton where Redfearn National glass plc (Rexam) has a large modern factory.

Joshua and Sam Redfearn had established their original glass and bottle works in 1862 at Old Mill, on a site bounded by the Barnsley Canal and Harborough Hill Road. In 1872 Wood Brothers and Co. erected glassworks between Pontefract Road and the Dearne and Dove Canal at the edge of the small mining community of Hoyle Mill, who were still suffering from the Oaks

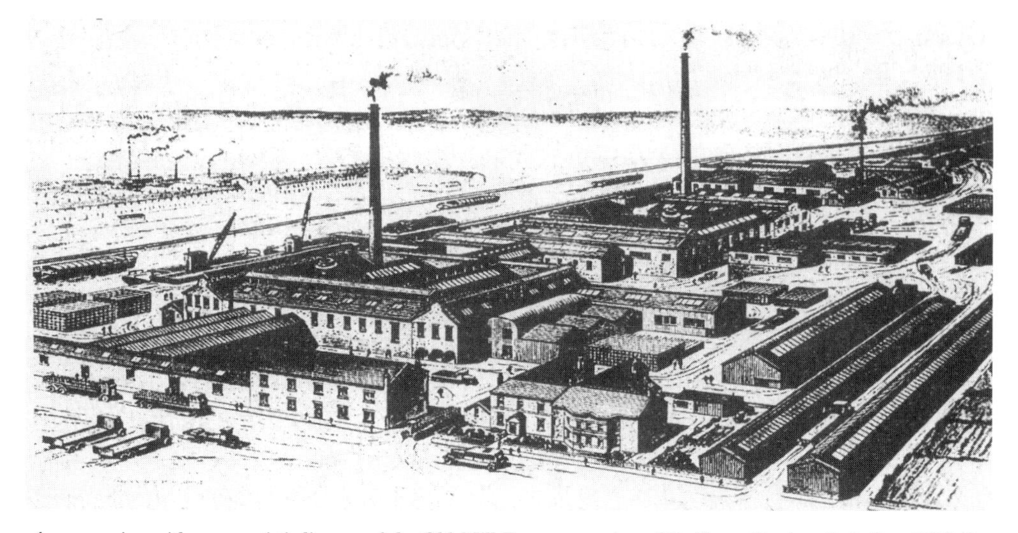

An engraving with some artistic licence, of the Old Mill Factory premises of Redfearn Brothers Ltd. (late 1930s?)

These marvellous photographs of Wood Bros, workers were taken in 1908, probably by Barnsley photographer, Warner Gothard. Sheffield Archives

Colliery disaster. Here the furnace produced pressed glass with labour imported from Newcastle-upon-Tyne and Gateshead but workmen were soon transferred from the Woods' Worsbrough Dale factory which had to be abandoned. The Worsbrough works was established in 1828 but within a few years was in the capable hands of brothers John and James Wood in partnership with Richard Perkes. As flint glassmakers, engravers and etchers the Wood Bros, factories made articles of outstanding merit.

The Hoyle Mill glassworks was closed and demolished in 1980, a sad end to a familiar industrial landmark which had served as a workplace for generations of Barnsley people.

Wood-cut illustration of a glass-furnace from Georgius Agricola's *De Re Metallica, 1556.* British Glass Makers Federation

Gawber

A public auction held at the *White Bear Inn* (Royal Hotel), Church Street on 7 March 1821 also marked the end of an era for a famous Barnsley glasshouse when 'that freehold estate, glasshouse and farms situate at Gawber Hall… in the occupation of Mr. Thorp' went under the hammer.

William Thorp, a grocer from the glassmaking centre of Houghton, near Ferrybridge, moved into the impressive timber-framed Gawber Hall during the 1730s and erected a glassworks about 200 yards north-west of his residence. Gawber was then part of the ancient parish of Darton and 'glassmaker' became a frequent entry in the church registers.

Business records do not survive for the Gawber works but excavations carried out by Denis Ashurst between 1964 and 1972 has shown that clear window glass and coloured bottle glass was

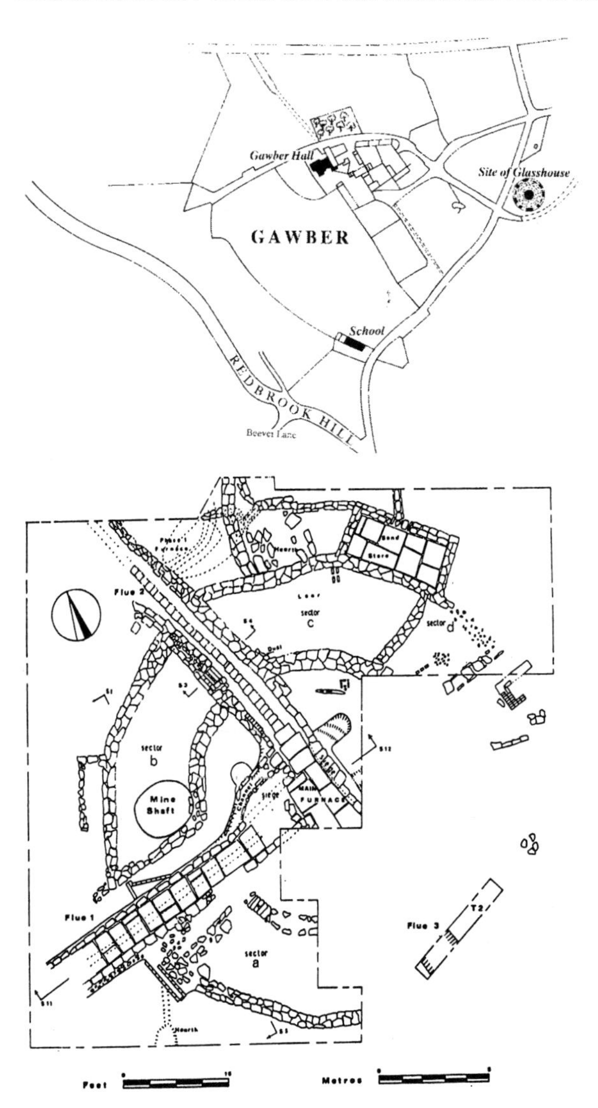

Map showing site of Gawber Hall and Glasshouse in Gawber.

Plan of the Gawber cone. Courtesy of Denis Ashurst and *Post-Medieval Archaeology*

The Catcliffe cone.

Examples of wine bottle seals found at Gawber. Denis Ashurst/Post-Medieval Archaeology

being produced. The cone coal-fired glasshouse must have been an impressive sight perhaps resembling the larger and unique example still visible at Catcliffe, near Rotherham which dates from about 1740.

An earlier furnace, of primitive construction, was also revealed during the excavations and was probably last fired between 1690 and 1735. The erection of the main cone destroyed most of its simple structure but it had once been housed under a heavy tiled roof on a timber frame.

The Thorp family leased the works during the eighteenth century, with sons Samuel and Richard in control from about 1774. Samuel Thorp, who became increasingly involved in coal mining ventures, had become a man of substance and moved to the country residence of Banks Hall, Cawthorne. Richard died in 1783, having managed the glasshouse on his own for several years. Samuel Thorp's lack of interest was understandable in the economic circumstances of the time. The Gawber glasshouse would have had to compete with more modern South Yorkshire works with better transport facilities. Also, the excise duty on glass was enough to discourage even the most conscientious of owners who had to pay tax on broken bottles and cope with ridiculous regulations concerning the collection of the tax.

Yet the Gawber glassworks, even in its twilight period, had a considerable reputation. An entry in the *Universal British Directory* of 1790 stated that 'A glass manufactury of black bottles is also carried on near this town [Barnsley] superior to any of the kind elsewhere'. Edward Miller, in his *History and Antiques of Doncaster and its Vicinity* (1804) referred to Barnsley as having '...a considerable linen manufactory and another of glass bottles'. As late as 1812 when John Bigland's *A Topographical and Historical Description of York* was published the author was still able to say that 'Barnsley carries on a considerable trade in making wire and also black bottles, which are here manufactured and are esteemed of an excellent quality'.

Evolution of the wine bottle from 1650 (left) to 1800. British Glassmakers' Federation

There are many problems that archaeologists have to try and overcome when excavating glasshouse sites and when interpreting finds. For example, items found on the site need to be distinguished from imported cullet (broken glass/waste). There is little chance of finding perfectly preserved articles; imperfect items would have been smashed and returned to the crucible rather than discarded. Denis Ashurst was able to excavate $1^1/_2$ tons of glass from the site, all in a fragmentary condition.

The colour of the glass found on the Gawber site ranged from various shades of green and brown to black and blue. An interesting variety of wine bottle shapes was apparent and some fascinating examples of bottle seals were found. Phials or pharmaceutical bottles were also produced, almost certainly before 1795 and though they may have been sold over a wide area provide an interesting link with the town's thriving apothecaries. Examples of clear (lead and soda-based) glass was also found and there were large quantitites of window glass of the crown type.

The glasshouse was in a ruiness state in 1823 and the cone appears to have been knocked down either then or shortly afterwards but the site is marked on the first edition of the six inch to one mile ordnance survey map surveyed in the 1850s. Surviving buildings were used as a Sunday School, then a Day School until bought and used as a joiner's shop between 1856 and 1874. Probably in further decline, it was then used as a cart shed and later as a tripe-dressing works, the structure falling down in about 1910. The building stone was removed for road making so that by the 1920s nothing remained above ground. The only remaining feature was the stone-flagged floor of the workshop. But for the archaeological investigation and research by Denis Ashurst little would have been known about a site which was clearly of importance in the context of English glassmaking history. Despite this even its local value has been lost since it is now obscured by modern housing.

Silkstone

William Morton, one of the glassmakers who worked at Gawber, had family connections in Silkstone where the early glassmakers had settled in the middle of the seventeenth century.

In about 1650 two brothers: John and Peter Pilmey and their sister Mary' established glassworks by a water mill in a pleasant wooded valley almost within the shadow of the medieval church. The Pilmeys were second or third generation immigrants, still referred to as 'frenchmen' in the church registers. With government encouragement, foreign glassmakers began to settle in England bringing with them family traditions from areas such as Normandy and Lorraine in eastern France. The Pilmeys had come to Silkstone via the English Midlands and Manchester. Glasshouses were often small family businesses, moving to wherever custom or fuel led them.

Two important developments occurred around the time the Pilmeys were setting up in business. In 1615 James I, concerned at the rapid disappearance of woodland, had banned wood as a fuel for glass furnaces. Sir Robert Mansell, a former MP for King's Lynn and Vice-Admiral of the navy, obtained a monopoly of the entire English glass industry but his domination ended in the mid-1650s. The way was then clear for independent glassmakers to set up in business. On the technical side, in the mid-1670s, George Ravencroft's experiments using oxide of lead and sand to make a new type of crystal glass was eventually successful although the term 'flint glass' continued to be used for many years. In recognition of his achievement he was allowed to use a raven head seal on his products and English glassmakers were leaders in the making of clear, colourless glass. The Ravenscroft patent expired in 1681, enabling glasshouses such as Silkstone to make new, fine glassware.

Regulation, innovation and fashion were obvious influences on the glassmakers but though Silkstone had favourable natural advantages: coal and clay and

Making window glass using the 'crown' technique. Roger Dodsworth/Broadfield House Glass Museum

Humorous print, after Rowlandson, showing interior of an English eighteenth century bottlehouse. Roger Dodsworth/Broadfield House Glass Museum

potash were plentiful but how the Pilmeys knew about the potential of the site may have been as much a consequence of luck than planning. Dennis Ashurst has uncovered the fact that the Pilmeys worked in the same Manchester area glasshouses as Francis Bristow who had moved to Wentworth in 1631 on a site provided by the first Earl of Stafford. The Wentworth enterprise was short-lived, ending in 1642 but the Pilmeys may well have gained local knowledge from Bristowe.

Whatever the reason, the Pilmeys integrated with the local community. John married Abigail Scott, widow of a local well-to-do farmer and Mary married John Moore, a respected citizen of Barnsley.

By 1695 Abigail Pilmey was almost certainly in sole charge of the glassworks and had probably been the main driving force behind the business for several years. She was widowed for a second time and her brother-in-law, Peter Pilmey was probably in poor health. Her feelings about the crippling excise duties on glass were publicly expressed in 1696 when, along with William Clifton of Houghton, she petitioned parliament. Despite the careful packing of fragile glass products there were bound to have been many breakages – all subject to tax – on the hazardous and mostly uphill journey to Barnsley and beyond.

Abigail Pilmey died on 10 December 1698 and her probate inventory, taken just ten days later, provides invaluable information about glassmaking in Silkstone. In the 'glass houses' she had:

	£ s. d.
11 greenhouse pipes	*11.00*
10 whitehouse pipes	*08.00*
Tools belonging to both houses & all the old Iron	*2.10.00*

Details of the kind of glass made are found in the final inventory items under the heading 'In all the warehouses'. The stock of glass 'both flinte, green ware & ordinary (£40)' refers to common green window glass and the flint (or 'crystal') of the new type of clear sparkling glass. Further evidence of crystal glass production is apparent by the listing of 'Breeley', a high quality sand from Brierley in Staffordshire and 'Red Lead'. A large quantity of rape ashes, valued at £20, provided a source of alkali for green bottles and a stock of salt petre (potassium nitrate) was used as a flux for crystal glass. 'Blew powder' and 'Manganeese' were employed as colouring agents. Reference to 'Vyall metall' shows that the Pilmeys were actively involved in making phials for the expanding medical trade. The overall impression is of a multi-purpose glassworks producing high quality goods as well as everyday items.

A group of seventeenth century medicine bottles. Victoria and Albert Museum

By 1700 a small complex of buildings had developed at the foot of Church Hill near to the old mill. There were two glass-houses, two warehouses and various farm buildings. Part of the site, known as Pot House from at least 1706, was sketched by Nattes in about 1810, when, like many

'Pottery at Silkstone', from a drawing by John C Nattes (1765–1822). Barnsley M.B. Council Dept. of Leisure and Amenities

Pothouses at Silkstone in 1937. Barnsley Chronicle

other small ex-glassworks, it was used as a pottery. The site was also photographed in 1937 by the *Barnsley Chronicle*, shortly before the demolition of the house. The gabled dwelling in the photograph was almost certainly the old Pilmey residence, having 'A.P.' (Abigail Pilmey) and 'Memento Mori' (Remember You Must Die) inscribed over the main doorway. Most of the Pot House was removed in 1965 and the land excavated for drainage improvement but a few interesting items have been found. The site, now occupied by a modern garden centre, remains of considerable historic importance.

After Abigail's death Pot House passed to her son (by her first marriage), John Scott who in his own will of 1706 left the house 'wherin my mother Pillmey lately dwelt', glassworks, tools, stock of 'glass ware & bottles' and 'all other ingredients for making glass wares' to his eldest son, also named John.

It is not known for certain if the new owners had the inclination, or perhaps more importantly if their workmen had the necessary skills to continue glassmaking in the Pilmey tradition. The secrets of the trade were not handed on lightly. Reference is made to the 'old

Site of Pothouses in 1988. Part of the Old Mill can be seen on the right. Alan Billingham

Glasshouse with a tiled shelter, from Ars Vitaria Experimentis *by Johann Knunckel, 1679.* Collins

Glasshouse' in John Scott senior's inventory and the former Pilmey residence is very poorly furnished, perhaps even empty. The Scott family established a pottery and were also busy working coal on or very near to the site, although the glasshouse was still mentioned in a deed of 1720 when the younger Scott conveyed it to his brother, William.

The Silkstone and Gawber glassworks serve as very interesting examples of early industrial enterprise near to Barnsley. The Pilmeys brought with them traditional Lorrainer skills and adapted them to English conditions using new technology. At Gawber traditional skills were also evident though the venture involved considerable investment, closing at a time when mass production methods were beginning to appear. Both works were attracted by the pull of Barnsley coal, and, along with a few other Yorkshire sites, were able to supply a large part of northern England with window glass, common bottles and fine table ware.

The Silkstone glassworks site, researched by Dr Denis Ashurst, is now recognised as being of world-importance, following excavations by English Heritage in 2003. Part of rose grower Tom Horsfield's 'backgarden' site has been protected for future generations and scheduled as an ancient monument.

Dr Denis Ashurst (left) and Tom Horsfield at Pot House, Sept, 2003. Barnsley Chronicle

10 Tanning

When John Hobson returned to his Dodworth Green home after a busy day at the tanyard there is little doubt that his household were immediately aware of his presence. Tanning could be a lucrative business, even though Hobson's tannery was probably on the wane towards the end of his life, but all tanners had an unmistakable occupational hazard: foul smells.

The finished pelts were quite pleasant, in fact the aroma of newly tanned leather was very attractive, but it was the various solutions in which the skins were placed that really did reek. The tanyard labourers must have had a very strong constitution when working long hot summer days. Vats or pits containing nauseous brews of anything from water to urine, and the dung of hens, pigeons and dogs were used. Excrement from hunting kennels were much in demand for a process known as 'baiting' which softened the pelt and resulted in a fine pliable leather suitable for purposes such as glovemaking. However, the basic process of converting raw hides into leather was by soaking them in solutions of oak-bark. The vegetable tanning liquor produced by bruised or ground oak-bark worked very slowly but it provided a leather with strength enough for saddlers and harness makers. Tannic acid gradually leached out of the bark, slowly transforming an almost white skin into the yellow-brown colour we now call 'tan'.

The tanning process took place in an open-sided building with a series of large pits in which pelts were suspended from wooden poles and immersed in oak-bark liquor. The pelts were moved from pit to pit at regular intervals as they made their way through solutions in which the tannin content became stronger and stronger. The tanner was able to gauge the strength of the liquid by experience which included dipping a finger into the solution and tasting.

Tanyards were usually associated with other farm buildings. A Dodworth tanyard was described in a sale of 1811 and could have been the one that Hobson and his forebears had worked:

> *TO BE SOLD BY AUCTION at Mr. Kelly's, the Bank Top Inn, near Barnsley … A very valuable Freehold and Tithe-Free Estate.*
> *Lot 1: Capital Messuage at Dodworth Green now in possession of Mr. Richard Perkins … and garden, orchard, barn, stables … and 65 acres of tithe-free land.*
> [4 lots, consisting of 9 closes or fields amounting to 50 acres were then listed].

Stripping the bark from oak woods and stacking it to dry.

Lot VI: A messuage at Dodworth Green ... lately occupied by Mr. Thomas Lambert, with a well-stocked garden and orchard, a good barn, with stables and other convenient outbuildings. Also an excellent Tanyard, with suitable erections and conveniences, now employed by Mr. Perkins, and wherein a very extensive Business has been carried on for many years: The neighbourhood affording a very ample supply of Bark. Also about 18 acres of rich tythe-free land, divided into convenient closes, and contigious to the Homestead and Tanyard'. There were 3 further lots, about 21 acres offered and 9 dwellings, all occupied and there was one final encouragement for any prospective buyer:

'All the lands ... contain very valuable Mines of Coal and Ironstone, capable of being worked at an early expense'.

A bark 'peeler' on display in Cawthorne Victorian Village Museum. Alan Billingham

[The above sale notice was printed in a provincial newspaper, the *Wakefield and Halifax Journal*].

A tannery demanded a large site capable of supporting a lengthy and integrated manufacturing process, preferably near a reliable source of water. A Barnsley tannery of 1717 was described in a deed as 'one Tann yard Tannpitts and a house and buildings there erected' and would have been a distinctive landscape feature. A tanyard meeting these requirements was sited at the fringe of town, by the River Dearne near to the later junction of the Wakefield Turnpike Road and Old Mill Lane. Another may have been established near Keresforth where a field called 'Tanpit Ing' (i.e. marsh or wet land) was located. In the 1630s, a Barnsley tanner, John Lyle, appears to have had difficulty in finding a suitable town site, moving from Old Town to another property but selling to a local ironmonger within three years. The compact nature of the town centre and lack of suitable water supply meant that Barnsley did not have a recognisable 'leather-producing' zone compared with Doncaster, Sheffield and Hull. The most important tanneries were located in or near villages such as Cawthorne, Silkstone and Dodworth.

The rural locations were not due to any fear of upsetting residents in more crowded places but was mainly because of requiring ample raw material, preferably close at hand, for the tanning process. There were plenty of oak woods near by where bark could be relatively easily transported. Also, many South Yorkshire 'spring woods' were coppiced to supply fuel for the local iron industry; the prior removal of the bark not only saved weight and reduced the cost of haulage but also had value when sold to the tanners. Another important advantage for our area, especially to the west, was the type of farming practised. Nearer to the Pennines, farmers specialised in keeping animals rather than growing crops, notably beef cattle, so there was, at least originally, a plentiful supply of hides.

Tanning is remembered in this evocative place-name in Hoyland Swaine. Alan Billingham

Another reminder of tanning – at Cawthorne. Alan Billingham

By the 1730s Hobson journeyed considerable distances in search of good hides and many tanners were soon having to rely on imported sources. There was certainly a good local market for the finished products; Barnsley had a variety of leather-workers providing essential goods and services for farmers and craftsmen. The Barnsley cordwainers (shoemakers) must have been regular customers, but the wealthy tanners would have been involved in selling their wares to more distant markets, including London. It was a trade that demanded considerable capital investment so sales had to be in large quantities.

The choice of the hide was very important. The state of health of the animal, its recent food etc. was reflected in the quality of its skin. Hides could arrive from considerable distances, so were salted or cured in order to remain fresh. As soon as possible after stripping from the animal the skin was sprinkled with salt on the flesh side and the skin piled in a heap, the salt working through and reducing decay. The purpose of soaking in water and lime was to loosen the roots of the hairs, making them easy to remove by a two-handed knife, sometimes called a 'scudder'. Liming also made it easier to remove the fleshy layer. At this stage the hides became 'pelts' and the tanner could then decide for what purpose they were best suited e.g. sole leather, harness leather etc. The pelts were cut into sections, after removal from the lime pits. The largest piece was known as the 'butt' and flanked by two belly sections, while above it were the shoulder and cheeks. Each half of the butt was called a 'bend'.

The most crucial, and longest stage, took place when the pelts were immersed in the oak liquor; here such

Hide selected
Skin removed
Cleaned and soaked in water
LIMING (3 months or more)
soaked in slaked lime liquor
Cut into sections e.g. 'butts' 'belly' 'bend'
'Fleshing' of underside
Hair removed
CLEANING
CURRYING
FINISHING
'Pelts' soaked in successive pits of oak-bark liquor
TANNING (10 months — 2 years)

Traditional Leather Production

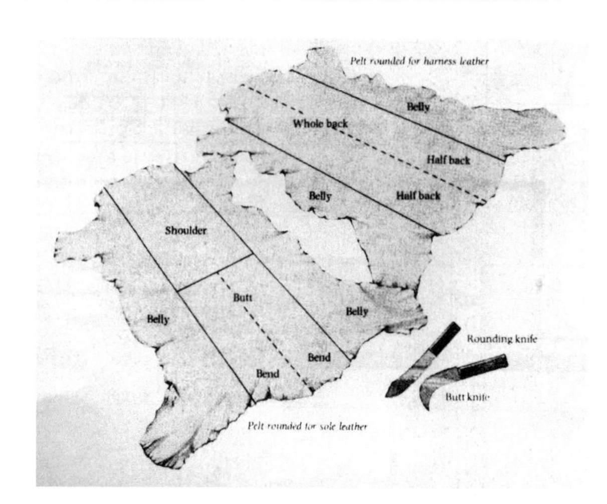

Sections of hides selected by the tanner.

Removing the hides from the lime pits, prior to removing unwanted hair.

factors as the strength of the solution and even the weather had to be carefully considered. It was a long and expensive process; large thick skins could be on site for up to two years. Eventually the pelts were dried, cleaned and could be passed on to the currier for further treatment.

Another very important and interesting reason why tanneries were established at Dodworth and Cawthorne relates to family tradition. Hobson was carrying on the work of several generations; for example the Brooke family of Dodworth carried on the trade from at least the seventeenth century. At the Quarter Sessions held at Doncaster, in 1640, Edward Crawshaw of Dodworth, shoemaker, Thomas Rawson of Barnsley, tailor and William Rayner of Cudworth, shoemaker were accused of stealing three and a half hides, valued at forty shillings, the property of John Hobson, probably the diarist's grandfather. Rayner was also accused of stealing 'six beasts head of tanned leather', valued at twenty-four shillings, the property of William Brook.

The Brooks prospered as a result of the tanning trade and it is remarkable that two families could do so well from the same business activity based from the small village of Dodworth. John Brook was described as 'gentleman' in his probate inventory of 1694. He lived in a substantial house containing a hall, dining room, parlour chamber, kitchen chamber, meal parlour, buttery, kitchen, cellar, granary, servant's chamber and there was also a malthouse, barn and fold.

His property included a number of interesting personal possessions including a silver tobacco box and a watch. He was certainly actively involved in trade with the capital for his appraisers noted the following item: 'In money returned to London for buying hides... £20'.

Brook's tanyard was leased at £7 per annum and his farm stock consisted of 4 oxen (£24), 2 cows and a calf (£7.10s.), 4 horses (£14) and 2 pigs and sheep (£1.15s.). His stock of leather in the

The unwanted fleshy matter is next stripped away from the underside of the hide in this machine – a process that is known as fleshing.

Immersing the hides in a succession of tanpits containing increasing concentrations of oak bark 'liquor'.

The fine Georgian facade of Cinder Hill Farm, Cawthorne, home of the Fretwell family in the eighteenth century. The author

Remains of the Cinder Hill Tannery. The author

tanyard shows a considerable scale of production: '90 stright Bends 20, for Bends, 3 heads (£10), 19 hides of the fourth shutt (£20.10s.), 31 hides of the first shutt (£39), 80 heads (£10), 20 strong Bends of the last shutt (£10), 25 hides in the scouring (£33.10s.)'. There was also 'one lead one dragnet, one trough with certain horns and hair, and three bark sacks (£1.5s.)'. The inventory also included a list of debts owed by seventeen persons, totalling about £25, in a valuation of a substantial £363.

A less prosperous Dodworth tanner of a generation earlier got into trouble in 1637. He appeared at the Doncaster Quarter Sessions for keeping and using 'harepipes' for destroying hares and rabbits. It was illegal for ordinary folk to keep greyhounds or any other dog to hunt or ferret, use nets or harepipes 'to destroy deer, hares or conyes, nor any other gentleman's game'. Offenders could be imprisoned for up to a year but Walker was pardoned.

The great length of time and considerable expense involved in the tanning trade meant that tanners had to be shrewd businessmen. At a time when there was no formal banking system they also had to trust customers, many of whom would not pay for their goods until many weeks or months had passed. This was often the way transactions took place and one can easily imagine the problems and difficulties of obtaining cash. Customers must have been 'vetted' according to their character as well as 'credit worthiness' and yet at the same time larger orders from relatively unknown merchants could not be easily turned down. Not surprisingly, probate inventories of tanners sometimes included 'desparate' debts, outstanding

A recycled tannery ... The stone footbridge once formed the sides of one of the many tanpits of Cinder Hill. The author

A fragment of 'bulls-eye' glass with 'John Child' etched on the surface; It came from the tanyard drying shed windows. The Childs were a West Bretton family and had close links with the Fretwells of Cinder Hill.

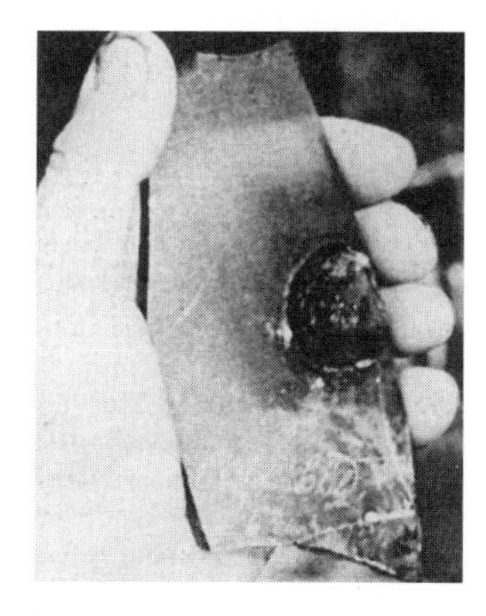

Dean Hill, Cawthorne, probably re-built in about 1760, shortly before being bought by John Spencer of Cannon Hall. The author

Sketches of Dean Hill Farm and Tanyard by John C Nattes, c. 1807. Barnsley MBC Dept. of Leisure and Amenities

sums, unlikely ever to be honoured. The entire operation was a delicate balancing act.

The Book of Trades, published in 1821, had no doubts about such an important matter as finance:

> *The trade of a tanner cannot be carried on without considerable capital; and a roomy yard, sheds and pits with plenty of water are indispensible requisites.*

Yet tanning could be a very lucrative business, and one which could reward a hard-working exponent with elevated social status. William Smith, son of a Cawthorne farmer of modest means, rose to become a much respected and important figure in the local community.

William Smith lived at Dean Hill, a farm which still exists today. In his will of 1 May 1722, his son, Thomas, received 'all my Real Estate, Houses, Lands and premises ... within ye realm of Great Brittain'. Smith in fact also had business interests in Barnsley and probably other places. He was also able to make generous provision for his three married daughters, each receiving £90. Hannah, probably his second wife, was well looked after; she received a small amount of cash but was given the right to 'enjoy' part of Dean Hill: (a parlour and chamber over it, on the west side of the house) along with certain furniture and fittings: 'One Chist and paire of Bedstocks with sufficient Beding to them of her own choyce Also one seel'd Chaire'. However, the widow had these advantages for only 'Two full years next after my decease'. If still alive, she would presumably be at the mercy of the eldest son and heir.

William Smith's probate inventory, compiled in February, 1724, contained goods and chattels in excess of £1,000, an exceptionally high figure, by the standards of the day. A substantial proportion of this related to his tanning interests. One item alone consisted of 'Certain Tan'd Lether Calfe Skins Tan'd part Tan'd and otherwise with Bark', valued at £660. This suggests an extremely large and important stock in trade, only rarely surpassed by tanners from other parts of the country. Smith was also owed £200, probably an estimated figure, from his customers, had investments totalling £50 and £180 made up of 'inward debts' and 'Redy Cash.'

Such apparent prosperity, however, needs handling with some care, in view of the comments expressed above concerning the hazards of the tanning trade, but the Smiths certainly lived in some comfort when compared with many other families. Dean Hill had been extended into a fairly substantial dwelling containing four ground-floor rooms as well as a buttery and cellar; above could be found four 'chambers,' three of them used as bedrooms and one as a storage area. There was, in addition, a 'Salt Chamber. The possessions listed in the inventory suggests a working farmhouse rather than the genteel residence of a wealthy gentleman.

Thomas, William Smith's son and heir, probably found life difficult during his own tenure at Dean Hill. In 1761, the farm became part of the Cannon Hall estate of the Spencer family and from about the middle of the eighteenth century onwards an increasing number of rural tanners found it difficult to prosper. Imported hides, government regulation and eventually the use of machinery transformed the ancient industry.

One or two local tanners such as the Russell family of Upper Hoyland continued to operate throughout much of the nineteenth century. Surviving place-names such as Tanyard Farm (Dodworth). Skinpit Lane (Hoyland Swaine), Bark House Lane, and Tanyard Wood (Cawthorne) remain as interesting reminders of one of our region's most important and almost forgotten rural industries.

Part Four: Crafts and Trades

11 Cordwainers

James Winter, one of my maternal great great grandfathers, was born in Barnsley in about 1824. The son of a bleacher, James became a shoemaker or cordwainer by trade, living and working from modest premises in Silver Street and eventually New Street.

The cordwainer's skills were passed on to his eldest son, Albert, who in the census of 1881 was aged seventeen and described as a 'Boot Rivetter'. Great grandfather Albert moved to Royston where he lived until his death in 1934.

Albert was, by all accounts, quite a character and was certainly proud of his craft. His wife, Eliza Anne, died in 1920 and her death certificate describes Albert's rank or profession as 'Boot and Shoemaker (Master)'.

I can well imagine the registrar being prompted to add 'master' to the otherwise undistinguished title. The Winters were carrying on a trade which had existed in most villages and every town for countless generations, but from at least the mid-seventeenth century Barnsley was a noted centre of shoemaking.

Unlike the tanners, the shoemakers were generally poor. They worked from tiny 'shops' and had few luxuries. Most were part self-sufficient, perhaps keeping a cow, a pig and growing a little corn and vegetables. The value of their stock and tools was usually very low.

John Woodcock was a cordwainer who lived at Old Barnsley during the 1720s. Despite his modest status he was in frequent demand as an appraiser of probate inventories for which he probably received a small fee. He was literate enough to write his own will, made in 1728, although the spelling was delightfully wayward. After describing his condition as 'being weake in body but of sound mind' his first bequest was to his son, Richard, who got 'My best sute of Close ... that is coate, Waste coate and Bretches and new hatt (and) my sekend sute of Close that is Cote waistcote and Bretches greate coate and Bootes and spores (spurs!)'. Daughters Elizabeth and Mary were promised three pounds in cash whilst a third daughter, Elizabeth, had the benefit of 'my Stock and Long Tabell and Cupboard and lether Cobard formes ... and a Livery (table: a store cupboard, ventilated with holes, for food) and three Chares ...' A few other modest items went to three daughters-in-law, the remainder of the estate (if anything in fact remained) went to his widow, Anne.

Woodcock's own inventory was drawn up a few days after his death, in December 1729. On the ground floor his dwelling consisted of 'House', which served as living room and kitchen, 'Shop' (workshop) and parlour containing a bed with red 'hangings' and no other furniture. Above could be found two chambers, the one over the 'house' containing a bed with green hangings, a portable or 'trundle' bed and a few other items including a desk. The chamber over the shop just contained a chest and an old spinning wheel. Outside there was a Cowhouse which housed a cow and a mare. He also had some hay stored in the 'Laith' or barn and there was 'muck in the fold'. An acre of 'hardcorn' had recently been sown on 'Wood bos feild'. Goods listed in his workshop provide us with an interesting picture of his stock and tools:

12 pairs of Shoes little and big ... 12 shillings.
Butt Leather ... 8 shillings.
Calfe Leather ... 5 shillings.
Wood Lasts old and new 2 seats 2 hammers & a pair of pinsors a pair of nippers & a rasp & a cutting knife 2 blocks ... 17 shillings.

Albert Winter, Master Boot and Shoe Maker. Author's collection

The room also contained three loads of beans, valued at one pound ten shillings! The total value of his goods and chattels amounted to little more than £21 but there would have been many other shoemakers far worse off.

Woodcock probably knew James Gledhill, a Barnsley cordwainer who died in 1722. Gledhill did not make a will, or at least did not go to the trouble of having it proved, but his modest inventory has survived. There is no mention of tools or stock in trade but the document does give an insight into the house and possessions of a relatively poor Barnsley resident, the latter valued in total £9.5s.6d.

Joseph Rushforth who died in 1731 had goods and chattels worth more than £30 but a large proportion of this was for 'money upon notes' and his mare and gelding were valued at £2.10s. Rushforth had, certainly for his own use, but probably to supplement a meagre income, a Brewhouse containing a lead, four tubbs and a range. The cellar contained six barrels. In his will the cordwainer left 'one house kitching and Bruhous with ye backside Stable thereto ... which I now liveth' to his son, James. Rushforth had some property interests since his daughter Elizabeth was to have 'ye next house of Robert Coward live and the two that my mother Firth lives in and the house of John Wilkinson doth live now'.

Henry Derby, another Barnsley cordwainer, died in 1737, his simple dwelling consisting of 'house', 'parlour', 'shop' and 'chamber' with goods and possessions worth little more than £15. In the chamber he had a stock of 44 pairs of shoes described as 'great and small' in size, valued at £2, less than one shilling (5p!) per pair. In the workshop there were the following items:

> *Two hammers two pairs of Nippers and other instruments belonging to the trade ... 1 shlling.*
> *Five calf skins and a Hide ... £1.4s.*

William Crofts serves as a final example of one of Barnsley's poor cordwainers. He died without leaving a will in 1751, and the complete list of his goods and chattels, appraised by Thomas Denton, Thomas Morton, Edward Midlane and Thomas Turner, was valued at £5.16s.11d.

Shoemakers, corvisors or cordwainers were terms used simultaneously for the same craft though cordwainers, having the benefit of an organised membership, aspired to a higher status. The name originated from Cordova in Spain where a special type of leather was developed and called 'cordovan'. The peculiarity of the leather was that it was dressed with alum and salt, a process known as 'tawing'. It was white leather and makers were called 'whitetawyers'. When finished it was soft, usually dyed with bright colours, especially red and sometimes was gaily decorated with gold and silver, in which form it was used for hangings and upholstery.

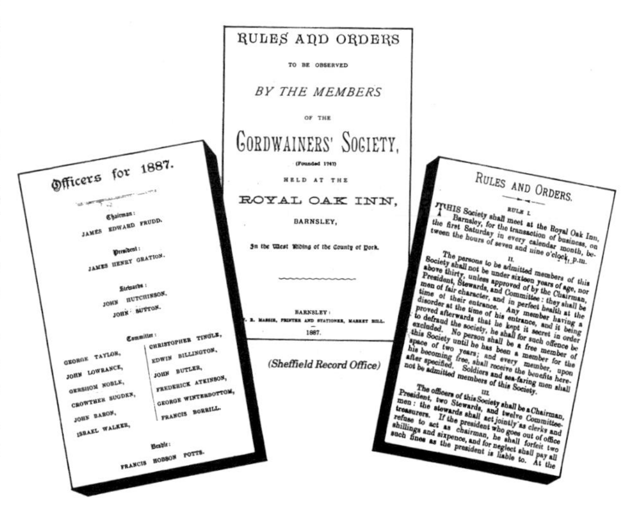

Officers for 1887.

Chairman:
JAMES EDWARD FRUDD.

President:
JAMES HENRY GRATION.

Stewards:
JOHN HUTCHINSON,
JOHN SUTTON.

Committee:
GEORGE TAYLOR,
JOHN LOWRANCE,
GERSHOM NOBLE,
CROWTHER SUGDEN,
JOHN BARON,
ISRAEL WALKER,
CHRISTOPHER TINGLE,
EDWIN BILLINGTON,
JOHN BUTLER,
FREDERICK ATKINSON,
GEORGE WINTERBOTTOM,
FRANCIS BORRILL.

Beadle:
FRANCIS HOBSON POTTS.

RULES AND ORDERS
TO BE OBSERVED
BY THE MEMBERS
OF THE
CORDWAINERS' SOCIETY,
(Founded 1747)
HELD AT THE
ROYAL OAK INN,
BARNSLEY,
In the West Riding of the County of York.

BARNSLEY:
[illegible] MASSIE, PRINTER AND STATIONER, MARKET HILL.
1887.

RULES AND ORDERS.

RULE I.
THIS Society shall meet at the Royal Oak Inn, Barnsley, for the transaction of business, on the first Saturday in every calendar month, between the hours of seven and nine o'clock, p.m.

II.
The persons to be admitted members of this Society shall not be under sixteen years of age, nor above thirty, unless approved of by the Chairman, President, Stewards, and Committee: they shall be men of fair character, and in perfect health at the time of their entrance. Any member having a disorder at the time of his entrance, and it being proved afterwards that he kept it secret in order to defraud the society, he shall for such offence be excluded. No person shall be a free member of this Society until he has been a member for the space of two years; and every member, upon his becoming free, shall receive the benefits hereafter specified. Soldiers and sea-faring men shall not be admitted members of this Society.

III.
The officers of this Society shall be a Chairman, President, two Stewards, and twelve Committee-men: the stewards shall act jointly as clerks and treasurers. If the president who goes out of office refuse to act as chairman, he shall forfeit two shillings and sixpence, and for neglect shall pay all such fines as the president is liable to. At the

(Sheffield Record Office)

There was no distinction between left and right feet until the end of the eighteenth century and sizes could be as vague as 'little and big'.

The heel was an Elizabethan innovation and had an especial appeal to ladies, adding an inch or two to the wearer's height. The shoemaker worked with one pattern or 'last', crafted out of wood and used to shape the shoes for both feet. The standard pattern was a shoe that had a plain front with a wide tongue over the instep. The whole front part of the shoe was made in one piece. There was a back or 'counter' also in one piece, with two projecting portions overlapping the tongue on the instep and tied or buckled together.

One of the main tasks of the shoemaker was cutting the leather to shape, followed by stitching the uppers and then the 'making' of the shoes. Imagine the skill involved: leather will stretch more in one direction than another and some parts of the shoe must 'give' whilst others must not. All the processes were completed by the craftsman, with simple tools in his little 'shop'.

The Cordwainers' Society of Barnsley came into existence on 5 March 1747/8 as a Friendly or Benefit Society. In return for weekly subscriptions the members got cash benefits in times of need. Members were also provided with a social life, comradeship and a sense of identity. They were one of the few working class organisations that escaped the repressive laws of the French Revolution period. They combined sick insurance with convivial club rights and annual outings or 'feasts'. Members were originally artisans and not from the middle classes.

For some the Friendly Society was nothing more than an engine of sedition but such views failed to understand basic human needs such as the cost of burial for the poor.

Rules and regulations of Friendly Societies were very strict. Penalties often exceeded those of an employer. There was even a fine – comparable to 'huffing' at draughts – for members failing to take the opportunity to fine other members for misdemeanours. The rules and orders of the Cordwainers' Society of Barnsley included the following:

> *Any member having a disorder at the time of his entrance, and it being proved afterwards that he kept it in secret in order to defraud the society, he shall for such offence be excluded.*
>
> *Soldiers and sea-faring men shall not be admitted.*
>
> *No member shall receive the benefit of this Society in the veneral disease nor for any hurt or sickness occasioned by fighting, wantonness, intoxication or irregularity … or he shall forfeit five shillings or be excluded.*
>
> [if] *any member has received benefit out of the fund of this Society under fraudulent pretences … such member shall be summoned by the president or stewards to appear before one or more of His Majesty's Justices of the Peace …*
>
> *If any member … be convicted of felony or embezzlement of money in the discharge of any of the offices of this Society, he shall forever be excluded: And* [if] *found guilty of self murder, the money payable at death shall be forfeited.*
>
> *If any member of this Society reflect upon another member, for having received any of the benefits heretofore specified, or shall circulate abroad the transactions of the Society, so that any member shall be prejudiced by, he shall be excluded.*

The social historian E P Thompson views early Friendly Societies as precursors of the working class:

> *And in many towns the actual nucleus from which the labour movement derived ideas, organisation and leadership, was made up of such men as shoemakers, weavers, saddlers and harnessmakers, booksellers, printers, building workers, small tradesmen and the like'.* [The Making of the Working Class].

The social history of Barnsley during the first half of the nineteenth century largely confirms this analysis.

On the Feast of St. Crispin (25 October) the shoemakers would celebrate their special day amid great festivity and rejoicings. Brethren of the craft would represent 'King Crispin' and members of his court in a grand procession. The banner, held high, and proclaimed with music and song, displayed a motto for all to see:

May the Manufactures of the Sons of Crispin be trod upon by All the World.

CAUTION.

THE COMMITTEE OF THE

CORDWAINERS' SOCIETY

GIVE THIS PUBLIC NOTICE,

THAT if any Member of their Society enters into any Secret, or other Society, for the purpose of receiving Relief, such Member will be excluded from the CORDWAINERS' SOCIETY, (agreeable to the twenty-second Rule,) and for ever forfeit all Claims and Benefits arising from the said Society.

BARNSLEY, OCT. 1ST, 1839.

P.S. It is reported that there are several Members who are now in Secret Societies, and have received Benefit from them, as well as from the CORDWAINERS' SOCIETY; it is particularly incumbent on them to be *aware.*

G. HARRISON, PRINTER, MARKET-PLACE, BARNSLEY.

Sheffield Record Office

This public notice, posted in Barnsley in 1839, was a stern warning to all members:

EXTRAORDINARY CHEAP
BOOT AND SHOE WAREHOUSE,
May Day Green Barnsley.

JOSEPH WOODRUFFE'S Stock of Ladies Gentlemen's and Children's Boots, Shoes, and Slippers is very extensive and well selected, which for workmanship, style and material will, on inspection, purchase and trial, be found at the respective prices as cheap, if not cheaper, than any offered to the public.

Bespoke orders and repairs executed on the shortest notice. N.B.–The address:
J. WOODRUFFE,
May Day Green, Barnsley.

12 Clockmakers & Ropers

John Hallifax

The third son of a Barnsley man was elected Lord Mayor of London in 1776, the momentous year of the Declaration of Independence by the United States of America. It was the most prestigious municipal office in the land and vested with political power superior to most of the ministers of George III. A fourth son was Mayor of Doncaster in 1775 and 1792. The fifth son carried on his father's trade in Barnsley and served as the town Postmaster.

The progenitor of this notable brood had, by the time of death, gained a considerable reputation of his own. His name was John Hallifax and his skill was in horology: the art and science of making timepieces.

By the early 1700s English clockmakers were the best in the world. The ingenuity of men such as Thomas Tompion meant that seconds and minutes on a dial could be registered with reasonable accuracy. Colonies of craftsmen grew up in the towns. Bustling market centres such as Barnsley were ideal locations for newcomers to set up in business.

The demand for fashionable timepieces meant a steady trade from the wealthier residents and from well-to-do yeomen farmers and gentlemen from the small country houses and manors of the district. A town location also provided the maker with a recognisable 'tag' to place under his name when 'signing' his clock.

Country clockmakers were at a disadvantage; a village name would mean little to a customer from distant parts, indeed it was probably not mentioned on the clock face.

Clocks were luxury items and status symbols despite their obvious advantages. Of the 71 inventories extant for Barnsley from 1685 to 1765, mostly of the better-off families, just 17 households had clocks. The earliest (1692) was in the house of widow Mary Green. The curate, William Denton, was the only person with a watch recorded.

Some residents such as innkeepers and the town postmaster-grocer Anthony Rhodes had 'clocks and cases' as important parts of their occupational and social roles. The clocks were usually kept in the best downstairs room or 'house' and varied in value from a few shillings to £8 but most of them priced around £2.

For most ordinary people a clock was unnecessary as well as too expensive. They rose with the sun and went to bed when it was dark; the time between was fairly arbitrary and geared for mealtimes and also prayer. Some households would keep a 'glass' for monitoring the hours and there would always be the cries of the watchman and the sound of the church bells.

John Hallifax was one of a handful of watch and clockmakers working in Barnsley during the golden age of the trade. He may well have known John Harrison of Nostell, son of the estate carpenter, who after 30 years of experiments created a marine chronometer of such accuracy as to merit the accolade of one of the greatest examples of mechanical engineering in history. Following a succession of maritime disasters the government of 1713 offered a reward of £20,000 for the first person to invent an accurate method of recording longitude at sea. Harrison eventually claimed his prize though it was said that this took almost as much ingenuity as the invention itself.

Sir Thomas Hallifax, Knight, Lord Mayor of London.

Hallifax descended from a wealthy family called Waterhouses who once held part of the tithes of Barnsley and had property and shopkeeping interests in the town. The Waterhouses lived in Halifax and it seems that one of John Hallifax's ancestors substituted the family name in favour of their place of residence.

A fine John Hallifax clock still in working order: Cannon Hall Museum. Courtesy of Barnsley MBC Dept. of Leisure and Amenities

John Hallifax was born in about 1695, moving to Barnsley as a young man where in 1717 he married Anna, daughter of George Archdale of Pilley. He was, at the age of 23, already making clocks, his marriage entry having 'Horolog' after his name.

The extent to which John Hallifax actually 'made' clocks is impossible to say. Some early clockmakers literally made everything – dials, movements, weights, hands and case – but others assembled ready-made parts, even in the early eighteenth century. Whether or not he used the services of a local woodworker and engraver John Hallifax's clocks were very handsome affairs. A few surviving examples are still around, two of them on view at Cannon Hall along with a superb walnut case barometer. Having a 'Hallifax' soon became synonymous with a clock that kept good time.

John Hallifax's third son, Thomas (1722–1789), grew to become a man of great intelligence, ability and ambition. He soon tired of his apprenticeship to a Barnsley grocer and, like Dick Whittington, packed his bags and headed for the streets of London. Thomas really did find the streets 'paved in gold'. Working his way through a banking career so rapidly, by the age of thirty this unsung hero of Barnsley was given the Freedom of the City. He became a member of the Company of Goldsmiths and was soon elected as alderman and sheriff. After his year as Lord Mayor he was duly knighted. On his death, aged 68, he was said to be worth £100,000, a former 'millionaire' MP for Aylesbury.

George (1725–1811), son number four, settled in Doncaster where, according to the 'Historical Notices of Doncaster' he was said to be 'far in advance of his age in the manufacture of clocks'. He married a Darton girl in 1748 and two years later was Freeman of Doncaster. George Hallifax provided a watch and later a clock for the Mansion House, each priced at seven guineas and no doubt enjoyed his two-year mayoral stint. He employed workers to assemble his clocks and watches.

John, the second son, was living in Barnsley at the time of his father's death and may well have been skilled in the clockmaking trade but moved to Warwickshire. The youngest son, Benjamin, after an academic career, was rector of Cublington, Bucks. It was left to the fifth son, Joseph, to carry on the Hallifax clockmaking tradition in Barnsley.

John Hallifax's signature (from an original will). Borthwick Institute of Historical Research

Joseph Hallifax (1728–1762) produced some fine clocks during his short life and also had the dual and appropriate occupation of postmaster. One can visualise him looking up at one of his own timepieces, waiting for the

John Harrison. Hamlyn

Above: *John Harrison's famous marine chronometer.* ***Inset:*** *A long-case clock of Harrisons can still be seen in Nostell Priory.* Hamlyn

Left: *Eighteenth century clock face by Joseph butterworth on display at Cawthorne Victorian Jubilee Museum.* Alan Billingham

arrival of the mail coach. A grandfather clock, by 'Jo: Hallifax' made £800 at an auction at Hoyland Common in September, 1986. Kath Parkin of the *Barnsley Chronicle 'Collectors Corner'* reported the sale of a mahogany long-cased clock, made by Joseph Hallifax, which realised £1,150 in May, 1987. The prices reflect a growing interest in long-case clocks, especially when they have local connections.

An old gravestone rests in Barnsley churchyard and the crumbling inscription can just about be made out:

Mr. JOHN HALLIFAX late of this Town whose Abilities And Virtue Few in these times Have attained His Art and Industry were such as His Ingenious Inventions will be a Lasting Monument of his Merit Such as recommended him to the Favour and Esteem of all good Men that knew this life Septr 1750

A fitting tribute to one of the most remarkable families of old Barnsley.

The Fletchers

The name Fletcher appears fairly frequently in Barnsley records during the eighteenth century. Occupations attributed to them include that of collier, nailmaker, whitewasher, plumber and glazier, plasterer and bleacher but it was as clockmakers that one branch of the family gained local fame.

John Fletcher, born in 1739, was making clocks in Barnsley, possibly succeeding Joseph Hallifax as the best known clockmaker in the town. An oak-cased longcase clock signed by John Fletcher fetched £600 at a sale by auctioneers Wilbys in September, 1986. Fletcher died when aged only 39 in 1778. He had four sons born between 1769 and 1774 but it is not known if any of them carried on his trade. His wife, Cecilia survived him for nearly forty years, and died at the age of 75 on February 8th 1819.

Tobias or 'Toby' Fletcher worked as a clock and watchmaker from premises in Church Street. He may have been a nephew of John. His shop was a brick structure on the site of what is now the entrance to Royal Street, and adjoining the *Royal Hotel*, then known as the *Old White Bear*, kept by the Roper family. Tobias married Eve Fletcher (same surname) in 1773. Tragically, two children, Hannah and Tobias died within weeks of each other during the smallpox epidemic of 1777.

Tobias was called upon to service and repair the clock of St Mary's:

> *Mr. Taylor and Mr. Raywood, churchwardens of Barnsley, to Tobias Fletcher, clock cleaning and looking to, one year .... £1.11s.6d.*

And also at St Mary's, Worsbrough:

> *1800 – Toby Fletcher for clock .... £0.18s.0d.*
> *1804 – Tobias Fletcher, 1 year for dressing and mending clock .... £0.18s.0d.*

One of Tobias's clocks once graced the Sessions Room of the old Moot Hall and was later moved to the Reading Room of the Harvey Institute (Civic Hall).

By the mid-1790s Toby Fletcher had become a local character, largely as a result of a what was to become a well-known incident involving one of His Majesty's soldiers from the 21st Light Dragoons. Four troops, each containing 60 men were enlisted from the Barnsley area with the understanding that they would serve abroad. Within a year they were sent to the West Indies, under Abercrombie, when he attacked and took St Lucia. By the end of a bloody campaign, made worse by malaria, only fifteen men from the regiment answered the roll call, the rest were dead or dying.

One of the surviving dragoons, John Helme, from Barugh, limped into Barnsley, having recently suffered from a kick from his horse and, being off-duty decided to refresh himself at the *King's Head*, an old inn near the bottom of Market Hill. Around a welcoming fire in the kitchen of the hostelry were a jovial group of locals, enjoying jugs of ale served by Mrs Johnson. Among the party was John Hydes the barber, whose shop was under the Moot Hall, George Watts, the tailor, and stonemasons George and Joseph Milner.

Into the midst of the friendly but peaceful company came Toby Fletcher, clockmaker

A clockmaker's workshop. Hamlyn

who, seeing the injured dragoon, began to take the mickey by stamping and limping about the room much to the great hilarity of the assembly, apart, of course from John Helme. Toby apparently exclaimed in exaggerated fashion 'Oh, dear! I shall never be able to rejoin my regiment' amid increasingly uproarious laughter. The more that the soldier showed his irritation then the more Toby emphasised the mimicry. Helme warned the clockmaker that he would put him on the fire-back if he continued his limping and mocking.

Old Toby only continued with his act no doubt encouraged by the company. The dragoon lost all patience, leaped from his seat and 'with arms extended like the sails of a windmill' picked up the offending mimic, lifted him over the fire and placed him on the hot backstone. For a few seconds the clockmaker tried to remain cool, the sweat pouring from his perturbed brow and in danger of being 'done brown' until his position became unbearable. At last he cried out 'So, quietness is best. Take me off, lads, take me off! Quietness is best'

The above story was recounted by John Burland in his 'Annals' of Barnsley and apparently the saying 'Quietness is best' later not only brought notoriety to Toby Fletcher but became a saying used by local folk when ever there was a rumpus in the town.

At least three of Toby Fletcher's sons carried on the clockmaking trade. In his will of 1811 he left his son, John, a pair of clock vices. His stock in trade and tools went to son Charles and another son, Tobias also received a pair of clock vices. Tobias Fletcher was buried on Christmas Eve, 1811.

According to Edward Baines's directory of 1822 Charles Fletcher had his father's shop in a Church Street and there was also a Thomas Fletcher with clockmaking premise on Shambles Street. Other clockmakers at this time were Augustine Allen (Market Hill) and Thomas Stainrod (Cheapside).

Barnsley emerges as a noted centre of clock and watchmaking during the eighteenth century and the horolgists, along with local craftsmen, helped to bring a certain amount of prestige to the town.

From the Fletcher family Bible. Author's collection

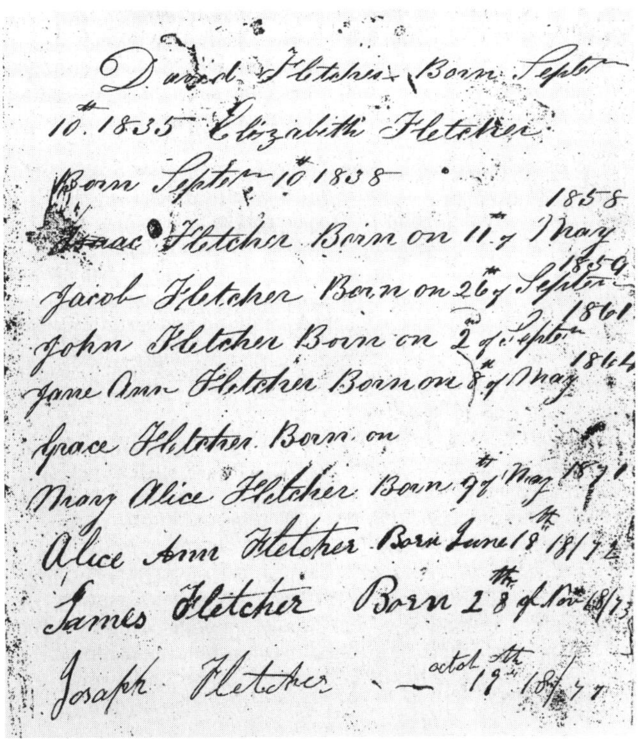
David Fletcher Born Septr 10th 1835 Elizabeth Fletcher
Born Septr 10th 1838
1858 Isaac Fletcher Born on 11th of May
1859 Jacob Fletcher Born on 26th of Septr
1861 John Fletcher Born on 2nd of Septr
1864 Jane Ann Fletcher Born on 8th of May
Grace Fletcher Born on
Mary Alice Fletcher Born 9th May 1871
Alice Ann Fletcher Born June 18th 1872
James Fletcher Born 28th of Novr 1873
Joseph Fletcher — octobr 19th 1877

An interesting family Bible, loaned to me by a *Barnsley Chronicle* reader and once owned by David Fletcher (b.1838) may well relate to the clockmakers of the same surname.

The Crawshaws of Worsbrough & Barnsley

It was once quite common for a man to have two or even three occupations. Most people had some farming interests as well as a craft or trade. In the days before standardised working patterns people laboured from dawn to dusk on a variety of tasks according to the season, weather conditions, the day of the week and so on. The Crawshaws were an interesting local family of ropemakers who also turned their hand to the making of clocks.

The family history of the Crawshaws is complex and, like the rope that some of them made, takes some untangling. They were resident at Worsbrough from at least the 1650s, but by the early eighteenth century a branch of the family were in business as ropers in

A traditional rope-walk.

Barnsley. A few years after the roper's death the Worsbrough Crawshaws (who were ropers and clockmakers) set up business in Barnsley, probably in 1736. During the early 1700s some of the Crawshaws also worked as filecutters in Sheffield and one of them worked as a cordwainer in London.

The Crawshaws had business, property and social links with a variety of Barnsley residents, including shopkeepers and innkeepers. From 1710 to 1750 some eleven agreements relating to property in Barnsley were registered at Wakefield.

William Crawshaw of Barnsley died in 1728. He did not leave a will but his probate inventory gives the impression of someone who lived in style, may have kept a small inn and certainly made rope on and near the premises.

Ropemaking involved the use of natural fibres such as hemp, flax and horse-hair. Inland roperies in country towns such as Barnsley provided very important products for local farmers. Crawshaw made halters for cattle and horses and probably cow bands for tethering cows. He would also have been involved in custom-made plough lines, reins, wagon ropes, twine, rabbit snares, clothes lines etc. Some ropers made nets, sacks, bags and tarpaulins.

The Barnsley ropery must have been a very distinct building. Its length was more important that its width and there would also have been an open-air rope walk; some rope walks were 80 to 100 yards long. The length of the rope depended on the length of the 'premises'.

The first task of William Crawshaw, and probably of his wife, Anne and their children, was to clean and 'dress' the fibres. This was done by 'hacking' or drawing the tangled hay-like mass through a series of prongs on a work-bench. The fibres or skein of hemp would be wrapped around the operator's waist during this process, oil would be added to the material and the combing out resulted in fine slivers; the 'hay' became yarn.

The skilled part of the operation took place next with the spinning of the yarn. The roper walked backwards along the rope walk, drawing out fibres as he moved and throwing yarn over T-shaped stakes embedded in the ground. A good spinner would walk many miles every day. The final process involved the twisting and tightening of stands in the 'shop' via hooks and revolving wheels, probably operated by children. Ropemaking was therefore a family affair employing few hands.

William Crawshaw had some of his equipment and stock listed in his probate inventory. In 'ye Shopp' could be found 'one pair Loomes with some haire cloth 3 pieces of Garthwebb 2 stone of hemp 2 pr. traces and 6 halters' and in an upstairs storeroom there were 'Turn hookes for making ropes and other, tooles wth. a Small pcell of hare'.

Crawshaw's premises consisted of 'house', dining room, pantry, low parlour, kitchen and workshop on the ground floor. Above were three 'chambers', including a long chamber, perhaps a further indication of his ropemaking craft and a closet. Although his inventory was valued at a modest £55 he lived in well-furnished accommodation and his furniture and furnishings were rather grand for a humble craftsman, perhaps a reflection of his family's status. He had a coloured bed with hangings, silver 'pints' and spoons, curtains and pictures in the dining room. There were also a surprising number of tankards, pewterware etc. and since he had twenty barrels and sixty gallons of ale stored in the cellar it seems likely that he was also an inn or alehouse keeper.

Ropemaking was so geared to agriculture that it was a seasonal occupation so there was opportunity and necessity to work at another 'occupation'. Crawshaw also had a small farm, keeping pigs, a cow and growing a little corn at Churchfields. It is not known whether he made clocks but he did have a 'clock and case' valued at two guineas in the dining room.

A series of family deeds relating to the Worsbrough and Barnsley branches of the Crawshaws include frequent references to an old Barnsley inn which they may have kept. An indenture of 1710 refers to the 'tenement or dwelling house commonly called and known by the name of the Sign of the Cross', along with shops and cellars. *The Cross* was probably an inn sign, perhaps named after the market cross of Barnsley, suggesting a location near the market place or Church Street. A deed of 1716 also mentions the *Black Bull* in Kirkgate or Church Street but this may have been kept by Cornelious Wood who was involved in an agreement with the Crawshaws.

Another William Crawshaw, born in Worsbrough in 1694 but living in Barnsley in the 1730s is listed as a clockmaker in Brian Loomes' book *Yorkshire Clockmakers* (1985, publ. Kelsall). His longcase clocks were apparently signed 'without place-name', perhaps because of the family link with Worsbrough. His father, Edward, who died in 1726, was also a ropemaker who apparently cared for the Worsbrough church clock in the early 1700s.

A deed of 1745, relating to William Crawshaw of Barnsley, clockmaker, also had a Thomas Crawshaw, clockmaker as a witness. This was William's son, possibly born at Worsbrough in 1727. Another Thomas Crawshaw (son of Thomas?) also a clockmaker, may have moved from Barnsley to set up business in Rotherham during the late eighteenth century.

Three or four generations of the Crawshaw family were therefore involved in either making clocks or ropes (sometimes both) in Worsbrough and Barnsley during the eighteenth century. They also had agricultural and property interests in Barnsley probably relating to innkeeping.

The Crawshaws emerge as a very interesting local family, contemporary with the Hallifax's though perhaps not as well-known. Another obscure Barnsley clockmaker, Henry South, along with John Hallifax, witnessed a deed of 1730 though, according to Mr Loomes, married and lived in Rotherham in 1731. The movement of clockmakers from Barnsley at this time may be an indication of a little too much competition combined with a search for new opportunities in nearby towns.

13 SOAP & CANDLE MAKERS

Richard Richardson

In the late seventeenth and during the eighteenth century there were several Barnsley families associated with the making of soap and candles. Inhabitants such as William Smith, together with two or more generations of the Methley family, made a living from the trade. Yet many townfolk would have bought supplies of these essential commodities from the shop of an extraordinary entrepreneur who lived in considerable comfort well away from the hustle and bustle, amid the pleasant surroundings of Brierley Park in the ancient parish of Felkirk.

We will never know how many people either through business or pleasure visited the home of Mr Richard Richardson but one fact is certain: they would come away with an indelible impression of a grand household, substantial farm and the memorable sight and smells of an unusual manufacturing process.

The Company of Tallow Chandlers was formed in 1462 and it became common for members to visit homes, collecting fat from kitchens to make candles to order. These mobile craftsmen also took opportunity to sell pots and pans, brooms, packthread etc whilst on their doorstep travels. Chandlers also had control over soaps and oil but stock was subject to inspection and could be destroyed if not of sufficient quality.

Though candles were fairly expensive items they were a commodity in great demand, used for both domestic and business purposes and even for street lighting. An act of 1599 ordered every householder from 1 October to 1 March to 'cause substantial lanthorns and a Candle of Eight in the Pound to be hang'd without their Doors.' It is unlikely that the Act was adhered to by many Barnsley residents but inns, shops and especially the market place would have been illuminated by lanthorns and cressets ('grease' baskets, made by the blacksmith, mounted on poles).

Nowadays we tend to think of candle light in a romantic sense but in the days before the use of paraffin wax (pre-1850s) candles gave off a most unpleasant smell and a tallow chandler was not a popular neighbour. John Evelyn, the famous seventeenth century author and diarist actually petitioned parliament against chandlers and butchers 'because of those horrid stinks ridorous and unwholesome smells which proceed from the tallow.'

Sweet smelling beeswax was almost exclusively used in churches and for seals on legal documents. The Worshipful Company of Wax Chandlers were an even more ancient and more powerful guild. The Elizabethan will of John Storye of Burton Grange included a gift of 'one bee hyve to the church of Roiston and the commoditie therof to find way to make one candell to burne at the hie masse before the Sacrement.' His widow, Alice, left three 'of my best chandles and one great candlestycke' to a nephew as heirlooms. Wax candles were luxury commodities.

Richard Richardson made his will in the winter of 1728 and was proud to describe himself as 'sope boyler,' and therefore distinguishing himself from an ordinary chandler. Richardson was a major manufacturer of soap and candles and the situation and scale of his empire allowed control of retail outlets in Barnsley and Doncaster. It is also likely that he supplied his products to a range of South Yorkshire shopkeepers, including other chandlers.

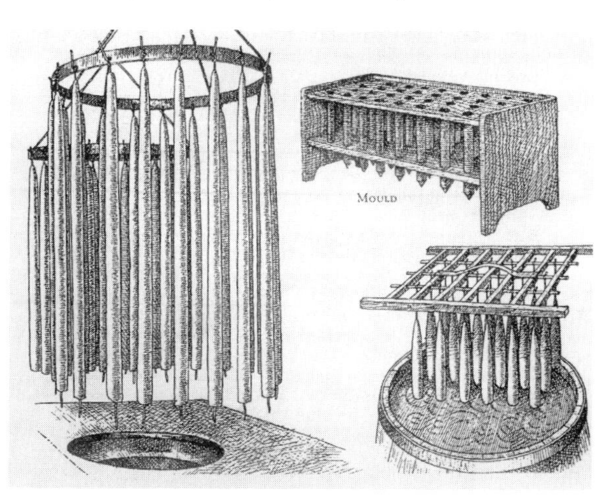

Candlemaking by 'dipping' and by the use of moulds.

To some extent the soap side of his business contrasted with the production of tallow candles. Soap for personal hygiene was a relatively new development though more basic soap products were used in washing and cleaning in the home. Early soapmakers began working in Bristol at the end of the twelfth century and a small community soon became established in the Cheapside area of London but it took time for manufacturers to be established in northern England. Richardson's soap works probably had its origin in the second half of the seventeenth century, one of the earliest and most important for miles around.

Soapmakers had to pay a duty on all the soap produced, a tax which reached horrendous proportions after the Napoleonic wars when boiling pans were fitted with lids that could be locked every night by the tax collector in order to stop any black market production at night.

Early soapmakers used ashes and animal fats. Wood or plant ashes were dispersed in water, and fat added to the solution. The mixture was then boiled, with ashes being repeatedly added as the water evaporated. A slow chemical splitting of the neutral fat occurred and the fatty acids reacted with the alkali carbonates from the plant ash to form soap.

'Modern' manufacturers such as Richardson used slaked lime to improve the process. The mixture was boiled in a large circular open pan, with separate vessels to receive the 'lye.'

An inventory of the soapmaker's goods, compiled shortly after his death gives us an interesting insight into the manufacturing process. The soap workhouse contained an iron pan, presumably the main boiling container which was heated by a coal fire, having an 'Iron Grate' and 'Coal Rake ec.' listed. Nearby were two brass ladles for stirring the mixture and adding the ashes. There were also various tubs, troughs, and 'A Table to make Soap on and Work it up.' Two 'Brewing Vessells' and 'Washing fflasks' completed the list of items in this special purpose building.

Nearby was the 'Ash Chamber,' a small warehouse containing an unspecified number of ash sacks and 20 loads of ashes at one shilling and sixpence a piece. Two loads of 'Knottingley Lime' (£1.5s.) were stored in the Limehouse along with a long table, panniers, rakes and oak boards.

A 'Soap Chamber' was a convenient storeroom for the finished cakes of soap. It housed '2 Large Chests of Soap' and various bowls, tubs, panchions, buckets, a churn and even two frying pans.

A guild sign of 1579 showing soapmaking 'tackle'.

Next door to the soap workhouse was the candle workhouse. This also contained a large iron pan in which the animal fat would be heated to produce tallow, a chopping trough with three knives and the main candle making apparatus; an iron mould, a wooden mould and two dozen pewter moulds. There was also a frame, 'dippin' and a table, suggesting that candles were being produced by a multitude of methods, perhaps dependant upon their purpose and customer preference. They could be made in moulds, by pouring molten tallow down wicks suspended from circular frames or by traditional hand dipping.

Candles were sold by the pound so that 'a dozen candles' usually meant twelve pounds of candles. In the candle workhouse Richardson had a pair of large weigh scales with lead and iron weights and a pair of 'Little Scales to Pound Candles' and brass weights, perhaps used for 'packaging' the candles into pre-determined bundles. There was also a piece of equipment called a 'Cooler,' a valuable item at more than £2, tubs, boxes and a pot for the moulds.

He had a substantial stock of candles awaiting sorting: some 11 'dozen,' valued at five shillings per dozen or five old pence per pound, a price which compared favourably with the price of candles in other parts of the country at this time. If a single candle weighed half an ounce (the weight of a modern candle) then there were about thirty candles to the pound. Richardson thus had somewhere in the region of 4,000 candles in the workhouse, illustrating a considerable scale of production.

Stocks of tallow were also stored in the workhouse awaiting processing into candles. There were eight packs of rendered tallow i.e. already treated in his furnace and valued at a very substantial £30 which would have bought about six cows. This may, in part, have been sold to chandlers who had not the facilities to heat their own tallow.

If Richardson had lived in the centre of town he would have been an offensive neighbour. However, the pollution aspect was by no means the chief locational factor for his business. Indeed it may not have even been considered. At Brierley Park he had limestone and woodland nearby and was well-placed for obtaining fat from the farming communities all around him.

There was also thirty stone of 'Rough tallow,' much cheaper, not fully processed, at four shillings per stone. The wick, processing and profits added about one third to the cost of the tallow.

The corn chamber and loft doubled as the storeplace for the material for making the wicks. He had sixteen pounds of cotton wool in store at one shilling per pound together with 114 'Candlew'(?) valued at the same rate, thirty six mould candles (5 pence per pound) and, puzzlingly, '12 Cowers Weak' at two pence per pound.

The appraisers of Richard Richardson's probate inventory also referred to his 'Sale house' at Doncaster and 'Sale Shop' at Barnsley. Both premises had weigh scales and weights and stocks of soap and candles. The value of the stock suggests at least 1,000 candles available to Doncaster and Barnsley customers.

A further clue as to the volume of production is provided by his debt book which contained a record of money owing from customers and amounted to almost £150. If the debts were listed within a twelve month period and his soap products were excluded then he would have an annual turnover of approaching a quarter of a million candles! Even allowing for soap accounting for up to one third of his business, he would still be producing somewhere in the region of 100,000 candles per annum.

A search at the Wakefield Registry of Deeds reveals that Richardson and his family were involved in property transactions in the town from 1714 when he was 'of Brierley Park' and already being described as 'soap boyler.' He made an agreement concerning a property 'at a certain place called Sowbridge.' One of the witnesses was a Sheffield tallow chandler.

By 1721 he was described as 'candler' and his eldest son, John Richardson, was also in business as a candler in Wakefield. The Barnsley property is described in more detail: 'three tenements or dwelling houses adjacent together in a certain street called Sowbridge Street one of which tenement is an inn known by the name of the three cranes inn, the Sowbridge being on the north of the said tenement, inn or dwelling house and Joshua Shaw on the south which said inn or dwelling house are in several occupations of Jonas Clarke, John Truelove and William Addy …'

Records relating to the enclosure of Barnsley in the late 1770s show that the Richardson family had, and recently held, at least six properties including two shops by the Sow Dyke at the bottom of Market Hill and near to the beginning of modern Queen Street. This may well have been his candle and soap shop.

Richard Richardson emerges as a very enterprising and interesting local character. His candle and soap making interests would have made him one of the most important chandlers of the West Riding and certainly responsible for providing many Barnsley folk with much needed commodities.

But for the survival of his detailed probate inventory his contribution to the life and times of Barnsley would have been long forgotten.

14 THE GARDENER

The term gardener was used to describe men of contrasting abilities and social standing. At the top of the tree were the landscape gardeners, professionals such as Richard Woods whose services, despite his distant home in Essex, was sought by the country landowners at Cusworth and Cawthorne.

In 1764 John Spencer of Cannon Hall recorded that he had signed a contract with Mr Woods whereby he engages to complete my next piece of water ... to make a Palladian Bridge and a head at the Park walls, to raise the water for 330 feet, to be completed in twenty weeks' time'.

Over 200 varieties of trees were planted in the park, enthusiastically supervised by Spencer, but probably put into effect by his own chief gardener, Thomas Peach.

The legacy of the estate gardener is reflected in some of the interesting smaller country houses and manors of our area.

Most ordinary Barnsley folk cultivated a kitchen garden, and for many the smallholding provided work for all the family in addition to a trade or occupation. Yet commercial gardening, either through the nurseryman who traded in living plants or the market gardener who sold crops off plants, was becoming increasingly important in provincial towns.

Thomas Johnson

Thomas Johnson was a Barnsley gardener who died in the early summer of 1735. His friends and neighbours had the formidable task of taking an inventory of his goods and chattels, including his rapidly growing plants. Fortunately they performed their duties with some care giving us a unique view of one of our earliest market gardens.

The smallholding was arranged into four main plots and the scale of his business was considerable:

	£. s. d.
In the ffirst garden, some herbs	*0.2.0*
In the second garden, seven hundred cabigas	*1.10.0*
Seven hundred yards of onions	*1.10.0*
Seven hundred yards of herbs	*1.10.0*
In the third garden, two hundred beds colyflowers and cowcumbrs	*0.15.0*
A parcel of onions	*1.5.0*
The cherrys upon eight trees	*0.6.0*
A small border of pease a score of cabbgs a row of beans	*0.16.0*
In the fourth garden, fifty young appletree grafts	*0.10.0*
Two thousand cabbages	*4.10.0*
A parcel of pease and beans	*2.0.0*
A parcel pottatas, carots and sallading	*2.0.0*
Eight glasses and frames for cowcumbers	

The size of each garden is difficult to estimate though the cropping does suggest a degree of planning and rotation. Perhaps related as much to the demands of the market place as weather conditions or soil. It is most interesting that he was using glass and frames for forcing early crops and protecting his cucumbers. Such care was hopefully rewarded with good prices.

Herbs were an important commercial plant. They were widely used for culinary purposes and were the basic medicines of the day. Herbal books containing medicinal remedies started pouring off the new printing presses. John Gerard's *Herbal* (1597) was translated, with many errors from a Belgian work. A generation later the book were corrected and enlarged by a man also called Thomas Johnson though Gerard continued to get all the credit.

Nicholas Culpeper (1616–1654) was a great English herbalist whose writings helped to popularise the use of herbs for a variety of dishes and ailments. It is likely that the Barnsley gardener supplied some of our town apothecaries.

The huge scale of planting must have meant that Johnson had some labour to help him. Even allowing for working an average 10 to 12 hour day he would have needed intensive help with all

Sixteenth century woodcut showing the use of raised-beds.

the demands of vegetable production. His wife Alice, and perhaps his children and part-time workers may have assisted, especially when doing jobs such as preparing the ground, weeding, thinning, planting and getting stock ready for market.

The tools that were available were obviously basic and were listed as follows:

One Wheel Barrow
Three spades, two dung fforks, one shovel, three hows
Two rakes, a potata setter.

Their number may give a rough indication of the number of hands at work at any one time.

Brassicas especially cabbages, formed the backbone of Thomas Johnson's eighteenth century Barnsley garden. The use of plenty of manure would ensure sturdy plants which even in the eighteenth century could be cropped during most of the year. Greens formed an important part of the diet, especially in winter and spring. The mass production of this crop reflected a widespread demand. Johnson's cabbages were valued, whilst in the field, between four shillings and three pence and four shillings and six pence per hundred. Cauliflowers would seem to have been given special treatment, perhaps in raised beds; they had heads much smaller than the modern plant, about the size of a golfball.

The onion was also a popular vegetable. Its location next to herbs may have been deliberate. The history of the onion has been more associated with medical than culinary properties. Gerard had no doubts about the value of the juice of an onion which 'annointed upon a bald head in the sun bringeth the haire again very speedily'. The herbalist was less enthusiastic about its gastronomic qualities: it causeth headache, hurteth the eyes, and maketh a man dim sighted dulleth the senses, and provoketh overmuch sleep, especially being eated raw'. In spite of Gerard, it did become a popular food and its magical properties declined.

Peas and beans were good rotational crops, had a steady demand and were also grown on many of the farms in our area.

The versatile potato was a relatively new crop and was once regarded as something of a delicacy, eaten mainly by the wealthy. 'Carots' and Sallading' provided Johnson with a good variety of vegetables.

Gerard advocated boiling cucumbers with mutton and mixing it with oatmeal. The concoction 'doth perfectly cure all manner of sauce flegme and copper faces, red and shiney fierie noses'. It had, in fact, been a popular food since Roman times. Emperor Tiberius was supposed to have consumed one every day,

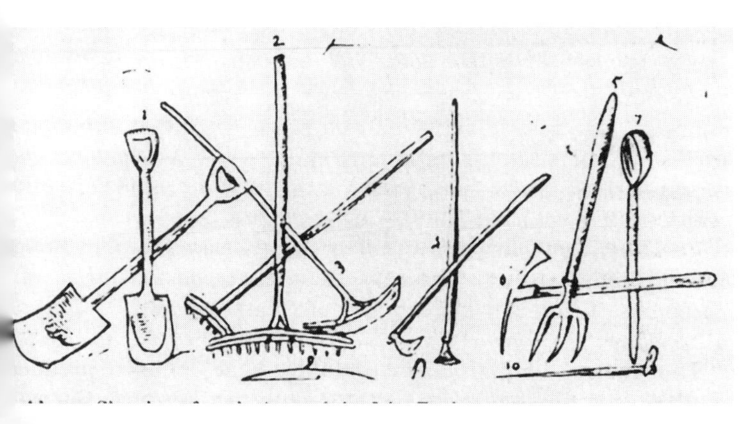

Sketches of gardening tools by John Evelyn (1659)

Another woodcut showing the well-dressed gardener.

helped by the skill of his gardeners. Johnson was therefore following a long tradition and using his skill to grow them in frames, under glass. They were obviously a valuable crop despite the view expressed by Dr Johnson:

> *The cucumber should be well sliced, and dressed with pepper and vinegar, and then thrown out, as good for nothing.*

Johnson's interest in soft fruit and recently grafted apple trees further emphasises his gardening skill as well as showing good business sense when the vagaries of the weather could ruin other crops.

The Barnsley gardener also had 'Some Berry Trees' in Robert Richardson's garden. Richardson's main trade was that of a carpenter. There was also an acre of potatoes grown by Johnson at Ardsley.

The variety of fruit and vegetables that Johnson produced dispels any misconceptions that eighteenth century Barnsley people had a poor and unbalanced diet!

Johnson must have needed a large quantity of seed for his garden. He could have produced his own but the time and effort involved was great so it seems likely that he obtain at least some seed from a nurseryman or even from a local estate.

Another very interesting feature of Johnson's inventory is that he appears to have kept a shop. Under the heading 'In the Shop' are listed a wheel, eight baskets, a pair of panniers, a wheelbarrow and a pair of scales. He was obviously retailing some of his own produce. The panniers' would have been a pair of bags or baskets slung on either side of a pack horse, used to carry goods to market and perhaps deliver to wealthy households. A horse is not listed but Johnson had a stable which contained a pack saddle, a further indication of his mobile trading.

With tending the gardens, running the shop and transporting his produce Johnson had an extremely busy life. The financial returns were fairly modest by the standards of the day. All his goods and chattels were valued at little more than forty pounds. His house only consisted of two ground floor rooms with a chamber above, a passage and a buttery. However, he lived in some comfort. In his 'House' or living room was a pewter case and dresser, a clock and a case, a 'seeing glass,' three tables, seven chairs and a good range of pots, pans and plates. Food was cooked on a range which had tongs, a shovel, spits, racks, ladles and other utensils nearby. The room also contained a pair of brass scales and weights and a seed box, perhaps kept in a dry spot by the fire.

The other ground floor room, the parlour, was used as a bedroom, contained a bed which had curtains around it and was probably where Johnson slept. It also had a seeing glass, a chest, a box and four chairs and a fireplace. In the sparsely furnished chamber were two less valuable beds, a chest with some bacon in store and a stock of joiner's tools.

Thomas Johnson emerges as an early market gardener, growing vegetables on a large scale, had interests in both soft and hard fruit and selling some of his produce from his Barnsley shop. His lifestyle was far removed from the romantic picture of the estate gardener in his fine clothes cultivating the master's kitchen garden. Johnson was in a very risky business, subject to market prices and demand and the effects of weather and disease.

Thomas Johnson's interesting inventory suggests that gardening was flourishing in the Barnsley area. Its origins may go back to medieval times when the monks of Monk Bretton and Pontefract had such an important influence on the making of the town. Interestingly, one of our aristocratic landlords, William Bentinck, (1645–1709) newly created Earl of Portland was, like the new king William III, from Holland, probably the leading gardening nation of Europe.

Part Five: Shops and Shopping

15 If You Want a Five-legged, Green Elephant With a Glass Eye ...

Many old-established family businesses have disappeared from the streets of Barnsley in recent years. Edward Tasker's painstakingly produced visual record of the town gives a vivid impression of the hundreds of small family concerns which provided so much character during the one hundred and fifty years before extensive re-developnent of 1974.

Some of the emporiums are fondly remembered. Generations of local couples have sealed their romances with engagement and wedding rings from the Eldon Street jewellers of 'Benjy Harrals.' Until the mid-1980s rows of rings could still be viewed through windows under a famous clock and sign proclaiming WATCHMAKERS TO THE ADMIRALTY. Established in 1898, its founder served customers until the day before his death, aged 95, in 1971. A purchase of a wedding ring was commemorated with a small but much appreciated gift; in our transaction it was a silver-plated cake knife. Benjamin Harral, his son and grandson, were far more than shopkeepers: they were public figures and their premises were well-known meeting places, in fact social institutions.

At the top of Market Hill stood the premises of one of Barnsley's most famous retailers, closed down in 1975. Above street level, and carved on an elegant stone facade is the surviving visual evidence of its former function: BUTTERFIELDS DRAPERY MARKET. Yet the place evokes many childhood memories such as its amazing overhead network of wires which when mechanically operated by an assistant zipped away capsuled customer cash and dramatically returned with any change – and a written receipt. The shop had been run by successive

Harral's and Eldon Street at the turn of the century. Author's collection

Now closed (1988), much of this magnificent facade has gone. (Brian Elliott)

Butterfields may have long gone but the upper part of an impressive facade remains. (Alan Billingham)

generations of the Butterfield and Massie family from the 1830s but the site has witnessed the comings and goings of a long succession of drapery bazaars from the fine mercery ware of the Ludlam's in Stuart Barnsley to the occupancy by drapers Henry and Joseph Clarke in the Hanoverian era.

A little further down the hill is 'Elstones', established, according to an early advertisement, in 1797, and still in private hands, selling newspapers and magazines and traditional products such as tobacco, cigars, walking sticks, chocolates and coffee.

Brammer's tobacconists in Regent Street closed down in December, 1984, Mr. Charles Brammer, then in his 86th year, had run the shop since 1937 but thought that the expiration of the lease was the right time to 'call it a day'. 'I have seen kids come into the shop as young office boys', reflected Mr. Brammer, 'and later return grey-haired. When I first came here, Players were 11 1/2d. for twenty. We used to sell chewing tobacco twists for 8d.'. A local saying was said to sum up Brammers: 'If you want a five-legged green elephant with a glass eye, then try Brammers. If they haven't got one in stock, they'll get it for you.'

About the same time, Mr. Eric Banks, proprietor of a sweet and tobacconist shop on Wellington Street retired, after fifty-two years in the business, serving sweets and biscuits to thousands of adults and children: 'I've seen many changes,' said Mr. Banks. 'I've seen people come into my shop as children and then watch them grow up over the years. Barnsley was full of characters in the old days. Shops like mine belong to the past, it's now the end of a lifetime.'

The Market Hill grocery business of the Guest family served discerning customers with fine teas, coffees, cheese and cooked meats from 1765 until 1973. The aroma from the shop fails to disipate with the passing of time. Next door, and just within living memory, was another drapery shop which in the 1770s was occupied by John Hall, ironmonger.

TALKING OF FOOD

WHEN IN TOWN TAKE LUNCH IN OUR CAFE.

—Dainty Meals served in pleasant surroundings.—

Morning Coffee 10 to 11-45 a.m. Lunch 12 to 2 p.m.

Afternoon Tea 3 to 5-30 p.m.

Open until 1-30 p.m. for Lunch on Thursdays.

BUTTERFIELDS

Butterfields & Massies Ltd., — Church Street, Barnsley.

REYNOLDS & WADSWORTH

LIMITED.

15, 17 & 19, Market Hill, Barnsley.

We have all the Lastest

COOKING UTENSILS including—

"PRESTIGE" PRESSURE COOKERS

Notice to Brides

Bring him along to Eldon Street to choose the Ring—

"You will be delighted."

BENJ. HARRAL

LIMITED.

THE RING SHOPS,

Mexboro'. BARNSLEY Pontefract.

Advert from St George's parish magazine of February 1950.

Henry Elstones, now and then. Tasker collection

Charles Brammer (86) outside his Regent Street shop which closed in December, 1984. Barnsley Chronicle

Photograph of Eric Banks (70), outside his Wellington Street shop which closed after 52 years in business, (1984). He started in 1932 and at one time managed four shops in Barnsley ranging from a small newsagents to a bakery. The author

Many of the emporiums which gave the town its identity have been replaced by the universally recognisable frontages of estate agents, travel companies and branches of building societies. The conversion of the old Harral's Jewellers by Lancasters has at least retained some architectural dignity but a marvellous frontage has been lost.

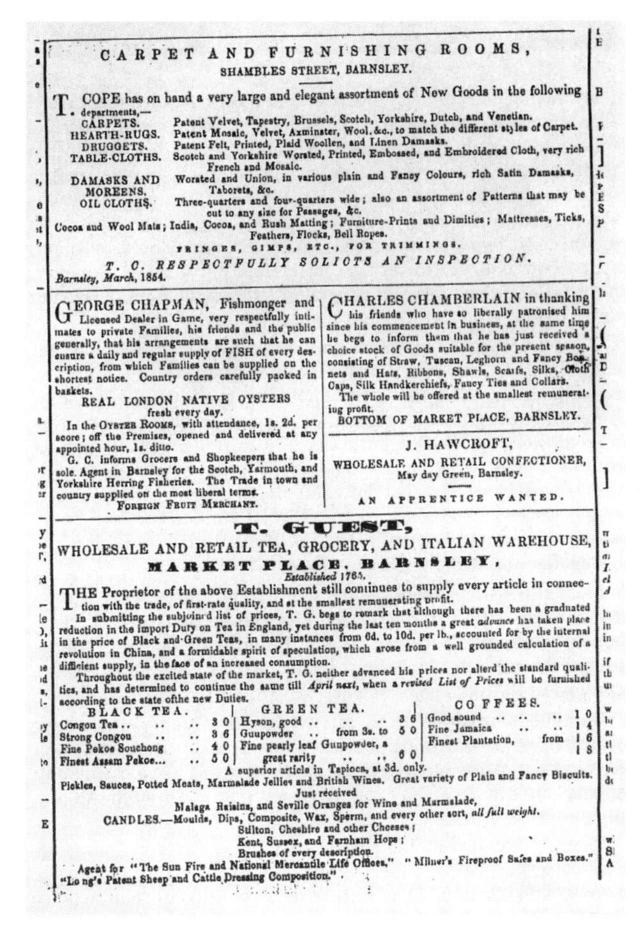

CARPET AND FURNISHING ROOMS,
SHAMBLES STREET, BARNSLEY.

T. COPE has on hand a very large and elegant assortment of New Goods in the following departments,—

CARPETS.	Patent Velvet, Tapestry, Brussels, Scotch, Yorkshire, Dutch, and Venetian.
HEARTH-RUGS.	Patent Mosaic, Velvet, Axminster, Wool, &c., to match the different styles of Carpet.
DRUGGETS.	Patent Felt, Printed, Plaid Woollen, and Linen Damasks.
TABLE-CLOTHS.	Scotch and Yorkshire Worsted, Printed, Embossed, and Embroidered Cloth, very rich French and Mosaic.
DAMASKS AND MOREENS.	Worsted and Union, in various plain and Fancy Colours, rich Satin Damasks, Taborets, &c.
OIL CLOTHS.	Three-quarters and four-quarters wide; also an assortment of Patterns that may be cut to any size for Passages, &c.

Cocoa and Wool Mats; India, Cocoa, and Rush Matting; Furniture-Prints and Dimities; Mattresses, Ticks, Feathers, Flocks, Bell Ropes.

FRINGES, GIMPS, ETC., FOR TRIMMINGS.

T. C. RESPECTFULLY SOLICTS AN INSPECTION.

Barnsley, March, 1854.

GEORGE CHAPMAN, Fishmonger and Licensed Dealer in Game, very respectfully intimates to private Families, his friends and the public generally, that his arrangements are such that he can ensure a daily and regular supply of FISH of every description, from which Families can be supplied on the shortest notice. Country orders carefully packed in baskets.

REAL LONDON NATIVE OYSTERS
fresh every day.

In the OYSTER ROOMS, with attendance, 1s. 2d. per score; off the Premises, opened and delivered at any appointed hour, 1s. ditto.

G. C. informs Grocers and Shopkeepers that he is sole. Agent in Barnsley for the Scotch, Yarmouth, and Yorkshire Herring Fisheries. The Trade in town and country supplied on the most liberal terms.

FOREIGN FRUIT MERCHANT.

CHARLES CHAMBERLAIN in thanking his friends who have so liberally patronised him since his commencement in business, at the same time he begs to inform them that he has just received a choice stock of Goods suitable for the present season, consisting of Straw, Tuscan, Leghorn and Fancy Bonnets and Hats, Ribbons, Shawls, Scarfs, Silks, Cloth Caps, Silk Handkerchiefs, Fancy Ties and Collars.

The whole will be offered at the smallest remunerating profit.

BOTTOM OF MARKET PLACE, BARNSLEY.

J. HAWCROFT,
WHOLESALE AND RETAIL CONFECTIONER,
May day Green, Barnsley.

AN APPRENTICE WANTED.

T. GUEST,
WHOLESALE AND RETAIL TEA, GROCERY, AND ITALIAN WAREHOUSE,
MARKET PLACE, BARNSLEY,
Established 1765.

THE Proprietor of the above Establishment still continues to supply every article in connection with the trade, of first-rate quality, and at the smallest remunerating profit.

In submitting the subjoined list of prices, T. G. begs to remark that although there has been a graduated reduction in the import Duty on Tea in England, yet during the last ten months a great *advance* has taken place in the price of Black and Green Teas, in many instances from 6d. to 10d. per lb., accounted for by the internal revolution in China, and a formidable spirit of speculation, which arose from a well grounded calculation of a difficient supply, in the face of an increased consumption.

Throughout the excited state of the market, T. G. neither advanced his prices nor alterd the standard qualities, and has determined to continue the same till *April next*, when a *revised List of Prices* will be furnished according to the state ofthe new Duties.

BLACK TEA.	
Congou Tea	3 0
Strong Congou	3 6
Fine Pekoe Souchong ..	4 0
Finest Assam Pekoe... ..	5 0

GREEN TEA.	
Hyson, good	3 6
Gunpowder .. from 3s. to	5 0
Fine pearly leaf Gunpowder, a great rarity	6 0

COFFEES.	
Good sound	1 0
Fine Jamaica	1 4
Finest Plantation, from	1 6
	1 8

A superior article in Tapioca, at 3d. only.

Pickles, Sauces, Potted Meats, Marmalade Jellies and British Wines. Great variety of Plain and Fancy Biscuits.

Just received
Malaga Raisins, and Seville Oranges for Wine and Marmalade,

CANDLES.—Moulds, Dips, Composite, Wax, Sperm, and every other sort, *all full weight.*

Stilton, Cheshire and other Cheeses;
Kent, Sussex, and Farnham Hops;
Brushes of every description.

Agent for "The Sun Fire and National Mercantile Life Offices." "Milner's Fireproof Safes and Boxes." "Long's Patent Sheep and Cattle Dressing Composition."

Advert taken from the Barnsley Record of 1854, a precursor of the Barnsley Chronicle.

Shopping in Stuart & Hanoverian Barnsley

As a shopping and commercial centre, Barnsley served a rural area of about fifty square miles. Its role as a retail centre is reflected not only in its innkeepers and carriers but also in the professional and commercial occupations of many leading inhabitants. The marriage registers from 1757, when occupations are recorded, identify six mercers or drapers, a grocer, an apothecary, two chapmen and a hardwareman. There were also six butchers, three saddlers, a currier, four hatters, a clockmaker, nine tailors, three breeches-makers, two staymakers, a hawker and a twenty-two cordwainers or shoemakers.

As an occupational guide the registers are useful but not exhaustive. There were also attorneys and surgeons, parsons and schoolmasters. The versatile Thomas Frudd cut hair, called himself dancing master, brewed on a considerable scale and kept a small-holding. Such a muliplicity of callings, particularly for ordinary folk was not unusual. Yet a small degree of specialisation was present, for example, Benjamin Micklethwaite was described as a tobacconist in 1730, John and Stephen Smith were mercers and booksellers in the 1740s and John Bent was a bookseller and stationer in the 1750s.

Most of the shopkeepers sold a much wider range of goods than their trade titles implied. Many services remained 'hidden' beneath an occupational label. Prominent dealers offered financial services, including loans. Grocer Anthony Rhodes doubled as the town post-master.

In 1706, Joseph Wilson, an immigrant Quaker, was busy establishing a hardware business on Market Hill and soon funding a dynasty of enterprise which was to have far reaching effects on the economy of Barnsley right through to the nineteenth century.

Thomas Wood and his attorney heirs were key figures in administering local business affairs. In 1672 he paid tax on six hearths and his detailed probate inventory confirms that he lived in one of the largest and most prestigious houses in town. His residence, later forming part of the *King's Head Hotel*, was well-sited for business, overlooking the market place. Wood enjoyed a high level of comfort in nine well-furnished rooms containing admirable quantities of pewter, silver, glassware and pictures.

The Rooke Coat of Arms.

Daniel Rooke's inventory included capital of £745 in gold, silver, cash and bonds. The will of this gentleman

A view of Burghley from across the 'Capability Brown' lake. The author

mercer and apothecary shows that he had also accumulated sufficient wealth to move out of a substantial property in Church Street in favour of a fine new house built on the outskirts of town.

In contrast, mercer John Littlewood's house was sparsely furnished but he was only twenty-nine-years-old when he died and had substantial farming interests with 'debts inward' of £65.

Francis Usher preferred to invest more than £700 from his mercery and apothecary trade in land securities and investment bonds. Usher had family links with the Ludlams, one of Barnsley's premier business families.

The Quaker draper Robert Leatham was successfully establishing a thriving business which a generation later was reflected in his son's huge personal estate of almost £3,000, overtaking Ludlam as the wealthiest shopkeeper in town and stocking one of the largest lists of fabric recorded in any English provincial town. The Leatham's shop and warehouse was probably situated at the far end of Church Street, near the present junction with Old Mill Lane. The family were successful business entrepreneurs over three generations. A Pontefract branch of the family continued to prosper after the Barnsley Leathams began to decline. John Leatham of Pontefract (1740–1823) was a partner in the Leatham, Tew and Company bank which remained in the family over four generations. A Doncaster branch opened and a third, at Wakefield, in 1808 which was to become the centre of a formidable financial empire. In 1906 the Leatham and Tew company was amalgamated into Barclays Bank. The history of this great multi-national company has therefore some Barnsley connections!

Postscript:
A Barnsley link with Burghley House

In 1988 the author wrote to Lady Victoria Leatham who lives at Burghley House, near Stamford, in Northamptonshire to see if there was any family connection with the Leathams of Barnsley who were an important family of Quaker shopkeepers. Lady Leatham, who had recently presented a television programme about country houses, was kind enough to confirm that her husband was in fact one of the last surviving members of the family. Burghley House, began by Lord Cecil in 1553, is one of the largest and certainly finest buildings of Elizabethan England.

16 John Ludlam, Mercer

There were many other important Barnsley shopkeepers who were in business over several generations. The Chappells and the Deykin family are notable examples but a detailed insight into the shopkeeper's world can be found by reference to Mr John Ludlam.

A mercer was originally a dealer in fine fabrics such as silk but by the seventeenth century provincial mercers stocked a wide range of fabrics and often diversified into grocery and stationery items.

The Ludlam's had shops in Barnsley – on and near Market Hill – from at least Stuart times. In 1664 mercer 'Mr.' (a sign of status) John Ludlam left instructions that he was to be buried

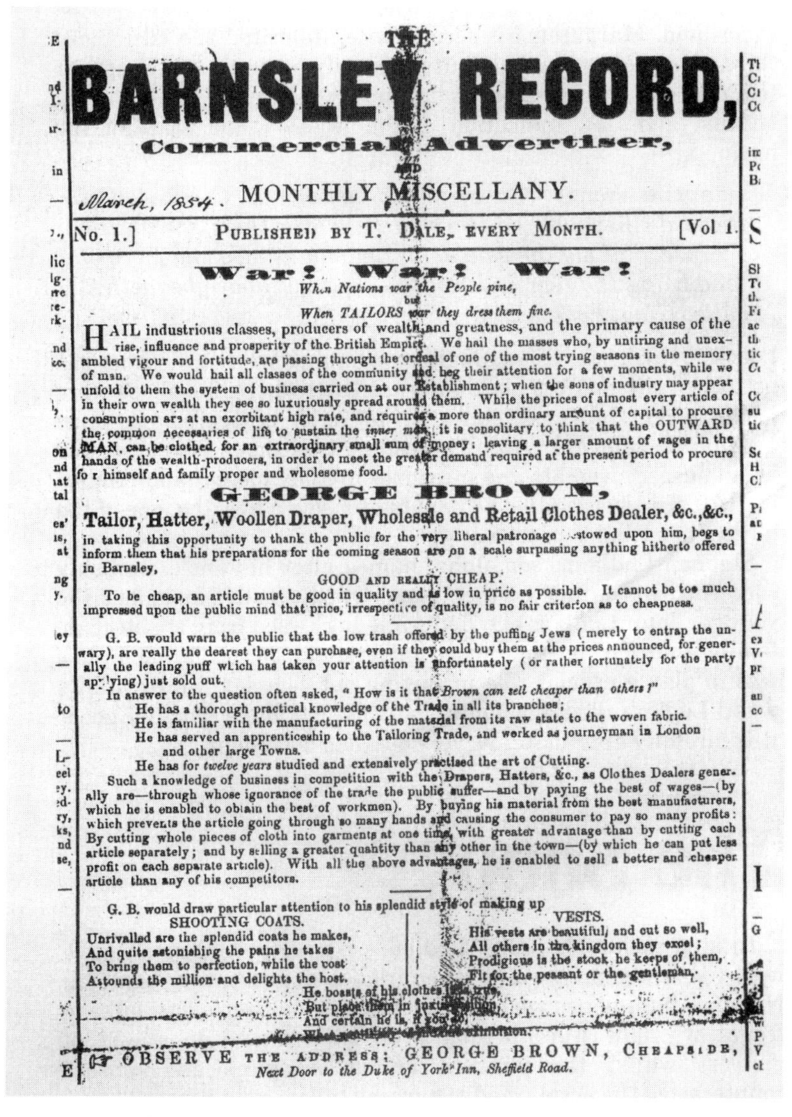

THE BARNSLEY RECORD, Commercial Advertiser, AND MONTHLY MISCELLANY.

March, 1854.

No. 1.] PUBLISHED BY T. DALE, EVERY MONTH. [Vol 1.

War! War! War!

When Nations war the People pine,
but
When TAILORS war they dress them fine.

HAIL industrious classes, producers of wealth and greatness, and the primary cause of the rise, influence and prosperity of the British Empire. We hail the masses who, by untiring and unexambled vigour and fortitude, are passing through the ordeal of one of the most trying seasons in the memory of man. We would hail all classes of the community and beg their attention for a few moments, while we unfold to them the system of business carried on at our Establishment; when the sons of industry may appear in their own wealth they see so luxuriously spread around them. While the prices of almost every article of consumption are at an exorbitant high rate, and requires a more than ordinary amount of capital to procure the common necessaries of life to sustain the *inner man*, it is consolitary to think that the OUTWARD MAN can be clothed for an extraordinary small sum of money; leaving a larger amount of wages in the hands of the wealth-producers, in order to meet the greater demand required at the present period to procure for himself and family proper and wholesome food.

GEORGE BROWN,

Tailor, Hatter, Woollen Draper, Wholesale and Retail Clothes Dealer, &c.,&c.,

in taking this opportunity to thank the public for the very liberal patronage bestowed upon him, begs to inform them that his preparations for the coming season are on a scale surpassing anything hitherto offered in Barnsley,

GOOD AND REALLY CHEAP.

To be cheap, an article must be good in quality and as low in price as possible. It cannot be too much impressed upon the public mind that price, irrespective of quality, is no fair criterion as to cheapness.

G. B. would warn the public that the low trash offered by the puffing Jews (merely to entrap the unwary), are really the dearest they can purchase, even if they could buy them at the prices announced, for generally the leading puff which has taken your attention is unfortunately (or rather fortunately for the party applying) just sold out.

In answer to the question often asked, "How is it that *Brown can sell cheaper than others?*"

He has a thorough practical knowledge of the Trade in all its branches;
He is familiar with the manufacturing of the material from its raw state to the woven fabric.
He has served an apprenticeship to the Tailoring Trade, and worked as journeyman in London and other large Towns.
He has for *twelve years* studied and extensively practised the art of Cutting.

Such a knowledge of business in competition with the Drapers, Hatters, &c., as Clothes Dealers generally are—through whose ignorance of the trade the public suffer—and by paying the best of wages—(by which he is enabled to obtain the best of workmen). By buying his material from the best manufacturers, which prevents the article going through so many hands and causing the consumer to pay so many profits: By cutting whole pieces of cloth into garments at one time, with greater advantage than by cutting each article separately; and by selling a greater quantity than any other in the town—(by which he can put less profit on each separate article). With all the above advantages, he is enabled to sell a better and cheaper article than any of his competitors.

G. B. would draw particular attention to his splendid style of making up

SHOOTING COATS.

Unrivalled are the splendid coats he makes,
And quite astonishing the pains he takes
To bring them to perfection, while the cost
Astounds the million and delights the host.

VESTS.

His vests are beautiful, and cut so well,
All others in the kingdom they excel;
Prodigious is the stock he keeps of them,
Fit for the peasant or the gentleman.

He boasts of his clothes [illegible],
But place them in [illegible],
And certain he is, if you do,
[illegible] exhibition.

☞ OBSERVE THE ADDRESS: GEORGE BROWN, CHEAPSIDE,
Next Door to the Duke of York Inn, Sheffield Road.

What would John Ludlam have thought of such an advert?

'at the Church of Barnsley at the discretion of my wife and kindred.' Through his first wife he had obtained a large town house and some land. Margaret, his second wife, inherited the customary third of his personal estate but the family business was entrusted to his brother, Stephen and the following bequest gives an indication of the location and scale of the business:

> *... two shopps with the standings now in Occupacon of Richard Chappell and two chambers over them now in the occupacon of me the said John Ludlam as also one piece of land being the remainder of the premises above bequethed called Great Peasehill.*

Peashill Nook was a narrow street running westwards from the bottom of the market place (Market Hill) where the shops were located. The business appeared to have prospered. Stephen Ludlam was one of twenty-five leading tradesmen who protested about suspect weights and measures used by mercer John Smith in 1670. Two years later he paid tax on seven hearths, one of the largest households in town.

Stephen Ludlam's son, John, named after his uncle, probably succeeded his father in the 1680s. On 18 November the younger John Ludlam married Anne Lockwood from a well-to-do family from Kirkburton, near Huddersfield. John's father-in-law was to play a crucial role in sorting out complex family affairs when Ludlam died, suddenly, in 1712. His huge stock of goods was carefully appraised in a very detailed document.

To step inside Mr John Ludlam's Barnsley shop must have been like entering a world taken from a story from the Arabian Nights. An immense variety of fabric ranging from exotic silks to frugal woollens were arranged on shelves and in chests of drawers whilst the pungent aroma of spices and tobacco counteracted the acrid smell of burning tallow candles.

Ludlam's stock of fabrics, listed in a very detailed inventory of 1712, consisted of more than four thousand yards of material and described through a bewildering welter of names. There were thirty-nine different types of fabric, many of them sub-divided according to quality, colour, use and state of production (e.g. bleached/unbleached).

Woollen cloth was kept in large quantities confirming a high demand for material used by working folk. 'Stuff', either plain or coloured was priced at between six and ten pence per yard and accounted for more than a quarter of the entire stock of fabric. Crepe, a much lighter fabric, was second in volume; it was available in scarlet or white and black crepe was in demand for mourning attire. At only a few pence per yard crape was more than four times cheaper than silk which it did resemble in appearance. Ludlam appeared to have done a good trade in supplying 'burying crape', an interesting response to the funeral customs of the day.

There were many fashionable garments on sale in Stuart and Georgian Barnsley – for those who could afford them.

'Tammy', originally made in Tamworth, Staffordshire and later produced in West Riding towns such as Wakefield, was stocked in large quantities. It was used widely by ordinary people for general clothing and for linings and undergarments. Tammy could be bought in qualities ranging from five to sixteen pence per yard, a similar price range being in force for worsted 'stuff'.

Waistcoats and breeches could be made from better quality woollen material such as 'calamanco', originally imported from Flanders, but later made locally.

Personal and household linen items were also stocked, headed

Pedlar with an assortment of goods from the Cries of London, 1711. Syndics of Cambridge Library

by 'damask' (table linen) and 'fancy ware' such as lace 'ruffell', used for decorative frills. 'camlet', once a costly oriental fabric but produced in seventeenth century England as a mixture of wool, cotton and hair, was also a valuable stock item; 'hair camblett' was the best grade, rivalling silk in value.

The coarser and heavier fabrics formed a distinct group in the inventory. 'Breeches stuff', along with other specialist materials such as 'grogram' (a coarse wool stiffened with gum), fustian (flax or cotton-based, used for frocks and jackets), and canvas (unbleached cloth of hemp or flax, used for sheeting, also for burials where the coffin was either too expensive or thought unnecessary) were popular items.

The fine 'Mantua' silks and 'alamodes' were the most expensive stock items at four to five shillings per yard and prudently stored in small quantities.

The cheaper and everyday special purpose materials such as flannel, buckram (linen, stiffened with gum or paste), 'drugget' (a coarse-grade woollen cloth used for outer garments), various grades of 'shalloon' (for linings) were grouped towards the end of the main list of fabrics. Small quantities of calico, 'Osnibruge' (probably home produced rather from the German town from which it was named) and 'tabby', a kind of taffeta, completed the list.

The emphasis of John Ludlam's business related to everyday dress and working apparel, with wool being the dominant ingredient. His choice of stock was a response to local demand and was therefore a reflection of the needs and tastes of Barnsley folk. The relatively small amount of linen in the inventory may have been due to the presence of several large and successful specialist linen drapers dominating this side of the trade.

Mr John Ludlam's shop emerges as an Aladdin's cave of goods with customers being given a wide choice of both traditional and new fashionable materials.

1. Haberdashery

The haberdashery side of John Ludlam's mercery trade only represented about one tenth of his turnover but the items he stocked were of tremendous importance to ordinary Barnsley people. The usual threads, laces, braids, ribbons and tapes were stocked along with newer items such as 'galloon', a narrow, gold or silver coloured ribbon used for trimming garments.

The mercer did not appear to stock hooks and eyes for fastening garments but buttons were available in some quantity, combining function with decoration.

A large quantity of playing cards was stocked but with a remarkable range of prices. The cheapest were sold at ten pence per dozen sets but luxury cards could be bought at ten shillings per dozen. Card playing was a popular pastime and by no means limited to the wealthy. Provincial mercers often stocked stationery items, especially paper and books but Ludlam did not appear to have had such interests. Perhaps this was due to the presence of John Smith's book and stationer's shop nearby.

Gloves and hats are the only examples of made-up goods for sale; both were obtained from Barnsley district felt and leather craftsmen and very large stocks would seem to have been kept. New gloves were often bought for mourning wear.

Despite the presence of several chandlers in the town, including the formidable Richard Richardson, Ludlam also stocked a few candles, perhaps for the convenience of the customers, more of a service rather than a serious stock item.

2. Grocery

'Groceries', despite the huge volume of fabrics, formed about one-sixth in value of John Ludlam's stock, one of the most obvious items being 617 pounds of tobacco, sold at ten pence per pound. Sugar was another basic commodity. Apart from the outrageously expensive sugar loaf, limited to the wealthy, the sugar was divided into grades such as 'powder' and 'bastard'. With more than eight hundred weight in stock this was obviously well within the reach of ordinary folk though 'Brown Candy' was a luxury item.

A good range of herbs and spices were available, stocked according to scarcity value and local demand. Ginger, pepper and carroway seeds were kept in large quantities whereas only a few ounces of mace and cloves were sold. Similarly, currants were in good supply but there were only limited amounts of nuts and rice.

A selection of household items were also sold. They included 'blew powder', (for washing clothes), sealing wax and corks.

Gunpowder and shot was available for firearms. Copperas and alum may have been bought to help with dying fabrics or tanning leather.

Mr John Ludlam emerges as a very important shopkeeper, someone who would have been well-known to fellow businessmen and most ordinary folk. He appears as one of the most successful and prosperous citizens of the market town of Barnsley, engaging in one of the most profitable but hardworking trades of seventeenth century England.

Ludlam was not alone in his enterprise; he was representative of a significant number of shopkeepers who formed part of a retailing revolution taking place in Barnsley.

3. Debts & Expenses

John Lockwood, Ludlam's father-in-law, was engaged in paying fifty-eight creditors sums ranging from a few shillings to over £100. The task must have taken a great deal of time and effort but was so necessary in order to sort out the late shopkeeper's affairs. George Usher's bill 'for physic the deced had in his last illness and several times before' amounted to £13.14s.11d., a fairly large sum and perhaps suggesting a prolonged illness. Ludlam certainly received a grand funeral since it cost a substantial £21.

Shop interior of the 1680s: a chapman, customer and debt book. Hambledon Press

Some expenses were offset by a sale of goods but Lockwood received £10 for 'apprizing the deceds and attending the sale of them for several weeks.' Ludlam owed at least thirteen Barnsley people sums either loaned or invested with him, some of them with considerable interest charges. A further twenty persons, probably not local, were paid a total of £200, perhaps in lieu of the recent provision of stock. Shopkeepers often paid partly in 'ready money' and the remainder paid later. It was quite common for a large amount of bills to be outstanding.

Legal expenses amounted to £15 and rent and taxes a further £33. Lockwood had to make several long journeys on horseback, round trips of 80 miles, to the busy port of Gainsborough which was an important source for fabric from East Anglia and the Midlands. He also had to make trips to Rotherham, Wakefield, York and 'other places' from his Kirkburton home in order to settle bills. Even outstanding postal charges to and from London where Ludlam also obtained goods, were duly paid. George Shillitoe, probably Ludlam's assistant, received £15 in wages and for helping to sell the deceased's goods.

The expenses and overheads amounted to £862, about £25 more than the value of his shops goods and personal possessions. Ludlam's demise was probably not unusual given the nature of trading practices of the time. What his inventory shows is a frozen picture of a busy shopkeeper with large overheads whose activities are revealed, warts and all, with the help of the meticulous attention to detail of a conscientious father-in-law.

In a sense John Ludlam was one of Barnsley's first urbanised citizens, at a time when the town was expanding and competition between shopkeepers was becoming more apparent. Mr Ludlam had social and business contacts with many other prominent local tradesmen; some, like the Leathams and Donfords, were Quakers, others such as the Ushers and Rookes had family connections. He was probably relatively young when he died; his son, Abraham being just ten years old.

PART SIX: PERSECUTION & PROSECUTION

17 WITCHCRAFT

Persecution, that most horrible of human characteristics, was rife in Barnsley during the middle decades of the seventeenth century. Yet groups such as the Quakers, inspired by fellowship and faith, successfully overcame the prejudice and jealousy that existed. Indeed many Friends, as we shall see, made remarkable contributions to the town.

However, another deep seated kind of mistrust continued which had even more hurtful effects on innocent individuals who could not call on the support of fraternal organisations. Witchcraft was thoroughly believed in and heavy and severe were the punishments meted out to those poor persons, usually old women, who became the objects of suspicion.

Even in supposedly more enlightened times, when witchcraft cases were not brought before the church courts or quarter sessions, old women could still be tormented and ill-treated by both children and adults, and some unfortunates became virtual tourist attractions. Gossip combined with rumour and superstition via home and market place and secret tales became amazing facts never to be questioned.

A faded gravestone forms part of the pathway of the porch of St Mary's, reminding worshippers:

You that on this do cast an eye,
Remember that you all must die;
There's few who live so many years,
For at all ages death appears.

Martha Watt lived to the grand old age of ninety-three. Her husband, Edward, passed away on Valentine's Day, 1746, almost 50 years earlier. Two of their children died in infancy and a third, a son, only survived to the age of sixteen. This poor widow barely made a living by selling sweetmeats and other produce from a little thatched cottage in Jumble Lane, near Beckett Square, with occasional treks to Penistone market.

Her later appearance, which was said to be tall, raw-boned, grim and ugly, together with her solitary and unfortunate life, made her an ideal victim of gossip and suspicion. Before she died the old lady was subjected to increasing abuse as she was branded with the title of the 'Barnsley Witch'.

It was reported that Martha's neighbours would not encounter her after dark if they could avoid her and when there was a chance meeting they expected no luck for the rest of the day. Her custom of fetching a 'kit' (wooden bucket) of water by balancing it on her head without touching it with her hands was thought to be highly suspicious.

One of her neighbours, John Widdop, gives a typically bizarre account of one of her doings, the kind of ridiculous tale which was, nevertheless, believed by some. He firstly described her small thatched house which was 'open to the ridge' inside. Then the story goes that one day she was sat in the house with her son, she knitting stockings by the fire, when she turned to him and said, 'Bill, you will neither say God nor Lord, I will show thee a touch' whereupon she threw her worstered ball upwards. It stuck to a roof timber and she seized the dangling loose end, climbed up, hand over hand until reaching the top. Bill acclaimed 'Ee God mother I did not think you could do that' which apparently broke the charm causing the lady to fall, breaking one of her legs in the process. The event was said to have been 'as true as Gospel,' since John Widdop's aunt had taken him many times to see the old woman who was laid in bed with a broken leg.

Another story in connection with 'Matty Watts' concerned her regular excursions to fetch water from a pump at the bottom of Graham's Orchard, then called Horn's Lane. *The Horns* was a licensed house which became the *Lord Nelson*.

The stream which fed the pump was unreliable in dry weather so she tried to obtain water from a yard behind another Barnsley hostelry – the *Old Royal Oak*, later the *Imperial Hotel.* This establishment was kept by a carrier called John Rycroft. One day he refused her water. Within the space of five weeks, five of his horses had been lost, and of course poor Martha was said to have 'bewitched' them. A witch-doctor was immediately consulted. There was a simple remedy. The heart of one of the horses was to be cut out, stuck full of pins and roasted before the fire.

Whilst this was being done an eager party was dispatched to Martha's house where they found the understandably frightened old lady huddled by the fire with beads of perspiration on her brow, a sure sign that the 'treatment' was working. Poor Martha was goaded into saying that Rycroft would not lose another horse – or at least that was the tale which was taken back to the *Royal Oak* and no doubt embellished further there. An unruly party of wiredrawers later waylaid poor Martha and pricked her with pins causing her great distress.

James I interrogating a group of potential witches. Weidenfeld & Nicolson

Martha was also said to have bewitched a child of John Siddons who occupied a cottage near what was later known as the Gas Nook. The child never walked until it was five years old but was said to have 'run across the floor' on 18 July 1795 when Martha Watts died. This day was also said to be memorable for its storm and thunder and lightning which did much damage and of course which Martha brewed.

Poor Martha must have had a miserable existence, a very sad reflection of a society which paradoxically could be very caring towards the poor.

Witches, Wizards & Scolding Women

In the late summer of 1674 two young women found themselves locked in a Barnsley gaol accused of witchcraft. Susan, the wife of Joseph Hinchliffe, and Ann, the wife of Thomas Shillitoe, both of Denby, were examined by a local magistrate.

Depositions or sworn statements were taken before Darcy Wentworth, JP. Mary Moor, a girl of sixteen, was an accuser and her evidence alleged that she had overheard Susan Hinchliffe and Ann Shillitoe talking together. Hinchliffe had said to Anne:

> *If thou canst but get young Thomas Haigh to buy three pennyworth of indigo, and look him in the face when he gives it thee, and touch his locks we shall have power enough to take life.*

Susan Hinchliffe was also said to have directed Ann Shillitoe to go and make hay at Thomas Haigh's farm:

> *If thou canst but bring nine bits of bread away and nine bits of butter in thy mouth, and we shall have power enough to take the life of his goods. We shall neither leave him cow nor horse …*

Two further pages of similar so-called evidence followed. At a time when reputation counted as much as facts, scarcely anyone could hope to have a fair hearing. The unfortunate women, as was the custom for such cases, were duly committed for trial at the next assizes to be held at York.

To make matters even more incredible, Thomas Haigh in his evidence to Wentworth, declared that Mary Moor, the principal witness, 'did vomit a piece of bent wire and also a piece of paper with two crooked pins.'

The women were, however, given considerable local support. A petition, signed by fifty persons who had known them for ten to twenty years, vouched for their sober, honest and unblemished characters.

A very early wood-cut: 'Ducking' a witch. Batsford

At the assizes, Joseph Hinchliffe, who was also indicted, and his wife, were bound over to answer the charge at the next assizes. The eventual outcome remains a mystery but there was a cruel twist to the story. Eighteen months after the accusation Joseph Hinchliffe hanged himself in a wood near his home. Susan, his wife, had recently died, apparently praying on her death-bed for her accusers.

Not everyone believed in witchcraft even during the anti-witch mania years of Puritan England. Yet gossip and plain ignorance permeated local society fired by both church and state. Punishment could be very severe. More than four thousand men, women and children were executed for witchcraft in Scotland between 1563 and 1722. The last execution of a witch in England took place at Exeter in 1682 when three women were hanged. Trials of suspected witches continued until 1712 and, as evident from the sad case of Martha Watt, the so-called 'Barnsley Witch', the belief continued until at least the end of the century.

Another curious case was heard at the quarter sessions held at Barnsley in October 1677. Michael Woodhouse, of Wadsley, tailor, was indicted for 'professing to declare where stolen goods were to be found, being a breach of statute concerning witchcraft.' Woodhouse had failed to find sureties for good behaviour and was therefore sent to York gaol. Margaret Rayner of Wentworth was summoned to answer the charge that she had gone to see Woodhouse to ask him to tell her who had stolen a spoon and was then given the description of a young man. The 'wizard' demanded a shilling for his services but she gave him four pence which was all she had.

Women could also be severely punished and certainly humiliated if they were thought to be guilty of using abusive or harsh language. Persistent offenders were likely to find themselves before the magistrate's bench. Ann Green and Ann Anderson, both of Cudworth, were indicted for 'issuing common scolds and disturbances of his majesty's peace'. Again no sureties were forthcoming so they were placed in York Castle gaol until evidence of their good character was received by the court.

Wearing the 'brank' was a common punishment for scolding women. The scold's brank was a kind a bridle made of iron bands, with a sort of tongue or gag that fitted into the mouth. The witch's brank had a gruesome addition: a spiked collar.

The 'cucking stool' or ducking stool was also a popular remedy. This consisted of a chair or stool in which the woman was tightly strapped and then swung over some water in which the offender was 'ducked', presumably until her temper was subdued.

Mr E Oxley in a letter of 25 August 1823, provides us with interesting information about local ducking stools:

> *I have heard my father say that at what is called Cuckstool, a little way below Wombwell on the way to Darfield, there existed a curious mechanical contrivance not infrequently used in his day. It consisted of a strong pole, probably thirty-feet long, one end of which was fastened to the ground, and to the other was fixed an arm chair, which was suspended over a deep pool. I recollect seeing nearly forty years ago* [i.e about 1783] *on Birdwell Common between Sheffield and Barnsley a ducking stool of the kind described.*

Local parish accounts often include items relating to the expense of repairing cuckstools and ducking stools.

18 The Quakers

On top of Burton Bank, almost encroached upon by modern housing, lies a small neglected burial ground, a hidden memorial to a group of people who have played a prominent part in the making of Barnsley. The Quakers or Society of Friends were never numerically strong in our area but they were a remarkably active section of the local community. Some of the early converts, such as shopkeeper John Leatham, spearheaded a wave of business activity which boosted the local economy and fuelled Barnsley's fame as 'a flourishing market town.' Others, such as Gamaliel Milner, had industrial interests and there were many country folk who were attracted by the unashamedly radical Christian voice of George Fox and his followers.

George Fox (1624–1691), the son of a Leicestershire weaver, left home at the age of nineteen and wandered the countryside 'thirsting for God.' Fox was soon imprisoned for daring to question orthodox views but, in the early 1650s, his influence began to spread and his message was quickly accepted by small groups of Barnsley people.

Friends suffered much persecution in the pursuit of their right to speak to God 'directly from the heart' and also because they refused to take oaths, or to pay tithes or rates to the Church of England. Locally, they became a race apart, as 'the people called quakers,' a highly distinct group not only due to their peculiar style of dress but also because of a strict puritanical belief that music-making, play-acting, sports and other worldly pastimes were contrary to Quaker teaching. Discipline within the Society of Friends was severe. A member could be excluded for drunkenness, bankruptcy or for marrying a non-Quaker. One of their greatest strengths was in their willingness to do business with each other in confidence and also help each other in times of distress. The regular local, regional and national meetings provided a superb basis of contacts.

Quakers believed in the immediacy of Christ's teachings, thought of churches as irrelevant 'steeple-houses,' ordained ministers as unnecessary but believed in the applications of first-hand experience. Consequently, they gathered together with little or no pre-arrangement or any preacher, certain that out of an energetic and expected silence God might use any one of them as ministers.

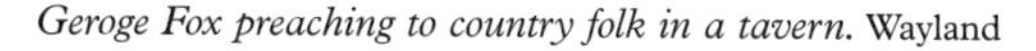

Geroge Fox preaching to country folk in a tavern. Wayland

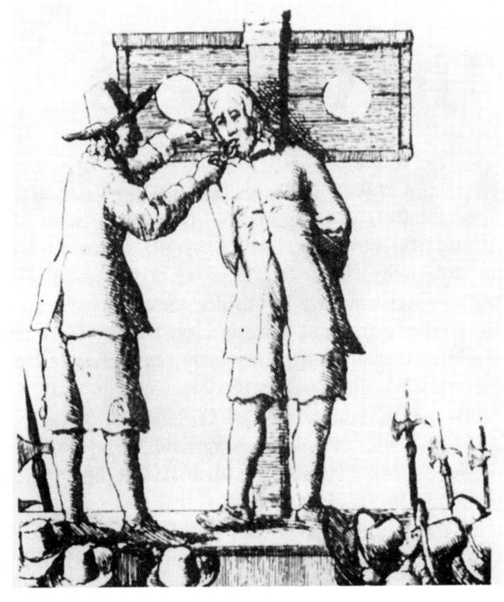

'Friends of Truth' were tortured, pillorised and imprisoned. Wayland

The Quaker burial ground at Burton Bank occupied a ledge of land near to the top of a precipitous slope. Although a bleak setting, one of the rewards was a most spectacular view of the Dearne Valley, which served as an extremely important routeway, and of the town of Barnsley rising boldy from the opposite hill top. The land at the rear of the site would have been at best marginal pasture, more likely waste. The eastern side abutted common land. The Barnsley-Burton roadway passed within twenty- five metres to the west and a packhorse route ran almost parallel to the burial ground. Access was either by foot or horse from the north or by a track, a route carefully described in the Monk Bretton Enclosure Award of 1778:

> *One other private road or way leading from … Old Mill Road near the west end of the village of Monk Bretton … thence eastwards in the direction towards the north-east corner of the burying ground of the people called Quakers leaving sufficient room before the west side … to turn a hearse, coach or other carriage which said road we have started and set out of the bredth of five yards and do order the same to be called Meeting House Road.*

In spite of the close proximity of the village, with relatively easy access, the rugged nature of the land meant that the burial place was hidden from the Barnsley side, and well out of sight of travellers.

By 1656, over one thousand Quakers were imprisoned, the number increasing to over 4,000 during the first two years of the reign of Charles II. The transport of a coffin from outlying areas such as Darfield, Darton, Notton, Woolley and Sandal must have been fraught with danger during the persecution years. An interesting story, often repeated down the years, and in fact recounted to me by a local resident in 1972, concerns the reason for the foundation of the Burton Bank Burial Ground. The following example is taken from the *Life of Thomas Shillitoe* (1807):

> *An aged man, a member of the Society who now occupies the house adjoining the premises, told us his family had continued to reside there for three generations, and related the following anecdote, showing how friends came into possession of the property. In the commencement of the Society in this neighbourhood, a young man who had embraced the principles of Friends died and when they were taking the body to the graveyard for burial a number of rude people assembled, and became so tumultuous, that they threw the coffin down, broke it, and rolled the dead body into the road; the owner of the property which the meeting-house and burial ground now occupy, being present, was so affected at this conduct, that he said he would prevent such outrages in future; and marked out the ground, and gave it to Friends for the purposes for which it is now used.*

The Quaker benefactor was said to have been one George Ellis. Documentary sources tend to support at least part of the story. According to two fragments of information, noted from minutes kept in Ackworth School safe, a certain George Ellis 'by a

Executors of this my last will & Testament, in witness whereof I have hereunto set my hand & Seal this twelfth day of May in the year of our Lord One thousand and seven hundred & forty ...
Signed Sealed published & declared by the Testatrix as her last Will in our presence who were desired by her to be Witnesses hereunto — Ann Leatham
... Leathom
Mary Eccles
John Will...
May 7. 1742. I gave the Affirmation to Mary Eccles Witness of this Will being a Quaker, and also to William Leatham and Boswell Middleton the Executors being likewise Quakers, Benjamin Wilson

Extract from the will of Ann Leatham, a Barnsley Quaker.

Deed of Gift in 1657 conveyed to several trustees a Piece of Ground for a burial place of the people called Quakers' and an agreement was made between Ellis and Gamaliel Milner, Thomas Storey, Thomas Aldham and John Kilham. Aldham was one of the first Quakers to be imprisoned in York Castle; he was buried at Warmsworth in 1660 where a former Meeting House still exists. In a gazeteer of Quaker Meetings, kept at the Library of the Religious Society of Friends, in London, Ellis is identified as one of the early Quakers of our area. He was a prominent citizen of Monk Bretton listed in tax returns taken in 1660 and 1672.

Women had equal rights with men at Quaker meetings.

The burial ground's position, right at the edge of the extensive and ancient parish of Royston must have made parochial control difficult to enforce. It was also out of administrative reach of Silkstone parish and yet was but a short journey from Barnsley whose fleeting parsons probably had little influence. Burton was also well-positioned in relation to the Pontefract Monthly Meeting group; it became a focal point from which the movement could spread. The presence of a very active group of early converts in the Burton Grange area, quite near to the old priory or 'Burton Abbey' as it was locally known, finally rooted Quakerism in the region.

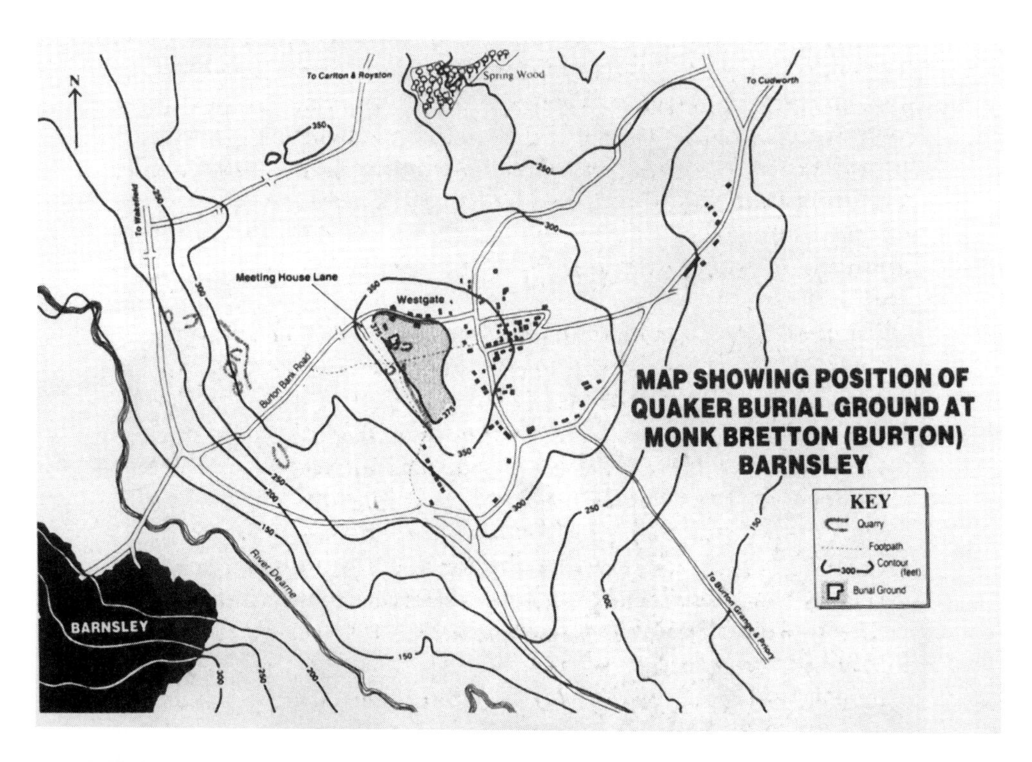

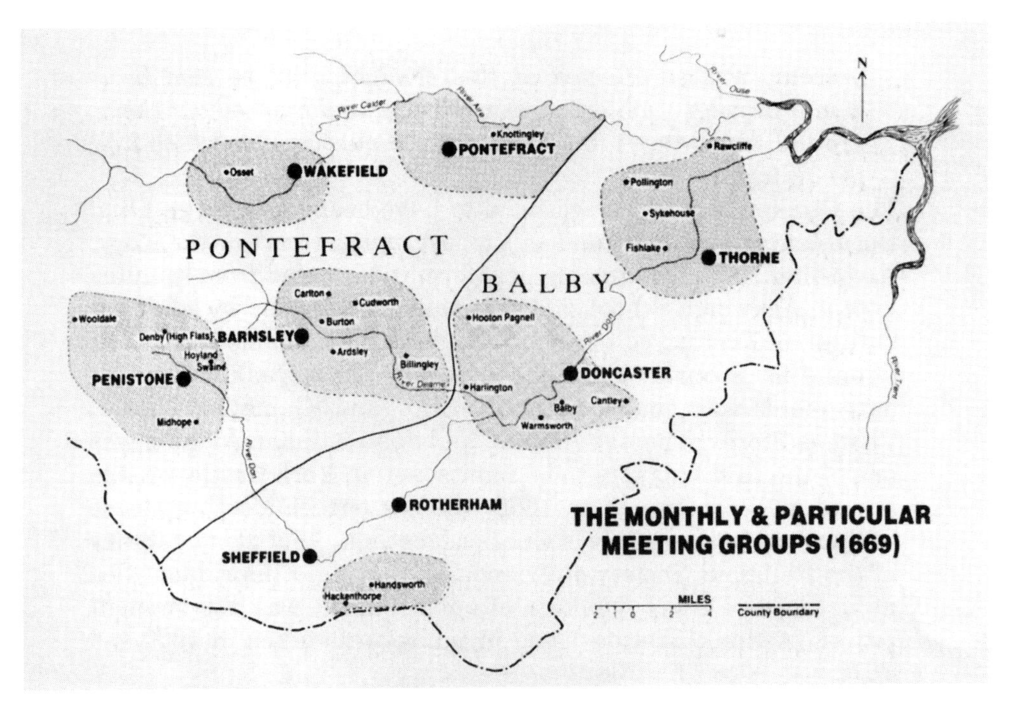

The old quaker Meeting house at Warmsworth (now a private home) where the Aldhams attended.

The Royston parish registers for the year 1657 contain the first recorded burial at bleak Burton Bank when 'Hellen wife of Gamaliel Milner of Monckbretton Abbey was buryed the 12th day of August in the burying place at burton a quaker.' The Dodworth diarist John Hobson made reference to the Milners in 1728:

> *10 September. That day, Michael Milner, a noted quaker, buried at the buriing-place at Burton, in the same grave that his father, Gamaliel Milner, and his mother were buried, who occasioned that place to be inclosed for that use; and she was the first to be interr'd there.*

The Milners, with Nottinghamshire and Northamptonshire connections, came to Burton Grange probably because they knew Lady Mary Armyne, the owner and sometime resident at the priory; she was a daughter of Henry Talbot, the younger brother of Gilbert, Earl of Shrewsbury. It was Lady Armyne who founded the Talbot Almshouses in 1654 for six poor widows who each received an annual allowance of forty shillings and a new gown.

Gamaliel Milner's Quaker neighbours included William Silvester who worked the old 'Abbey Mill' across from the ruined priory. Silvester was one of staunchest of the Burton Friends, frequently cited in civil and ecclesiastical courts for not attending church, refusing to have his children baptised, refusing to pay church assessments etc. The mill, almost certainly on a twelfth century site, is one of the most interesting buildings in the Barnsley area. J W Walker, writing in the 1920s, stated that Sir William Armyne's initials and a date of 1635 was carved on a door lintel. Unfortunately weathering appears to have obliterated this inscription but the date probably refers to a rebuilding of the structure. The Priory Corn Mill was converted into a public house and restaurant by Barnsley – born architect Malcolm Lister who had to overcome many legal and engineering problems prior to its construction. The entire building was raised above the flood level, a considerable engineering feat, and therefore ensuring that it could be not only preserved but enjoyed and used by future generations. In the course of renovation many names and dates of past millers, including William Silvester (1686), were found carved in stone and form most interesting features.

Gamaliel and Helen Milner had at least five children. After Helen's premature death Gamaliel remarried: to Isabel Jackson of Barnsley, and though there were four more children born, only one survived infancy; sons Joseph, Tobias and David were buried at Burton between 1660 and 1664.

Gamaliel Milner was one of the leading freeholders of Monk Bretton. In his will, made on 29 November, 1675, he described his status as 'gentleman' and his condition as 'aged in years and infirm in body.' He openly instructed that he was to be buried 'in the graveyard at Burton.' Other Friends tended to use the safer expression 'to be buried in a christian manner' or 'at the discretion of my executors.'

Gamaliel Milner's monetary bequests exceeded £1,000, a large sum for the period, and he had property in Darfield (Tyers Hill) and Worsbrough (White Cross). He also had industrial interests, especially coal mining. Some of the family maintained a high social profile in later years. A grandson, also called Gamaliel, left £2,000 in his will of 1733 whilst a Michael Milner lived in some style at Rockley Old Hall in Worsbrough township.

Quakerism is usually portrayed as the extreme left-wing of the Puritan movement but the leading members of the Society of Friends tended to be men of substance. In 1662 nonconformists were barred from public office and hundreds of dissenting ministers were expelled. Such repression may have made the Quakers even more determined to do well in trade and commerce and it did not stop enterprising Barnsley Friends from acting as charitable trustees for the town of Barnsley or serving on juries. Quaker traits such as frugality and discipline must have helped them in business affairs. Customers were more likely to patronise someone who was known to be honest and trustworthy.

In 1662 churchwardens were unsuccessful in getting the Burton Quakers to attend church, a situation probably common to all local parishes where Friends lived. In 1688, Royston farmer George Bramhall, who was a Quaker, was summoned to appear before the church court 'for uttering words of defamation at Mr. Dutton,' the parson. Another one of the Bramhalls was accused of a 'clandestine' marriage. In 1682, John Turner, a Cawthorne Quaker, was indicted at the Quarter Sessions 'for absenting himself from Church three Sundayes.'

Edward Pitt, constable of Monk Bretton reported to the Barnsley Quarter Sessions in October, 1683, saying that he had:

Made diligent search and enquire for all conventicle and unlawful meetings and hath not found any within our Constabulary sine the time limited in the warn't nor are have not any persons that absent themselves from church and devine service, except
Jonathan Broadhead and Jane his wife
William Broadhead and Hannah his wife
William Silvest and Elizabeth his wife
Henry Ellis
Joseph Sanderson
Alice Hall widdow and which is called by the name Quakers

There were frequent attempts made to make the Quakers pay local taxes. In 1661, for example, the following order was made at the Barnsley quarter sessions:

Wheras most of the Inhabitants of Munckbreton pettioned this corte that William Milner Gamaliel Milner William Silvester Richard Egborrow widdow Johnson and sevrall others within the parish refuse to pay their assessments to the Constable and for repairing the Church and dutyes thereunto belonging as formerly they have done and plead of late time priviledge that they are free by law yet that the service of the Kinge may be not neglected this corte do order that all and any inhabitants pay equall assessmts due to the Constable and above all the Church dutyes and upon the faylor of any this corte desires the next justices to bind over those that are refraining to answer their refusal…

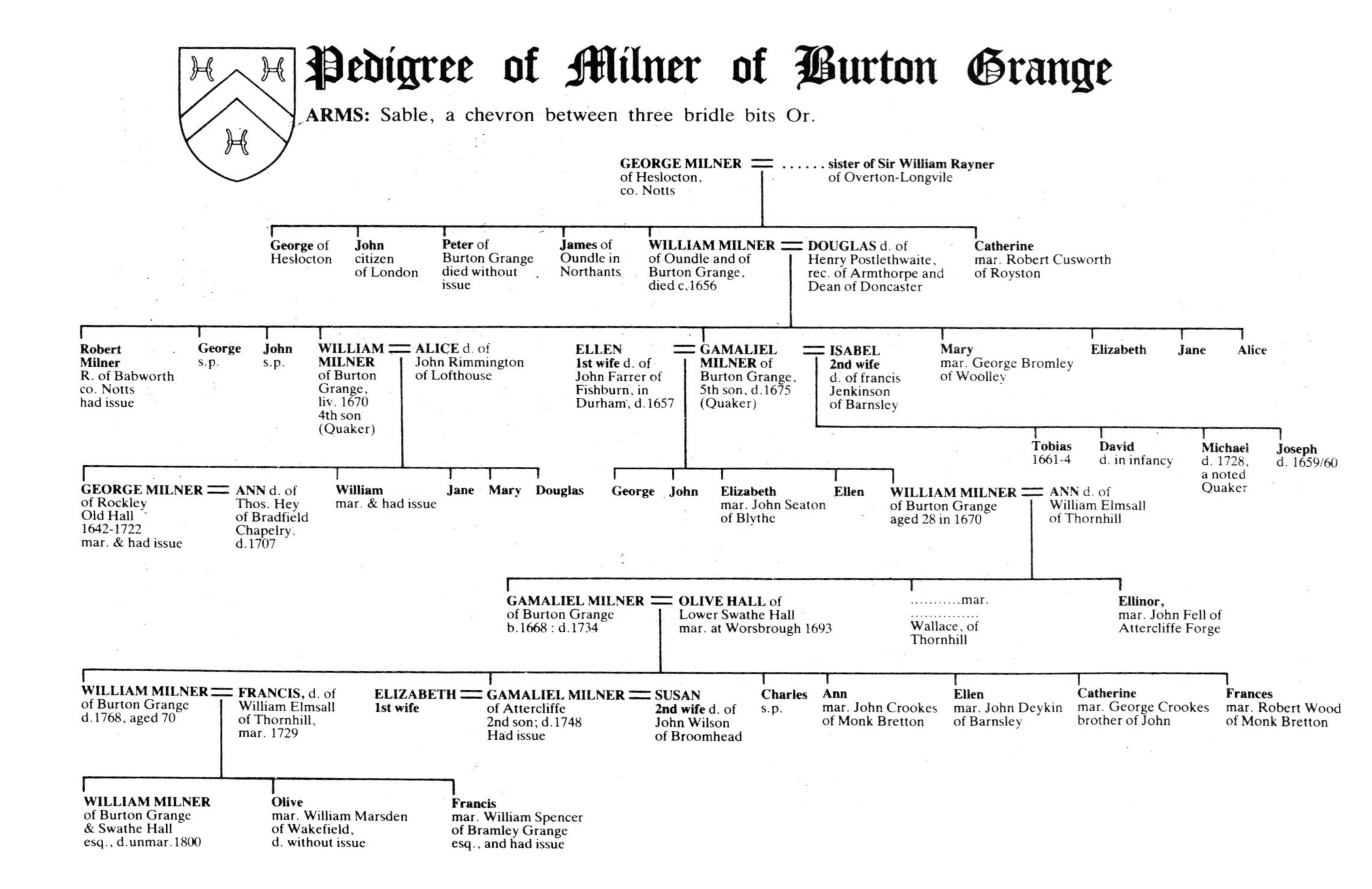
Pedigree of Milner of Burton Grange
ARMS: Sable, a chevron between three bridle bits Or.
GEORGE MILNER of Heslocton, co. Notts
...... sister of Sir William Rayner of Overton-Longvile
George of Heslocton
John citizen of London
Peter of Burton Grange died without issue
James of Oundle in Northants
WILLIAM MILNER of Oundle and of Burton Grange, died c.1656
DOUGLAS d. of Henry Postlethwaite, rec. of Armthorpe and Dean of Doncaster
Catherine mar. Robert Cusworth of Royston
Robert Milner R. of Babworth co. Notts had issue
George s.p.
John s.p.
WILLIAM MILNER of Burton Grange, liv. 1670 4th son (Quaker)
ALICE d. of John Rimmington of Lofthouse
ELLEN 1st wife d. of John Farrer of Fishburn, in Durham, d.1657
GAMALIEL MILNER of Burton Grange, 5th son, d.1675 (Quaker)
ISABEL 2nd wife d. of francis Jenkinson of Barnsley
Mary mar. George Bromley of Woolley
Elizabeth
Jane
Alice
Tobias 1661-4
David d. in infancy
Michael d. 1728, a noted Quaker
Joseph d. 1659/60
GEORGE MILNER of Rockley Old Hall 1642-1722 mar. & had issue
ANN d. of Thos. Hey of Bradfield Chapelry. d.1707
William mar. & had issue
Jane
Mary
Douglas
George
John
Elizabeth mar. John Seaton of Blythe
Ellen
WILLIAM MILNER of Burton Grange aged 28 in 1670
ANN d. of William Elmsall of Thornhill
GAMALIEL MILNER of Burton Grange b.1668 : d.1734
OLIVE HALL of Lower Swathe Hall mar. at Worsbrough 1693
..........mar. .... Wallace, of Thornhill
Ellinor, mar. John Fell of Attercliffe Forge
WILLIAM MILNER of Burton Grange d.1768, aged 70
FRANCIS, d. of William Elmsall of Thornhill, mar. 1729
ELIZABETH 1st wife
GAMALIEL MILNER of Attercliffe 2nd son; d.1748 Had issue
SUSAN 2nd wife d. of John Wilson of Broomhead
Charles s.p.
Ann mar. John Crookes of Monk Bretton
Ellen mar. John Deykin of Barnsley
Catherine mar. George Crookes brother of John
Frances mar. Robert Wood of Monk Bretton
WILLIAM MILNER of Burton Grange & Swathe Hall esq., d.unmar.1800
Olive mar. William Marsden of Wakefield, d. without issue
Francis mar. William Spencer of Bramley Grange esq., and had issue

A packed Quaker meeting in London.

Such orders had little effect. In 1663 the Burton Quakers were again ordered to pay constable and church dues.

Quakers also had to face the wrath of the church courts of the day. In the twenty years after 1667 the Archdeacon's Court, meeting at York, made judgments on 156 individuals and families from the Barnsley area, all 'reputed Quakers.' Some clearly defied judgements which included penances, excommunication and were 'presented' to the court almost on an annual basis. The Burton Grange miller William Silvester, and his wife, Elizabeth were named on at least twelve separate occasions. The reasons for being reported included phrases such as 'not coming to church to receive the sacrement, being quakers,' 'for very seldom frequenting church to hear divine service and sermons', 'absenting himself from church' and 'not paying his proportion of assessments for repairs to the chapel'. Yet the authorities were waging a losing battle. In a sample year (1684) there were Quaker families present in Sheffield (15), Thorne (15), Adlingfleet (8), Whiston (6), Ecclesall (6), Attercliffe (4), Kirk Smeaton (3), Aston (2), Hatfield, Hooton Pagnal and Fishlake (1 each). In 1682 sixteen Quakers from Barnsley were reported for not receiving the sacrament.

Following the Religious Toleration Act of 1689 local Quakers continued to meet in the same way as they had done for the previous thirty years. The private dwelling house was still the main meeting place though it could now be registered by archbishop or Quarter Sessions as an authorised place of worship.

The establishment of monthly business meetings brought order to the movement and helped it from falling apart. The early post-toleration years represented the zenith of Quaker strength. By 1699 Friends were known to be living in at least 464 Yorkshire towns and villages. Membership was at its highest level.

A small meeting house was erected at the side of the burial ground in 1697. Quaker travellers, passing through the area, were now able to call at Burton for worship, companionship and, if necessary, lodgings. Quaker diaries show that the Burton Meeting House, attracted Friends from a wide area:

> *Thence we went to Sheffield, and so to Burton, to Francis Harrison's, where we lodged.* Life of Thomas Storey, circa 1696.
>
> *I went to Steeton and had a meeting; from thence to Bradford, and had a meeting two miles off; so to Burton, and had a meeting at Michael Miller's (probably Milner's) house on a first day; from thence to Pomfret and Selby* Journal of the Life of William Edmundson, 1697.
>
> *On the 29th I went forward to Harrison, where I had great peace and comfort in the blessed truth …* (Life of Thomas Storey, 1715).
>
> *We had satisfactory meetings at Burton … and later, … passed on to Burton … where I had meetings,* Life of Deborah Bell, 1709.
>
> *… From thence we went to Burton … which was large and a comfortable time …* Life of David Stanton, 1749
>
> *… on the 6th to Burton, where many of the neighbours came to the meeting, and it was an open favoured time. The burial-ground there is said to be first that was in the possession of Friends; and to have been given by a sober man who was moved with pity, on seeing a corpse indecently treeted.* Life of Sarah Stephenson, c. 1720.

I continued at home one whole year after I married, when I found drawings in my mind to pay a religious visit to Friends in some parts of Yorkshire ... had two pretty large and laborious meetings from whence we travelled to Burton and many more meetings in those parts. Life of Joseph Oxley, 1758.

When the Vicar of Royston completed a report requested by Archbishop Herring, in 1743, he stated that only two out of 185 families living in the parish (including Burton) were Quakers. He also noted that they 'assemble once every Sunday but are few in number and very rarely any teacher'. In 1764 John Mence, the curate of St Mary's informed the archbishop that there were only seven dissenters in the town of Barnsley 'of the people called Quakers' out of some 350 families. Such figures are likely to be under-estimates but Quakers were declining in numbers as the century progressed. The change reflected a national decline in Puritanism. It also coincided with a new and popular movement in our region: Methodism.

Meetings continued to be held at Burton, though apparently not without some discomfort:

First day walked to Burton; the meeting house being damp, the meeting being held in an upper room, and I was apprehensive, from Friends thus deserting (that) strangers might be prevented from sitting down with them, by supposing that Friends were occupied about some Society concerns ... and I therefore advised Friends to make some means of making the meeting-house safe to sit in. Second day attended the Monthly Meeting at Burton. Journal of Thomas Shillitoe, 1807.

Meetings of Quakers were also taking place in Barnsley:

Here [Burton] *I also met Thomas Shillitoe, who had recently returned from his arduous labours in visiting the drinking houses in some parts of Ireland ... In the evening we had a large meeting with the town's people in Barnsley and the following day rode to Sheffield.* Life of Henry Hull, 1811.

Shillitoe, a local man, made a number of 'missionary visits' to Barnsley alehouses:

In the spring of the year 1817, I laid before the monthly meeting a concern to visit the ale-houses in Barnsley. My friend Joseph Wood of Highflats, proposing to accompany me, we were liberated for the service. We were generally well-received, and many of those we visited acknowledged their thankfullness ... Journal of Thomas Shillitoe, 1817.

The minutes of the York Quarterly Meeting of December, 1813 show that plans were being made for 'the disposing of the Meeting House at Burton and the building of a new one at Barnsley'. By March, 1815 the building had begun and £300 was needed for its completion. The specifications of the new Meeting House included the provision of old panels from, or in the style of, those at Burton. Subscriptions for the Barnsley Meeting House exceeded £1,100 and the Huddersfield Road building replaced Burton as the main centre of worship for Barnsley area Quakers.

Information in the present Barnsley Friend's Library, probably compiled by local historian E G Bayford, suggests that the columns which were once at the entrance to the Burton burial ground were preserved by the builder who demolished the old stonework on the site and found a new purpose when adapted for use as the village war memorial. The two columns, on new bases, stood at the entrance to the Recreation Ground but a few years ago were moved across Cross Street to a new memorial garden.

Although a relatively small group during the nineteenth century, the Barnsley Quakers continued to be influential. At a time when the town was emerging as one of the most important linen manufacturing centres in England many of the new industrialists were Quakers. By 1800 there were nine Friends running independent linen establishments and many others were drapers, weavers, warehousemen and carriers. William Bayliss came to Barnsley to establish a linen factory in 1812 and became a Quaker, Charles Wood (later Lord Halifax) wrote to his uncle, judge George Wood that cousin William (Bayliss) 'had turned Quaker and gone mad'. The Wilsons, Harveys, Bradys, Taylors and Yardleys had considerable influence on the early industrial development of Barnsley and in promoting educational and social activities. The Friends Adult School, for example was established in Wellington Street in 1897.

By the nineteenth century Quakers looked the same and were interested in the same things as most other people.

Women Friends took an active part in Quaker activities and held their own business meetings. The following epistle was read at a women's meeting in 1714:

> *... we should keep clear from wearing long cloaks and bonnets with them, likewise refrain from having tea tables set with fine china being more for sight than service, and that Friends keep clear from the superfluous part in drinking tea. We thinking that some of the time and money might be better made use of.*

The War Memorial Garden, Monk Bretton. Brian Elliott

Later Quakers drank tea and wore cloaks with a clear conscience!

Writing in the *Journal of the Friends Historical Society* in 1906, Charles Brady stated that 'There are a few flat gravestones in the Burton Burial Ground, now nearly illegible'. Two of them that he referred to: William Fletcher of Barnsley and his daughter, Hannah (1689), and Samuell Nickleson of Darton (1688) were subsequently removed for safe keeping to the grounds of the Barnsley Friends on Huddersfield Road. Many other gravestones went missing during the 1940s.

The Quaker Burial Ground photographed in 1981. The author

When I surveyed the site in 1972 the perimeter of the graveyard (14 by 10 metres) and the outline of the Meeting House (9 by 7 metres) could be clearly seen. A disfigured late-seventeenth century gravestone lay in the south-west corner of the plot and the gravestone of Vernon Crank of Barnsley, who was buried there as late as 1851, was also visible. It appears that meetings and interments were still taking place at Burton long after the establishment of the Barnsley Meeting House. Wilfred Allott of York, writing in 1869, recollected that his aunts remembered Jane Allott, 'our grandmother,' who was born in 1815, walking to Burton for a Meeting all the way from High Flatts, near Denby Dale, where another remote burial ground existed.

By 1981 much of the site was obliterated by a track leading to a

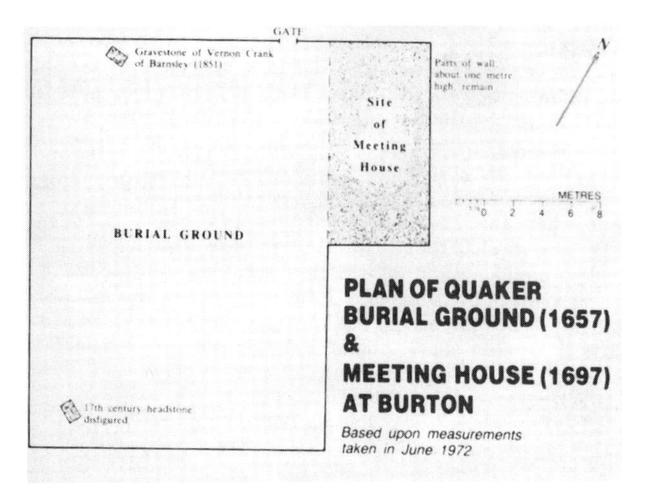

An aerial view of the Quaker burial ground (circled) taken in 1972. Meridian Airmaps

modern bungalow and vehicles from a haulage contractor. On a visit in the summer of 1988, when access was extremely difficult due to the partial blocking of a right of way, there was little to be seen above ground. Yet this site is of considerable regional and national importance, as one of the earliest Quaker burial grounds in the country and a key part of Barnsley's heritage. There is no doubt that if the site was rescued, perhaps even for future archaeological purposes, it would result in considerable interest, even from America where many people appreciate the importance of their Quaker ancestry. A vital link in a South Yorkshire Quaker Trail would then be secured.

The historian, G M Trevelyan, ably sums up the achievements of the 'quiet Friends' of later times as follows:

> *To maintain the Christian quality in the world of business and of domestic life, and to maintain it without pretension or hypocrisy, was the great achievement of these extraordinary people.*

English Social History, Longman, 1944, p267.

The Mill of the Black Monks

Above: *Portrait of Gilbert Talbot, 7th Earl of Shrewsbury (1553–1616), aged 40, uncle of Lady Mary Armyne; her father, Henry Talbot died aged 33 in 1595. Gilbert married Mary Cavendish of Chatsworth whose mother was the illustrious Bess of Hardwick. The Shrewsburys, from their Manor Lodge in Sheffield were the most powerful gentry family in South Yorkshire. Gilbert provided £200 per annum for a hospital for 20 poor people in Sheffield.* Christies

Below: *Lady Mary Armyne, founder of the Talbot Almshouses at Burton Grange.*

Above: *Map of the Priory c. 1925.*

Below: *Ruins of Monk Bretton Priory in 1840.*

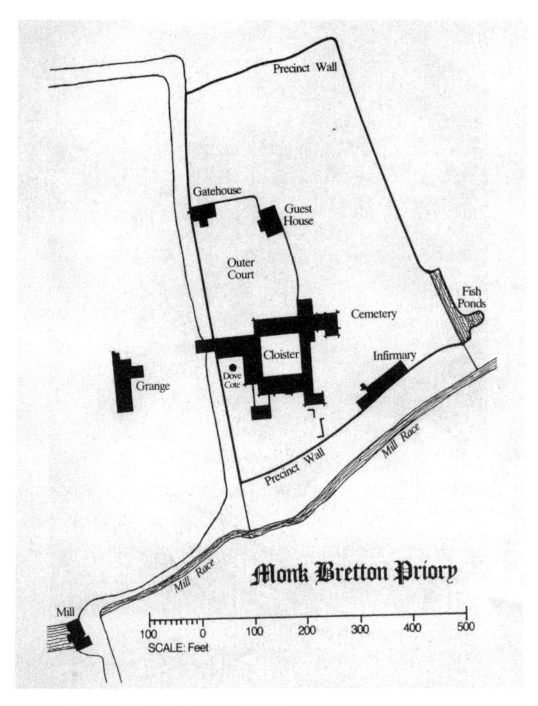

Map of the Priory c. 1925.

Architect Malcolm Lister and his plan for Priory Mill. Colin Fletcher

The Mill before major renovation. (1988). Colin Fletcher

The impressive East Doorway. Initials and dates of past millers are boldly carved on the door jamb masonry. Notice the huge lintel which once may have had inscribed features and the fine moulding with foliate motif. A two-light mullion window can be seen on the right. Masons' marks of fourteenth century origin are on the lower part of the building. RCHM

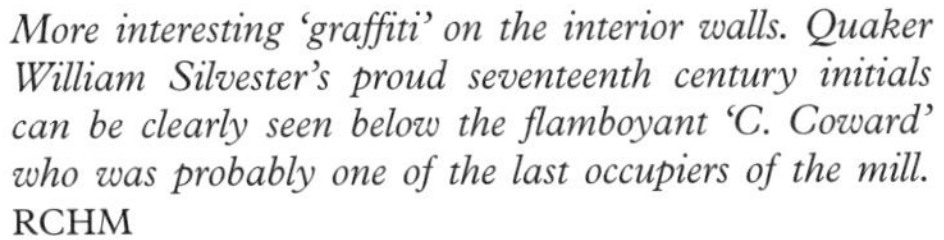

More interesting 'graffiti' on the interior walls. Quaker William Silvester's proud seventeenth century initials can be clearly seen below the flamboyant 'C. Coward' who was probably one of the last occupiers of the mill. RCHM

An interior view of the upper floor of Priory Mill shows that the surviving roof timbers – tie beams, queen posts, struts, rafters and ridge – are in very good condition.

The Mill four years on (August 1992), notice how much the building has been raised to bring it to the present road level. Malcolm Lister's extension to the Mill has also been completed. The author

19 *B*EFORE THE BENCH

The Quarter Sessions played a vital role in the life of our ancestors and the communities in which they lived. Although dealing with many types of what we now call criminal cases, it also had far-reaching administrative powers relating to roads, bridges, inns, alehouses, prisons, weights and measures, wages, apprenticeship, and was directly involved in dealing with the social problems of the day: bastardy, vagrancy, poverty and the mentally ill.

The Lord Lieutenant was supposed to preside over proceedings but rarely did. The key figures were the Justices of the Peace who had great independence and power. A justice could, without trial, send to the stocks a man for swearing, drunkenness, poaching or debt, whilst a mother could be sent to the House of Correction for bastardy and a poor vagrant could be ordered to be whipped 'until his back be bloody'. There was no appeal and although most ordinary, uneducated folk accepted judgement without question, surviving records show that some Barnsley people were not afraid to express their views – and in vernacular language. William Robinson of Denby, giving evidence at Woolley on 20 January 1668, stated that Matthew Crossland of Cawthorne did, on 12 January 'speak these treasonable words viz. that the King was a Bastard and his Mother a whore and he had more officers under him than was ought'. It is now known what judgement was made in this case which is taken from surviving depositions; these were in the form of statements and evidence collected and given in the locality, prior to any court appearance. The great joy of these examinations is that they do retain the vocabulary and phrases of ordinary people, virtually unaffected by legal terminology. In a real sense they speak to us directly across ten or more generations.

Local government, though superficially democratic, depended on the integrity of individual JP's. However, many cases show that some justices were men of genuine public spirit and honesty; and there was concern for the poor, the ill and the destitute.

The Quarter Sessions met four times each year, with Barnsley as one of the regular venues, usually in October. It was a convenient place for local affairs to be discussed but the justices also considered cases relating to other areas. When the justices were in town there would be an increased number of visitors who were either interested in a particular cases or perhaps wanting to hear about the latest scandal or punishment. One side-effect must have been the increased trade in the market, in shops and in inns and alehouses. Conversely, our local affairs could be affected by judgements in nearby session towns such as Doncaster, Rotherham, Sheffield and Pontefract.

The justices met in the most venerable building in Barnsley: the Moot Hall. The word 'Moot' was used in Saxon times to describe an assembly of people which formed a legislative court, so it was an apt name for the building. It was situated near the middle of the top of Market Hill, opposite the present Henry Elstone's shop.

The Moot Hall was the upper part of a short row of small shops and tenements that once divided Market Hill into two 'streets'. The width at the Church Street side was said to be only six yards, the other side measuring about fourteen yards. The building is described, probably from the notes of

Barnsley's Moot or 'town hall' may not have been as grand as this Leeds example but it was of similiar design and had the same function. Notice the market stalls in the foreground. From a print of 1816

Burland, in *Lodge's Almanack* for 1901/2. The property was made of stone in contrast to the adjoining brick structures. The colanaded lower storey was partly used for selling fresh produce on market days: eggs, butter and fowl. It was also used by the 'stall-setter' for storing the market stalls. A small extension to the lower part of the building was used as a shop. In about 1750 bookseller Joseph Smith occupied this prestigious spot and later Thomas Cockshutt, also a bookseller. Maybe the legal proceedings above encouraged a dignified use below.

The Justice Room was reached by a flight of thirty steps close to the wall, in the north-east corner, facing Church Street. Under the west face of the Moot Hall clock stood the pillary and under it, the town stocks. The clock showed the time to buyers and sellers on Market Hill. In 1646 Edmund Rogers gave £10 towards getting a clock to the benefit of the public. A second clock, locally made by Tobias Fletcher, was hung on a wall in the session's room during the late eighteenth century. At the same time the structure also housed a toll-bell which had the inscription 'T. Hylton, Wath, 1786', later removed to St. Paul's, Monk Bretton. Quarter Sessions continued to be held in the Moot Hall until about 1795 when the building was probably in a poor state of repair. Jackson states that it was 'pulled-down about the year 1820'.

The quarter sessions records are now housed at the Headquarters of the West Yorkshire Archive Service, Registry of Deeds, Wakefield. Countless hours of work has been carried out in order to conserve and catalogue the documents and the result is a marvellous source of information for the local and family historian. When the writer first consulted the documents, in the early 1970s, they were in Wakefield County Hall, some of the folios reduced to fragments, though others, apart from the accumulated dirt and dust of many years, were intact.

The following examples represent a small sample of session proceedings relating to Barnsley and the surrounding area.

The Poor

The justices received frequent petitions for financial help from the elderly, the infirm, old soldiers, widows and individuals who had been once well-able to support themselves but were now experiencing hard times. Here are two typical examples:

> *Robert Bray of Carlton … humbly showeth he hath for four years & upwards last past, maintained his mother … being a lame infirm woman of seaventy & two yeares of Age, & unable to help herself, And by reason of yor Petitioners poore condition, only farming a cottage & a small Yard of nineteen shills rent & having a family otherwise very chargeable upon him Humbly craves an allowance from the town towards the maintenance of his sd mother … And yor Petitioner shall ever pray for you* [1687]
>
> *That your petitioner was late servant to Mr. Dutton* [vicar of Royston] *and having lately married a wife within the sd towne the Inhabitants thereof refuse to let us there remaine we not requiring any thing from them but for our moneys in which case we have remained hawberlesse for the space of seven weeks to our great loss by reason we cold satle to noe imployment we therefore your poore petitioners humbly intreat this Honrable Bench to comisserate our Condition and by your Gracious Order soe help us to an habitation in the sd towne & as we are bound shall ever pray for you.* [Signed] Nathan Hoile (1674)

The churchwardens and overseers of the poor petitioned the court in 1680:

> *in regard of the great number of people inhabiting within the said towne being in number five hundred and thirty one who stands need of releife and there being but a few able persons therin they are not able to mayntaine them without begging and wandering abroade to other neighbouring townes and pishes* [parishes] *for releife wch is contrary to Lawe.*

If the precise figure of 531 refers to the number of vagrants it represents a huge social

Woodcut showing a poor beggar seeking alms. Batsford

and administrative problem; according to the hearth tax of 1672 there were only about 130 households in the town, and the Compton Census of 1680, though not always a reliable source, puts the population of Barnsley as 638. The resident population would have been almost matched by itinerants, perhaps understandable given the magnetic attraction of market towns.

Illegal Settlement

Ann Stainton, 'a poore childe' was ordered to be removed from Barnsley to Doncaster by the Wakefield court in 1662 but at the sessions held at Rotherham it was said that she had been sent to Hatfield 'without any legal order' and was therefore ordered to be sent to Doncaster. At the October sessions (in Barnsley), the unfortunate girl was returned to Barnsley, 'where the child confesseth she was borne'. Such cases were quite common but must have been bewildering for children.

'The Bench' from a painting by William Hogarth, 1758.

Mary Harrison, 'a poor woman', had arrived in Barnsley in 1687 'great with child with an intent to settle'. The overseers of the poor of Barnsley successfully objected to her presence since 'back to Greasbrough' was written at the bottom of the document.

In 1642, Francis Clayton, 'late of Barnsley' had moved to Darfield and was therefore 'likely to be chargeable to the parish'. The Pontefract court ordered him to be returned to Barnsley.

An unusual settlement problem arose in 1640. Edward Wilby of Royston had married a Darfield widow, Elizabeth Strafford, 'who refuseth to remove from Darfielde and live with the said husband', causing the Darfield inhabitants to be 'fearful she should bring a charge' to them. Elizabeth was ordered to remove 'forthwith' to go and live with her husband.

Such judgements seem very harsh but public funds for helping the destitute were limited. Great care was sometimes given to deserving cases. In 1638, for example, Jervas Sherlocke, a destitute labourer from Monk Bretton was to be provided with a house, 'to be built upon the waste there' and the overseers were ordered to 'provyde for him according to his necessities'. In another case, from the Barnsley sessions of 1639, Edward Harrop, 'a poore lame and infirme man' who was homeless had stayed at Brierley and Carlton but had fallen lame at Monk Bretton in the service of Nicholas Wood, yeoman. The Justices ordered that he was to stay at Monk Bretton 'and provided for as one of the poore', with the inhabitants of Brierley and Carlton making a reasonable contribution to his upkeep.

Inns & Alehouses

Robert Benson, Clerk of the Peace for the West Riding, in a letter to Sir Robert Berkley, Judge of Assize (1638), estimated that there were 2,000 alehouse keepers in the West Riding but there were at least 500 who brew without a licence.

In January 1661 Sir Francis Wortley informed the Barnsley court that 'there is more Alehouses in Carlton than is requisite for so little a towne'. Accordingly, the court decided that two alehouses were sufficient, giving approval to John Ford the elder and Eliza Ackroyd, with 'all the rest Suppressed'.

In 1674 George and Elizabeth Mabson of Darton were summoned to appear before the next Quarter Sessions 'to answer such matters touching brewing without a licence'. William Horsley, a Silkstone clothier also had to appear 'for keeping a Coman Alehouse or Tippleing house since Easter last not thereunto lawfully licenced'. When David Archer, a Bradfield labourer, was found guilty of 'keeping a common tipling house and there selling beare and ale ... to diverse Leige subjects of the King contrary to the Statute' he was fined twenty shillings which he paid in court.

The following report appeared in the *Sheffield Register*, 20 October 1787:

> *We hear from Barnsley that a J.P. near Wakefield, who was chairman at the Quarter Sessions held at Barnsley, on Wed., fortnight, received an anon. letter threatening his life; for having joined with two other magistrates in witholding the licence of an alehouse keeper.*

A reward of £100 was offered by the magistrates for the name of the offender.

Assault

Cases of alleged assault were often heard at the quarter sessions, keeping the local constables busy but there must have been many instances where physical attacks were not reported. In 1641, Henry Green, mercer (dealer in fine fabrics), and Peter Robinson, saddler, both of Barnsley, were accused of 'assaulting, imprisoning and maltreating' Robert Denton, 'detaining him against the law and custom of England for the space of five hours'. No reason is given for their alleged actions. The two accused were reported as being 'At large' but later they put themselves at the clemency of the court and were fined.

In 1641, three Dodworth 'woodcolliers' (charcoal burners), John and William Lyndley and Robert Hirst were accused of assaulting and maltreating John Perry at Worsbrough. Initially 'at large', they also later put themselves at the clemency of the court and were each fined six shillings and eight pence.

Robert Elliott, tailor, and John Elliott, husbandman, both of Royston, were accused at the Rotherham sessions of 1651 of assaulting George Clarke and his wife, Sarah:

> *and there did beate wound evill entreat and drewe blood from them soe their lives was in greate despaire & other injuries to them did doe to the great damage of the said George and Sara and contrary to the publike peace.*

A particularly vicious assault took place in Royston in 1771 when labourer John Walker and his wife, Hannah, described to the court as 'being persons of wicked barbarious inhuman and diabolic dispositions' ill-treated Elizabeth Owen, their thirteen-year-old servant. An amazing sequence of cruelty started when the girl was beaten 'with certain Rods Whips & Sticks' and she was compelled to 'strip from her body her cloathes … and was naked …'; she was then forced to labour continuously for thirteen hours, followed by confinement without food and without relief, 'contrary to the course of nature'. The unfortunate child received constant assaults for a further fifty days, including being forced to 'go into a certan rivulet naked containing frozen water' and forced to wash, made to stay too close to a fire resulting in burns, was thrown to the ground and 'hurt and wounded'; and 'other wrongs' done. Three witnesses gave evidence to the court. The Walkers received a remarkably light sentence, perhaps a reflection of the 'right' of householders to be able to chastise their servants: a fine of £3 and two months imprisonment in York Castle gaol.

There was an unusual case involving the 'kidnap' of a pregnant woman heard at the Pontefract sessions of 1652. William Wilson, labourer, Robert Gawber, overseer of the poor for Darfield parish and John Walker, all from Wombwell were the accused. Ann Doyer 'a poore impotent woman then greate with child & in strange labour in ye said town of Wombwell' was … 'from there unjustly, forceably & inhumanly did remove and on horse-back did carry away to Rawmarsh', where she later delivered a dead child. This seems an extreme and cruel case of trying to pass to another parish some one who would be a burden to the local rates.

Theft

Theft was an even more common occurrence in the session papers and often related to items of relatively low value. In 1637, for example, Henry Dobson of Wakefield, labourer, was accused of stealing a peck of oatmeal, a cheese and a pair of shoes, at Worsbrough, all valued at three shillings, being the property of Agnes Cudworth. He pleaded not guilty but lost his case and was duly ordered 'to be whipped on his naked body until the blood flows, and then set at large'.

Labourer Henry Casson of Barnsley also received a whipping for stealing, on 1 November, 1637 half a pound of sugar (12 pence), and a piece of beef (4 pence), the property of John Burrows. Roger Genn senior was said to be at large in 1642 when he was accused of stealing 'one measure of coal valued one penny the property of Francis Wortley knight and Bart'.

A public whipping through the streets with the menacing gallows in sight. From Hollinstead's Chronicles, 1577

The 'property' of the Wortley family was a frequent occurrence in court proceedings, often involving minor offences. In 1640, Barnsley labourer Robert Harrison was accused of 'unlawfully taking and carrying away … (at Monk Bretton), certain tallow, value 1d, the property of Francis Wortley, Knt. and bart'.

In 1671, Ann Beardsall of Barnsley was summoned to appear before the court for the 'suspicion of stealing a Linin Smocke', the property of Alice, wife of William Smith of Barnsley, shoemaker. She must have been found guilty since the word 'flogged' was added to the document. Three members of the Ellis family of Monk Bretton (William, Ann and Mary) were taken to the House of Correction at Wakefield in 1666 'for feloniously takeing severall pcells of stuffes callicoes linen cloth and kerseys'. In another case, Ann Johnson was also accused of feloniously taking of one payre of shoes of the value of three shillings' from Thomas Lockwood of Darton, shoemaker.

An interesting case of felony was cited at the Doncaster sessions of January 1673 when John Jackson of Barnsley made a statement at Worsbrough claiming that 'on Martinmas last hee had feloniously taken from him one Goose of the value of Twelve pence (and) … found the Goose in the possession of one Michael Guest of Barnsley' who claimed the said goose was his own property. On examination, Guest, when challenged by Jackson, 'saith that he bought her (the goose) about the first of August last … with above six other geese' from Elizabeth Haselome. Various other locals were called to give evidence and although the judgement was not available, it serves as an interesting reference to the days when Barnsley was famed for its Goose Fair – and goose 'pyes'.

Punishment by whipping for petty theft was quite common. In 1656, labourer William Brooke of Wath was indicted for stealing 'a peck of Rye meal of the value of sixpence … contrary to the publique peace'; he pleaded guilty and was 'to bee whipped'. Another common punishment continued to be the sending of offenders to the Wakefield House of Correction. Jane Holgate of Barnsley was 'committed to the House of Correction for the felonious stealing of certain household goods from George Leggat' in 1699.

Another interesting case involved statements being taken at Cawthorne in 1674. Thomas Sidebottom, labourer stated, on oath, that William Basforth of Cannon Hall 'took fower glass bottles of Mr. Spencers … and hid the same in … the croft and fold and tould this inform(an)t that he would carry them home and they would serve him to 'carry drink into the wood'. The informant also claimed that Basforth had hidden other bottles, about ten pigeons, some meat – and two black puddings, 'carrying (them) under his coat homeward'. An unusual petition, served by the accused's wife, Martha, provides a sad postscript to the affair:

That wheras your poor petitioners husband William Basforth of Dodworth was lately a Servant to Mr. Spencer of Cannon Hall' upon certain misdemainers imputed against him … by Mr. Spencer was bound to appear before these sessions but it hath pleased god (in the interim) to visit him with sickness whereof he is dead & the said Mr. Spencer doth detaine his wages which comes to the some of forty five shillings …

The widow pleaded with the court for 'the moneys which was due to her husband', promising, as was usual in petitions, that she would 'ever pray for' the justices.

Many of the thefts cited in the quarter sessions relate to servants and farm workers at a time when the court's interpretation of 'personal property' was extremely comprehensive. Some cases could certainly have been sorted out where a good relationship existed between master and man (or woman). Other cases were undoubtedly a consequence of extreme poverty, even starvation.

Poaching & Trespass

No one was supposed to keep greyhounds or any other dogs, ferrets, nets or 'harepipes' (snares) for the hunting of deer, hares or 'conies' (rabbits), nor any other 'gentleman's game' and offenders could receive one year's imprisonment. Managed rabbit warrens were an important part of estates and were known to exist in Barnsley, Silkstone and Woolley.

In 1637, Henry Walker, a Dodworth tanner, was summoned before the sessions 'for destroying hares and conyes aginst the form of the statute' but got off very lightly; pardoned by Jervas Cutler.

Two other Dodworth tanners, Thomas Brooke and John Hobson pleaded not guilty in 1640 of 'breaking and entering the free park of Francis Wortley Knt. & bart, commonly called Wortley Park & there killing a doe with a handgun charged with powder & a bullet, without licence of the said Francis Wortley ...'

Man trap on display in Cawthorne Jubilee Village Museum. Alan Billingham

William Armitage, senior, of Wombwell, labourer, was charged on 1 May 1638 for 'chasing with dogs at Wombwell in a field called Aldham Field eight sheep pasturing there, value 26s 8d, so that the same were greatly deteriorated'. Armitage was said to be 'at large' and on the same day as the above offence was also charged with chasing with dogs seventy six sheep belonging to Thomas Taylor, John Husan and John Cowper. A few days later the intrepid Armitage admitted to chasing ten sheep in the same field, the property of Roger Schofield and was fined five shillings on both accounts. However he was still regarded as 'at large' for three other sheep-chasing offences much to the distress of a further three local farmers.

Those who dared to stray into the parks of gentlemen did so knowing that the punishment could be very painful. The fate of William Slack of Barnsley who was suspected of 'stealing of Deer out of Chevett Park belonging to Francis Neville Esquire' is not known but it is likely that he received a thorough examination before and during his court appearance. Four men were found guilty of 'plucking up several 100 ash plants from a wood belonging to John Galley, Knight, Esquire of Langold and were given a three month prison sentence and publicly whipped once a month on the market day through the town of Wakefield. As late as 1812 the following notice appeared in the *Wakefield and Halifax Journal*:

> *THIS IS TO GIVE NOTICE THAT MEN TRAPS are set in the gardens, pleasure grounds and woods belonging to Godfrey Wentworth, Esq., in the townships of Woolley, Notton, Cold Hiendley and Darton.*
> *August 5th.*

The Constable

Before the establishment of a police force the office of constable was of crucial importance to maintaining law and order and administering justice. He was usually elected annually, though in Royston the office would appear to have become hereditary. The constable of Barnsley had to be on hand during market and fair days which were particularly susceptible to brawls, drunkenness and quarrels. He was frequently called in 'to keep the peace' in a wide range of situations, including marital differences and had the power to arrest offenders 'by force of arms'.

It must have been a job that required a great deal of tact, especially when sorting out quarrels and, as intermediary, he could be subjected to physical assault; he also had to give up his time, and often his money, in order to contain and deliver to justice an offender.

Being a constable could have its drawbacks. Anthony Shaw of Worsbrough was charged with 'negligintly permitting one Isaac Firth to escape from his custody ... while conveying him to the house of correction' in 1642. George Clarke of Royston, when on watch 'in gods peace and in the publique peace' was assaulted by Lancelot Stubbins who 'then and there did beate wound & evil entreate (him) soe that his life was in many danger and other wrought injuries ... did doe ...' (1655). John Handley, an Ardsley shoemaker, was indicted for 'neglecting his office of a Constable' in 1682.

At the same time constables demand a certain degree of respect. In 1642, Thomas Spencer of Hooton Levit, yeoman, was summoned to appear before the bench 'for speaking publickly scandalous words to and concerning Anthony Stacey', constable of Laughton-en-le-Morthen, at Thurcroft and Rotherham, 'in the presence and hearing of divers leige subjects of the King, these English words following: Thou art a bankerupt, roaguish, and knaveish constable'.

The constable's duties included the right to search premises for possible stolen goods. John Dilch, a cooper by trade, was Barnsley's constable in 1698. When searching the house of Susan Brooke, spinster, he found quite a collection of supposedly 'hot property':

> *two new brasse pans ... 3 pecks of good old wheat ... a pair of new Body's ... a plow ... Hatchet ... 3 pair of new shows ... a man's cloth gray cote with a cape ... a pair of new leather britches ... a new blew linn* [linen] *apron ... two pairs of new stockings ... one new black hatt ... a seeing glass ... and a good new silk cap.*

When questioned, Miss Brooke supplied a detailed and ingenious defence: the pots were bought at Barnsley Fair from a Skipton tinker, the wheat she had 'gleaned' from a field after harvest, the 'body's' she had bought in Halifax market, the hatchet came from her brother who lived in Watling-in-Norland, shoes and breeches were obtained from a disbanded soldier, the apron came from Halifax, the stockings were bought from a Barnsley hawker – and so on!

John Fairburn of Swinton, husbandman, was in double trouble in 1678. He had 'unlawfully rescued' one Charles Hill from constable Richard Addy who had arrested the latter for a felony. On being fined forty shillings for this misdemeanor, Fairburn refused to pay; and he was accordingly ordered by the court to be detained in York castle until such time that he changed his mind.

In 1678 the court at the Barnsley sessions ordered 'all chief constables issue warrents to their petty constables to make diligent search within their respective consableryes as are suspected to keepe greyhounds Netts doggs & others ...' which represents another attempt by the landowners to keep down poaching.

Various other officials executed their duties under peril: Timothy Elam of Barnsley and his wife Jane; threatened the life of local collector of taxes, Christopher Haslam, in 1662; and Barnsley mason Thomas Coward 'hindered the execution of a warrent' to arrest two men, issued by John Wentworth Esquire, JP.

Apprenticeship

From 1563, when the Statute of Artificers and Labourers was enacted, apprenticeships should last seven years between the ages of sixteen and twenty three. In practice many poor, illegitimate and orphan children served as apprentices, kept by their master in lieu of wages.

There were many reported abuses of the system. Thomas Parker of Monk Bretton, mason, was indicted for assaulting James Jubb, his apprentice, in 1653. Parker was said to have beaten, wounded 'and evill treate with spade on his left thigh did lame soe that his [apprentice's] life was in much despaire ...' In another example, taken from 1668, William Turton of Silkstone was 'bound over by warrent' for assaulting and 'cruelly beating Matthew Robinson his Apprentice'.

Occasional broken agreements reached the bench for judgement. In 1737, for example, Thomas Broadhead, a Barnsley wiredrawer, had not kept his 'bargain and agreement' with George Thompson 'to serve him in the trade or occupation of Wyredrawer to the great damage of George Thompson and against the form of the Statute ...'

There were also regulations made to try and ensure that practising craftsmen had the right training and experience. In 1654, John Bilcliffe of Carlton had 'for the space of nyne months ...

used & exercised the act trade or occupacon of a carpenter ... whereas in truth & in very deed ... was never educated as an apprentice by the space of seaven years, contrary to the forme of the ... Statute'.

Bastardy

Anyone who has studied parish registers will know that bastardy was a fairly common social problem. It was also an administrative and economic problem for the overseers. The identification and status of the father was of crucial importance; maintenance payments would mean that the child was not a burden for the rates. Reputed fathers could face examination by the justices. In 1670, William Kirkby of Carlton, tailor, had to answer a charge of 'begetting a base child under the body of Mary Beale ... widowe ...' An order was made in 1676 whereby Thomas Ellison of Barnsley 'the ruputed maker of a Bastard child ... upon the body of Sarah Hague' was to support the child for two and a half years and 'a warrent of his good behaviour was issued.

A genuine feeling for the plight of the mother and child was evident in some of the quarter sessions bastardy cases. However, this was by no means the end of the affair; moral judgement was also cast in the church courts. Widow Susannah Musgrave of Chevet was excommunicated in 1738 for 'having a bastard child the father not known'. In 1763, Mary Horner of Woolley appeared before the archdeacon's court and confessed the 'crime' of 'fornication & bastard child' with John Hutchinson named as the father; Mary was required to do a 'penance' for her sins. Mobile fathers were hard to track down; a soldier was 'the reputed father' of the child of Mary Rock of Worsbrough who had the great ordeal of facing the churchmen in 1738.

More Moral Matters

The formidable presence of the church courts in the seventeenth century meant that there was a dual influence on the moral affairs of the day. On issues such as bastardy, defamation, witchcraft and the quakers there was an overlap between civil and ecclesiastical courts. Probably one of the most important differences was that the wrath of the archdeacon's court could be manifested in great personal embarrassment and disgrace for an individual and his or her family's standing in the community. So-called penances were designed to both humiliate the 'sinner' and discourage others. In a typical example from the year 1705, Sarah Lister had to be present in the parish church of Royston on Sunday the 13th or 20th of May, between the hours of nine and eleven in the morning; she was ordered to appear before the full congregation 'bareheaded, barefoot and barelegged, having a white sheet wrapped about her from the shoulders to the feet, with a white wand in her hand' and after the reading of the Gospel she had to stand on a form or seat near to the pulpit and pronounce the following words:

> *Wheras I good People forgeting my Duty to Almighty God, have committed the detestable sin of fornication with Robert Shillitoe and thereby have justly provoked the heavy wrath of God against me ... to the evil example of others, I do earnestly repent ... that I never fall into like offence again, and for that end and purpose, I desire you all hear present to pray with me ...*

Accusations relating to defamation and bad language could result in a court appearance, as in 1688, when William Poppleton and William Ibbotson, both of Cudworth, were reported to the archdeacon 'for common curses and sweares'. The Justices of the Peace were probably not too pleased with one Richard Oxley of Ardsley, feltmaker, in 1682, who was reported by Barnsley labourer Thomas Loss as saying that he 'cared not a fart for the [evidence] the Constable said against him ...' Loss had claimed that Oxley was guilty of 'assaultinge beatinge and abusinge Ann ...' his wife.

An interesting case of defamation was heard at the church court in 1780 involving the removal of a swarm of bees from the garden of John Horbury of Woolley, wheelwright. Ann Backhouse was reported by a witness, Isaac Hall, of calling Horbury's wife 'a whore and a Common Street Walker'. Elizabeth, the wife of the witness, confirmed the story. Ann Backhouse confessed her defamation to the court and was 'to be ecclesiastically corrected and punished and to be condemned in lawful costs'.

Coal Mines

Thomas Taylor, husbandman and Thomas Hudson, John Holles, John Walker and Richard Fosterd, all Wath colliers, were charged with breaking into a 'half-part' of a coal mine at Newhill, in the 'peaceable possession of Thomas Tyas and the freehold of William Tinley' in April, 1652. Tyas was removed 'by force & arms and unlawfully by strong hand'. The expulsers were each fined 1s. 6d.

On 7 July 1652 Thomas Stones of High Green in the parish of Ecclesfield was charged at Barnsley with 'sufferinge coale pitts to remayne open and unfilled neere adjoining to the ... highway (between Barnsley and Sheffield).

The Price of Justice

The cost of bringing someone to court could result in a drain on the local rates. The churchwardens' accounts of 1782, for Royston parish, suffered badly following the robbery of the church poor box. Firth, the culprit, was eventually apprehended following a public meeting (costing 7s. 6d), the promise of a £2.2s. reward and two newspaper advertisements (9s); further charges were incurred for wages and horse hire to Wakefield, the cost of the warrant, attorney's and other legal costs; and there was also the expense of attending the Quarter Sessions at Wakefield. Firth's arrest had cost the parish over £19, a considerable sum, and it did not include new locks for the poor box.

The Death Sentence, Transportation & Prison

At the close of the eighteenth century and during the early years of the 19th century many offences which would earlier have appeared in the local Quarter Sessions went to the assizes and punishment could be severe. *The Sheffield Iris*, in March, 1799, reported the death sentence being imposed for offences such as counterfeiting, horse stealing and highway robbery; another case of theft resulted in transportation (to the colonies) for seven years and one William Clayton was gaoled for one month for 'uttering seditious words'. At the Lent assizes of 1813 the death penalty was issued to three persons 'for uttering forged notes' and Henry Sutcliffe was sentenced to death for forging his name on a bond; death verdicts also arose for offences such as fraud, stealing a bay mare, house-breaking (four men), robbery and two women and one man were transported for stealing a sheep.

The Quarter Sessions at this repressive time were also issuing harsh sentences. At the Rotherham sessions of 1812 Thomas Rawden was 'confined in York Castle for two years' for stealing chickens from Robert Marshall of Cawthorne. There was an amazing acquittal, however at the Bradford sessions of 1813, when James Chapman was indicted for sedition, having said to have uttered the following words:

'Damn the King, he is superannuated and has been there 6 and 20 years. We are governed by a set of damned whores, rogues and theives.'

20 A CHRISTMAS CRIME

John Hugh Burland was born on 5 April 1819 at an old tavern in Sackville Street, attended school only until the age of ten years, where he was 'well caned' and yet became one of the most respected literary figures of Victorian Barnsley.

Mr. Burland wrote sketches of local characters and during the long winter evenings composed the epic chronicle *The Annals of Barnsley and its Environs*. Burland's Annals appeared weekly in the *Chronicle* from 1873 to about 1880.

Four superb manuscript volumes were produced, each containing about 500 pages of closely written matter together with a voluminous index. They are beautifully and legibly written and there is a remarkable amount of detail compressed onto every page, covering the period 1744 to 1864.

His writings continue to be a rich and valuable source of information for local and family historians. John Hugh Burland died at Prospect Place, Hoyland Nether, on 24 September 1902.

The following account is based on the 'Annals' for the year 1794:

At the corner of Shambles Street and Church Street and directly opposite the old Moot Hall once stood the shop, vaults and residence of Joseph Walker, grocer and spirit merchant. Mr Walker, a bachelor and regular churchman had established a well-known and prosperous business but he had a lot on his mind as Christmas approached. His stock was gradually being 'spirited away' by person or persons unknown. A load of sugar would make a mysterious exit. Then a fine cheese – and whatever happened to that keg of spirits?

Despite living on the premises not a sound was heard, and there was no sign of any forced entrance. Mr Walker was determined to put an end to these distressing pilferings. A private watchman was employed 'whose detective qualities he placed great reliance' and instructed to apply his ear frequently at night to the door of the vaults. Mr Walker slept in his clothes in readiness for any alarm.

In the middle of Christmas week, on a dark and threatening night, the watchman heard a slight stir in the vaults. Mr Walker was quietly informed and, with his assistants, the party assembled in the kitchen in order to await any further developments.

Soon, a dark shadow began to emerge from the vaults with a stealthy and noiseless tread. It slowly hugged the adjoining house end and went its way up Shambles Street. Walker's brave assistants followed and stopped the intruder in a gateway of the Cock Yard. The culprit really was caught red-handed, having a keg of rum concealed under an ample overcoat.

Meanwhile, Mr. Walker's other assistants had rushed into the vaults and caught two other burglars – also helping themselves to spirits. There was no resistance to their 'arrest' which 'would have done credit to a posse of Bow Street runners'.

Opposite Dog Lane and across Shambles Street was a low dark passage which led into Billy West's Yard (later known as Beehive Yard; Musical Tavern Yard and Court 5). William or 'Billy' West was a ropemaker who occupied a shop and house on the east side of the passage and also owned a small croft adjoining Roper Street, in which lay his rope walk. Halfway up the yard stood a thatched cottage, rather run-down, black on the outside and very dingy inside. This was the home of an elderly couple called Hobson. Despite their very modest domain and status, Mr Hobson being a labourer and therefore having but a small income, the couple never seemed short of victuals. In fact they became quite well known for their full larder and huge appetites.

During Christmas week the Hobson household was, perhaps understandably, visited by mummers, morris dancers and the like in search of 'grub and lush'. One night a party was invited in and neat spirits were freely

John Hugh Burland (1819–1902) Local historian and literary figure of Victorian Barnsley.

handed round in a basin giving each mummer a hearty draught and an unsteady walk to the next house.

Old Mrs Hobson delighted in a bit of gossip and when she received her visitors she usually made a pot of strong tea and was never known to be without something to heighten its exhilaration.

The crafty burglar was none other but old Hobson. His son, employed at Liddle's wire works at Pinfold Hill, was one of those captured in the vaults. James Ward, a canal excavator, who lodged with the Hobsons, was the other villain. They had been using a skeleton key to enter the premises at the dead of night and had been successful on many occasions.

The late-eigthteenth century was a time when punishment could be very severe for even petty offences. William Hobson, George Hobson and James Ward were thus sentenced to death 'for feloniously entering by means of a false key the premises of Joseph Walker, at Barnsley, and stealing therefrom a quantity of rum'.

All three were placed in a cell, along with several other condemned men, soon to be taken to Tyburn, near Micklegate Bar, where gallows were erected. It was the usual practice to transport prisoners by cart, along with their own coffins and they would receive considerable ribaldry from the furious rabble. Their horrible fate seemed sealed.

However, that was not quite the end of the story. A prison officer entered the condemned cell, as was the routine, in order to check that everything was in order, but was overcome by several of the desperate inmates and was in danger of being killed. The Barnsley convicts sprang to the officer's aid and probably saved his skin.

The incident was reported to the Home Office and the sentence of death was actually commuted for the three Barnsley rogues. Old Hobson was imprisoned for two years and the other two transported, probably to Australia, for life.

On returning to Barnsley at the expiration of his sentence Hobson was detected in yet another burglary and was also transported, so ending a quite remarkable series of events which began at Christmas, back in 1794.

21 The Resurrectionists

Go to High Bradfield and you will find one of the most interesting churches of South Yorkshire in the most dramatic of settings. The church of St Nicholas is built near the top of a steep hill and close to a spectacular Norman motte-and-bailey earthwork known as Bailey Hill. Until Victorian times. St Nicholas was a chapel-of-ease of the huge parish of Ecclesfield. High Bradfield overlooks a series of lake-like reservoirs and some of the most beautiful countryside of old Hallamshire.

The exterior of the church is mainly a mixture of fourteenth and fifteenth century architecture. In the churchyard there are an unusual number of very fine gravestones with remarkably clear inscriptions going back to the seventeenth century. A most unusual Gothic fortified tower guards the entrance to the old churchyard. This was no folly but a positive response by the folk of Bradfield to deter the gruesome practice of body-snatching.

The watch-tower was erected at a time when unscrupulous characters, known with black humour as 'resurrectionists', would enter churchyards at night, exhume recently buried corpses and sell them to equally unscrupulous doctors who required human bodies for 'medical research.' The medical schools needed a regular supply of human bodies for dissection in their anatomy classes and professors such as Dr Knox of Edinburgh employed men to meet the demand, at about £10 per corpse.

There was a notorious scandal in Edinburgh in 1829 when it was discovered that two Irishmen named Burke and Hare had not only been regular suppliers of corpses to the medical authorities but also murdered fifteen people when no bodies were available. The affair made an immense impression on the public imagination prior to the passing of the Anatomy Act of 1832.

Country churchyards in the Barnsley and Sheffield area had become centres for the supplying of dead bodies to Edinburgh for the medical schools. The following report, headed 'Rescurrectionists at Sheffield and Barnsley' appeared in the *Sheffield Iris* of February, 1829:

> *On Tuesday the town of Barnsley was thrown into a state of considerabe excitement by the discovery of a body of a male child packed with hay on a box, and directed to Edinburgh*

A Scotsman, known in Barnsley as William Yeardley, had taken a house in Beckett Square where he lived with his wife. Most of his neighbours were weavers but no one seemed to know of the newcomers occupation, though they did seem quite well-off.

Mr Carnelley, the constable, began to view the couple with some suspician, especially since he found out that they were in the habit of regularly receiving boxes by stage wagon from Sheffield.

On Tuesday, 30 February a man and a woman brought a box to the coach office and Carnelley followed them and demanded that the box was opened. Inside was the body of a child of about two years of age. Yeardley or 'Stuart' as his real name may have been, and his wife were arrested and taken to the Low Grate Prison in the Gas Nook; the child's body was sent to the workhouse in St Mary's Place for identification.

The Watch-tower, Bradfield Churchyard. The author's great, great grandfather, Joseph Elliott (1815–1901), a gamekeeper, is buried nearby. Alan Billingham

'Alls well ...' The night watchman or bell-man with his Tantern and dog. From The Bellman of London, 1608 by Thomas Dekker. British Museum

Understandably there was a great public outcry over this awful affair. A set of implements, suitable for digging and wrenching bodies from coffins was found in the couple's lodging house. Thousands of people came forward to view the body, as news began to spread but there was no immediate identification.

The crowd even went to St. Mary's churchyard and uncovered the most recently interred coffins. One unfortunate man who had buried his child about a fortnight before, found that the body was missing.

The prisoners were brought before the Rev. Dr. Corbett and Joseph Beckett Esquire and were then committed to trial at the next sessions at Pontefract. The couple were greeted by an indescribable din – hisses, hoots, yells, groans – and snow and mud was hurled at them. Yeardley's hat was knocked off in front of the King's Head (an old inn at the bottom of Market Hill) and it was filled with snow and mud and put back on his head again.

An inquest took place with regard to the dead child. The child had flaxen-coloured hair, with a ringworm on the left side of the head, about the size of a half-crown. After a few days it was found that the body had been brought from Sheffield to Barnsley in a hamper and a man – James Bradshaw of Attercliffe – identified the body as his child.

On Tuesday the 10th Peter Stuart, alias William Yeardley was taken before Sheffield magistrates and was again committed to trial – for violating a grave in Attercliffe churchyard by stealing the body of a male child, eighteen months old. The distressed father was ordered to go to Barnsley to see his child decently buried, all expenses paid by the county. At the Pontefract sessions, commencing on April 27, Stuart was sentenced to twelve months hard labour.

This little story dramatically reminds us of a time of only four or five generations ago when the churchyards of our ancestors were not safe from such hideous deeds – crimes which became part of the folklore of Black Barnsley.

PART SEVEN: LOCAL CHARACTERS

22 THE ATTORNEY

The concerns of a handful of local legal men touched upon the lives of hundreds of Barnsley people as the pace of commerce and speculation began to quicken during the first half of the eighteenth century. Buoyant interest in real estate was partly reflected in a steadily increasing number of deeds registered at Wakefield: twenty from 1703 to 1712, rising to sixty-two in the decade ending in 1752. About one in three related to land and or residential property but there was an increasing interest in enterprises such as shops, inns, tanyards and collieries.

The attorney's clients were by no means limited to town and country worthies since they were also advocates for any man or woman who wanted to make a will, lease property or borrow money.

As Barnsley was not a corporate town, lawyers did not have the chance to hold offices such as Mayor or become Freemen but they did hold important county appointments such as Deputy Lieutenant, Justice of the Peace and Clerk of Peace; and were powerful, wealthy local figures.

The legal profession formed an elite and very distinct social group. The vocational attraction of the law meant that competition was high between men of good social standing to article their sons to one of the few local attorneys or to leading London practices, despite fees as high as £300 for a five-year clerkship. The rewards, however, both financial and social, could be very considerable and are well-illustrated by one of Barnsley's premier attorney families: the Woods.

The Wood family dominated legal affairs in Barnsley from about 1660 to the 1720s and continued to be prominent right through to the nineteenth century. As minor gentry they were resident in Monk Bretton from Tudor times and a branch of the family had established a residence at Smithies where they had ironworks in the early seventeenth century.

When James Wood died, in 1662, shortly followed by his brother, William, who was Clerk of the Peace for the West Riding, it was probably left to the youngest son, Henry, to carry on the family legal practice. By the time of his death, in 1720, aged 75, he was Barnsley's wealthiest and most powerful citizen. Henry Wood was able to leave almost £6,500 to nine children and settle on his eldest son, Henry (1690–1741) an estate of about 2,000 acres in Hatfield Chase, together with smaller estates in Barnsley, Penistone and Masborough. Ironworking interests in Yorkshire, Derbyshire and Nottinghamshire were shared between sons Simpson (1698–1746), who may have been named after William Simpson, a prominent Sheffield attorney and ironmaster, and Francis (1696–1775), who took over the Barnsley legal business. Francis Wood was professionally even more in demand than his father and brothers, being involved with more than thirty deeds relating to Barnsley property between 1721 and 1751. By 1733 his articled clerk was also witnessing deeds and Wood's 'Attorney at Law' title gradually gave way to 'Gentleman' and eventually to 'Esquire'. From the family mansion at the bottom of Market Hill, which had a private carriage road leading into Back Lane, an ornamental lawn on the south side and the Sough Dyke flowing close by, he was able to survey the business activities taking place around him from an impressive town house – and with more than a passing interest.

Sir Francis Wood (1730–1795), son of Francis Wood, attorney (1696–1775).

Francis Wood was a leading spirit in local business affairs and public works, an initiator as well as a consultant. The Woods had family links with leading shopkeepers and along with leading tradesmen, Francis was able to establish the town's first workhouse in 1736.

Wombwell family memorial plaque: St Mary's Church, Barnsley. The author

Sir George Wood, 'Judge Wood', (1734–1824) eldest son of Rev George Wood, vicar of Royston.

There were other well-to-do families who established legal practices in Barnsley in the 1720s and 1730s. John Wentworth Wombwell (1672–1733) and Thomas Wombwell (1709–1740) also had offices in Leeds. The Marsdens of Burntwood and Barnsley acted for the Duke of Leeds's manorial interests in Barnsley and lived in the Manor House, in Church Street.

A network of attorneys and land agents was also emerging in the villages and countryside around Barnsley. Henry Carrington, who, according to Hobson, died in 1730 shortly after consuming a barrel of oysters in a Barnsley hostelry, had established a thriving practice from 'The Views' in Worsbrough township. William Fenton (1708–1788) was another important legal man, agent and steward to Lord Strafford of Stainborough. The West family had a prestigious law practice in Cawthorne. One of their clerks was a young man called George Wood of Smithies who certainly gained from his training; the young clerk moved to a London office, soon established his own practice, and was so successful that he was called to the bar in 1792, was made Baron of the Exchequer, knighted and died leaving a huge fortune of £300,000. The Wests had an office in Barnsley during the late eighteenth century. Other local attorneys included Jonas Clarke of Barnsley, William Crookes of Monk Bretton, William Elmhirst of Worsbrough and Joseph Smith of Wath. These extensive practices of fathers and sons, brothers and nephews helped to consolidate and strengthen the legal profession in and around the developing market town of Barnsley.

23 The Quaker Industrialist

Joseph Wilson came to Barnsley from Cheshire in about 1700 and started an ironmongery business in Market Hill. Wilson was a devout Quaker so his move may have been partly influenced by contacts with, or knowledge of, the Barnsley Friends.

In a deed registered at Wakefield in 1706, Joseph Wilson is described as 'yeoman' when he obtained a substantial house in Church Street which became the family home. He prospered sufficiently to make comfortable provision for four sons. Two of them, Thomas and Matthew, were to establish hardware and drapery shops in Pontefract and Gainsborough, places in which there were also strong Quaker communities.

The two remaining brothers, John and William, inherited their father's business but never married. John, the eldest, became increasingly involved in land speculation and by the 1770s controlled 360 acres of the family estate in Lincolnshire and 67 acres of prime freehold land in Barnsley and Monk Bretton. 'Red House', a fine town residence built in brick, with a pleasant view across to Peashills, was erected on Shambles Street, a gleaming symbol of success.

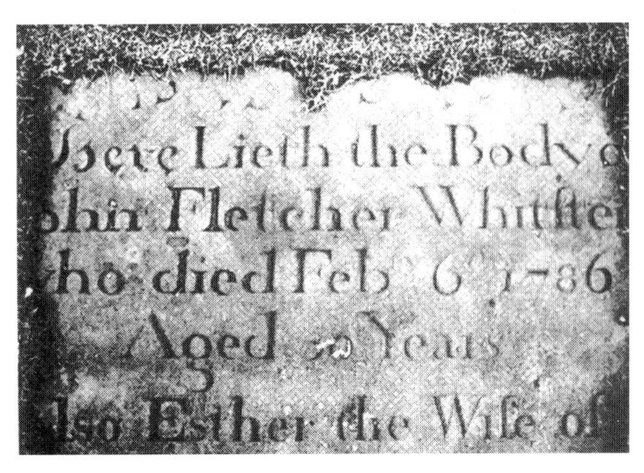

Part of the gravestone of John Fletcher of Barnsley, 'whitster' (bleacher). The author

William Wilson, the younger son, was described when aged thirty-seven as 'wever and linen-draper' but was soon to emerge as the acknowledged pioneer of Barnsley's famous linen trade. William began on a very modest scale, supplying bleached yarn to local weavers and sending linen yarn across to Cheshire, near to his parents' former home. The enterprise began to take off in 1744 when bleachers were brought across the Pennines and a bleach ground was established near Honeywell where there was a supply of spring water. By the 1750s further bleach grounds were established at Beevor Hole, Hoyle Mill, together with a large shop for weaving, run by John Lupton, also a Quaker.

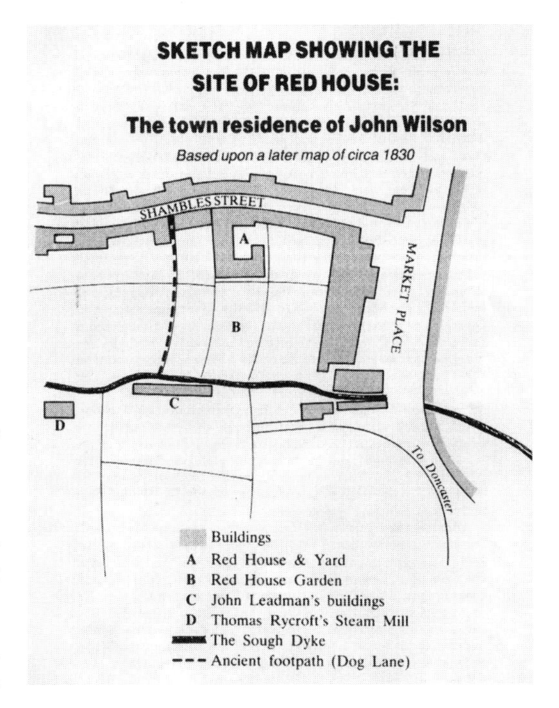

The Hyde brothers, William and Isaac, were also imported from Cheshire and proved to be most capable managers. Local men were trained by skilled migrants. Wilson originated a pattern of manufacture which was adopted by future linen pioneers: warehousing in town and bleaching in the nearby countryside. The occupational term 'whitster' (after 'whitener' or bleacher) started appearing in the church registers from the late 1750s.

William Wilson became a wealthy man but lived a lonely existence in a dilapidated and dirty house off Church Street. John Burland described him, unfairly, as 'one of those plain-dealing, plain speaking, plain-looking people commonly called Quakers' and went on to say that 'Like many of their fraternity, he was quaint in manner, curt in speech and shrewd in business ... an inveterate misogynist'. Even if Wilson really did hate marriage, or women, he was, in reality, and away from all the later gossip, probably a very shy man, certainly very hard working, an innovator who was reluctant to get involved in the inevitable financial side of business.

John, a favourite nephew, inherited William Wilson's industrial interests and by 1790 was one of Barnsley's premier linen manufacturers, supplying 500 handlooms with 100,000 bundles of yarn a year. Another nephew carried on the Market Hill ironmongery business.

William Wilson is rightly regarded as the founder of the Barnsley linen trade but his Quaker background and family shopkeeping interests were never far away. Even so, the abandonment of Red House by his nephew, in favour of a modest residence near to the Quaker Burial Ground at Burton is not easy to explain. The environs of the family home had become 'a hive of activity at all times of day and night'. The trickle of weavers coming across the moors from Cheshire and Lancashire was soon to be joined by Scottish and Irish immigrants in a wave which by the 1830s made Barnsley into one of the premier centres of the British linen industry.

24 The Collier & Alehouse Keeper

It would be a difficult task to describe the home and possessions of a 'typical' Barnsley family of 250 years ago but the use of surviving probate records, housed at the Borthwick Institute of Historical Research, York, helps to give a fair picture of everyday living conditions. Quite ordinary people made wills in order to distribute limited money and goods to family and friends and there was often a concern over the future occupation of property. Richard Fisher was by no means one of the wealthiest residents of Barnsley but when he died, in 1729, three of his friends and neighbours, led by Henry Armroyd, a long-serving schoolmaster, visited his home and compiled a list or inventory of the deceased's goods and chattels. This process was in fact a legal requirement, originally instituted at the time of Henry VIII in order to help safeguard probate. The survival of Richard Fisher's probate inventory gives us a detailed picture of a relatively modest household. The appraisers began upstairs, where there were two bedrooms or 'chambers' and in the 'best chamber' they noted a buffet stool, table, form, seven pictures and a range. Perhaps this was the room where Richard died. The adjoining room contained three beds, two chests, a 'close stool' or commode and a desk. The total valuation of the upstairs contents was just £5.12s. 6d.

Our three visitors then went downstairs into the 'Parlour' which usually served as a bedroom in small houses but in this example contained a clock, cupboard, table, eight chairs, a range together with eight pewter dishes and plates and four pewter pints and a quart. There was also a 'voider' or waste basket, the total value of the room's contents being exactly £4. The function of this room will soon become clear.

After venturing down the cellar, which contained ten small barrels, the party moved into the 'house' which served as the living room and kitchen. There was an open fire, used for most of the cooking, 11 pewter dishes, a pasty tin, dripping pan, four iron cooking pots, a few ladles, a saucepan and a warming pan. There was no mention of any furniture. The items in this important room were valued at only £1.10s. New additions to the home, referred to as the 'new parlour' consists of a bed, table, two chairs, a form and a range, all valued at only fifteen shillings.

Richard also had a brewhouse, quite unusual for such a modest cottage; it contained 'tubs', for mashing and a 'lead' for brewing ale together with various measures, all valued at £2. Outside the property, in the Fold, stood an old cart with some hay and a small stack of coal. Richard also owned a horse, sixteen sheep and three geese, together worth £6.10s. The total value of the goods and chattels amounted to £23.9s. 6d.

The survival of Richard Fisher's will give us further insight concerning his family and lifestyle. It was written in his own rather simple hand and quite a few words are expressed in phonetic terms with some very quaint spellings and little punctuation. The prologue is fairly typical of the form of the day and worth quoting in full:

> *In the Name of God Amen ye 30th day of May 1726 according to the computation of ye Church of England I Richard Fisher in ye County of York Colyar Being in perfit health and sound memory thanksbe to God. I therefore make or ordaine constitute this my Last Will and Testament in manner and form as following viz. First I bequath my soul into the hands of almighty God my maker hoping to be saved by ye meritorious death and passion of Jesus Christ my only Saviour and Redemer and as for my body to be buried in a Christian buriall at ye Discretion of my Executor hereafter named …*

Richard's first bequest was to his wife, leaving her 'all Debts that we have trusted in ye ale trade ever since wee begun to Brue'. Also 'I leave her those fifteen gines that she took out of my pocket with all ye interest for ye same in whose hands she put them I know not pray God forgive her'. Hardly an affectionate message so far! However, further intersting information begins to emerge:

> *allso I leave her half of ye Guds that is now standing in that house I first builded on ye Pinfold hill to be eakwelly devided betwixt her and my executor … and if she has a desire to brue and Keep those four Roomes in ye old hous and ye selar she shall have them while she doth Live.*

But this apparent concession was subject to an important condition:

> *... she pay my Executor twenty shillings every May day and If she have amind to Live with any of her Children and Quit ye House ye Executor shall pay to her forty shillings every may day.'*

The will concluded with the following small bequests:

> *I Leave my Brother John Fishers suns one shilling a pece and his daughter Elizabeth I Leave her twenty shillings' 'I Leave my sister in worsper dale one shilling and her daughter twenty shillings' 'I Leave my brother Thomas Fisher one shilling and his sun Richard that house that Lornae Cargill Lived on which I let to Sammuell Sinyer for eighteen shillings a year paying chief rent with Lornae Cargill Bond so if Cargill Cum to ye hous he must pay ye Bond*

The remainder of Richard's property, including 'ye hous at botam of ye pinfold hill and the houses at ye top of ye pinfold hill went to his brother, William Fisher, subject to him paying off outstanding debts, and William was made sole Executor of the will.

So here we have a fascinating picture of a local man, a skilled coal miner, who, along with his wife, kept what was probably a well-known alehouse in an area of Barnsley fairly congested with similar premises.

Pinfold Hill (part of modern Sackville Street) ran parallel to Summer Lane and could be reached via Pinfold Steps from Westgate (Shambles Street) which was one of the main thoroughfares of the town. The Pinfold, a small enclosure where stray farm animals were temporarily kept was found near the top right hand side of the steps.

It is interesting to consider that, squeezed between John Rideal House and a tyre service business may have stood one of Richard Fisher's properties.

Richard Fisher must have been personally known by many Barnsley people though how common knowledge was of his wife's alleged misconduct remains less certain. But for the survival of his will and inventory he would have almost certainly been forgotten.

25 The Country Doctor

One of the most familiar figures riding along the much trodden tracks and lanes in the undulating countryside to the south and west of Barnsley was undoubtedly Mr. William Elmhirst, apothecary and surgeon. 'Doctor Elmhirst', as he was often called, was the only son of William Elmhirst, who was born on 8th October, 1686 and died in 1746 in his sixtieth year. The elder William had settled at Elmhirst and later Genne House in Worsbrough township following the uncertainties of merchant adventure. His brother, Richard, was lost at sea, returning from Virginia.

The younger William was baptised at Worsbrough on 29 December 1721. When in his mid-thirties he married Elizabeth, daughter of John Wordsworth of Hermit Hill in the parish of Tankersley. He had then been in medical practice for about fourteen years and it was during the first couple of years of marriage that building work was being carried out at Genne House, a substantial barn having a datestone showing '1659'.

William may have been apprenticed in the medical profession to follow the worthy example of his great uncle, another William, who described himself as 'Batchellor of Physick' in his will of 1702 and who bequethed 'my Study of Books with the chest they are in to any of the thre sons (his nephews) that shall turn Student in either of the two universities or be an apothecary or surgeon ...'.

Ouslethwaite Hall in c.1900.

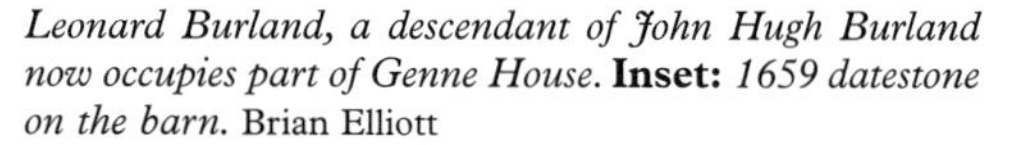

Leonard Burland, a descendant of John Hugh Burland now occupies part of Genne House. **Inset:** *1659 datestone on the barn.* Brian Elliott

Apothecary's storage jar from Cawthorne Village Museum. The author

Worsbrough Hall, the home of the Edmunds family c. 1900

William Elmhirst lived a very busy life as a Worsbrough doctor with a fairly extensive country practice. His rounds brought him into contact with many local families but he also had patients in Barnsley and journeyed as far as Grenoside, Whiston and Rotherham, competing with more local medical men. Such journeys, as we know from Hobson's dairy, were often very hazardous, especially in the depths of winter.

Dr Elmhirst's clients understandably included the local well-to-do families such as the Edmunds of Worsbrough Hall but he may have been called to treat servants in local households. He was also called upon by the overseers of the poor in places such as Worsbrough, Hoyland, Dodworth and Silkstone when paupers needed treatment. However, it was 'ability to pay' which was the main reason for his attendance, though people of fairly modest means – farm workers, wiredrawers, masons, weavers, etc., formed an integral part of his business. In some instances no charge was made. William would submit his bill 'as he saw fit' that is taking into consideration individual circumstances. Such discretionary judgements must have been difficult for a young doctor when treating wealthy patients, despite his own old-established family background. Sometimes goods and chattels were substitute for payment: a sheep, some cloth, some coal, a few candles or a load of manure.

William's medical ledger, extant in Sheffield Archives, gives some insight into how he made a living. Although most of his income came from medical care, he also received income from farming and rents from tenants who exploited the coal from under his lands. By 1768 he was able to buy the nearby Ouslethwaite estate for £3,000.

Compounds of various herbs were prescribed and powders 'to clear the system' were dispensed to individuals or complete households. There was also an array of ointments, cordials, plasters etc.

During the last four years of his life the Worsbrough doctor conducted 110 bleedings, a very popular though highly dangerous practice. Thomas Gelder, a pauper from Worsbrough Workhouse, had his leg amputated by the doctor on 28 January 1770 and would appear to have survived the operation. The overseers faced a bill of three guineas. Interestingly, he was also practicing inoculation recording at least twenty-seven between 1768–1773.

William Elmhirst was killed when thrown from his horse at Hangmanstone Toll Bar, Birdwell, in 1773. His son, yet another William, succeeded to his estates.

The Coat of Arms of the Elmhirsts of Elmhirst, Houndhill, Ouslethwaite and Genne House.
ARMS: *Barry wavy of six pieces argent and sable; a canton paly wavy also of six pieces argent and sable.*
CREST: *On a wreath of the colours, a mount vert, therefrom issuant rays of the sun, in front of a hurst of elm-trees proper.*
MOTTO: *In Domino Confido.*

26 THOMAS KERESFORTH & PULE HILL HALL

Pule Hill Hall is not mentioned in Nikolaus Pevsner's West Riding edition of *The Buildings of England* but is not without architectural interest and, more importantly, has a most interesting past.

My interest in Pule Hill began in 1975 when researching the smaller country houses and manor houses of the Barnsley area as part of an adult education class project. Initially it represented an intriguing name on an ordnance survey map, reached by footpath or track from the A629 at Thurgoland. The first sight of the back of the farmhouse and its yard and outbuildings proved to be of considerable interest but when the then owner, Mr Bockin, took myself and local historian Arthur Clayton to the front of the building we received a most pleasant surprise. Here could be seen the impressive facade of a small country house which, with its weathered coat of arms, was once the residence of someone of local importance. Mr Bockin, although born in the house and about to retire from farming, was unable to supply any information, saying that hardly anyone had expressed any interest in the building. A little research was obviously needed but what follows is by no means complete.

Pule Hill, according to A H Smith's *Place-Names of the West Riding*, is named from a small pool near the farm; Pule or 'Puel' represents the dialect pronunciation of 'pool' (i.e. 'puil'), so in early documents it was phonetically spelt 'Pule'. A house probably existed on or near the site in medieval times, 'Pulehill' being recorded in a deed of 1420.

For many years Pule Hill was associated with a family called Bamford. John Bamford lived there in about 1600. John married and had a son and two daughters. The son, also named John, was to marry three times; his first wife came from Bamford in Derbyshire, perhaps explaining the origin of the family name; his second wife, Alice, came from Bradfield, producing two sons, both dying young; his third wife, Priscilla, came from Roxby, Lincolnshire and had five children, three of them boys.

The triple-married John Bamford, esquire was a man of some substance, having purchased the manor of Thurgoland and serving as a Justice of the Peace. He also held the office of treasurer for lame soldiers during the reign of Charles 1. John's support of the Royalist cause was at considerable personal cost; he was to leave, according to Joseph Hunter, 'an embarrassed estate to his son and heir, whose own extravagance, and his losses in the civil wars, compelled him to dispose of what he had in Thurgoland ...'. Lyon Bamford sold Pule Hill, along with the neighbouring estates of Roper House, Cheesebottom and Thurgoland Hall with its manorial rights. It must have been a very distressing time for the family since two of Lyon's brothers had been killed in the Civil War and their affairs were in ruin. Mr W E Spencer's work on *Penistone and parts of South Yorkshire during the Great Rebellion* (in Sheffield City Archives) includes quite a lot of information concerning the winding-up of Bamford's affairs, including several begging letters.

Pule Hill became the residence of someone from one of the most ancient families of Barnsley: Thomas Keresforth. The Keresforths were one of only a few local families who were able to prove their right to bear arms

Mr Bockin outside Pule Hill Hall. The author

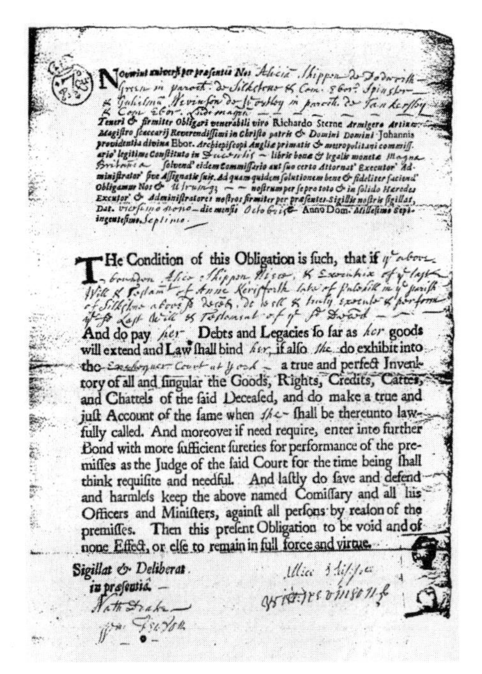

Noverint universi per praesentes Nos Aliciam Shippen de Dodworth Greene in parochia de Silkstone & Com. Ebor. Spinster & Gulielmum Wilkinson de Stodley in parochia de Tankersley & Com. Ebor. Yeoman Teneri & firmiter Obligari venerabili viro Richardo Sterne Armigero Artium Magistro Scaccarij Reverendissimi in Christo patris & Domini Domini Johannis providentia divina Ebor. Archiepiscopi Angliae primatis & metropolitani commissario legitime Constituto in ... libris bonae & legalis monetae Magnae Britanniae solvend' eidem Commissario aut suo certo Attornat' Executor' Administrator' sive Assignatis suis. Ad quam quidem solutionem bene & fideliter faciend' Obligamus Nos & utrumque nostrum per se pro toto & in solido Haeredes Executor' & Administratores nostros firmiter per praesentes. Sigillis nostris Sigillat. Dat. ... die mensis Octobris Anno Dom. Millesimo Septingentesimo Septimo.

THe Condition of this Obligation is such, that if ye above bounden Alice Shippen Spinster, Executrix of ye last Will & Testament of Anne Keresforth late of Pulshill in ye parish of Silkstone aforesaid deceased, do well & truly execute & performe ye sd Last Will & Testament of ye sd deceased — And do pay her Debts and Legacies so far as her goods will extend and Law shall bind her, if also she do exhibit into the Exchequer Court at York a true and perfect Inventory of all and singular the Goods, Rights, Credits, Cattels, and Chattels of the said Deceased, and do make a true and just Account of the same when she shall be thereunto lawfully called. And moreover if need require, enter into further Bond with more sufficient sureties for performance of the premisses as the Judge of the said Court for the time being shall think requisite and needful. And lastly do save and defend and harmless keep the above named Comissary and all his Officers and Ministers, against all persons by reason of the premisses. Then this present Obligation to be void and of none Effect, or else to remain in full force and virtue.

Sigillat & Deliberat in praesentia —

Administration Bond attached to the will of Anne Keresforth.

Part of the long 'prologue' of Thomas Keresforth's will.

at successive visitations. The main branch of the family lived at Keresforth Hill from medieval times until about 1620 when the estate was sold.

The Keresforth Coat of Arms.

Thomas Keresforth was the eldest of the three sons of Gabriel Keresforth who died in 1641. One of his aunts, Grace, married Robert Bower who was involved in the Barnsley wiredrawing trade. Thomas, born in about 1597, married Anne who came from Abingdon in Berkshire.

There were no children from the Keresforth marriage which may explain why he was keen to establish a school in Barnsley. A school house was built in the 1660s, endowed with farm rents. St Mary's House, owned by Thomas, and situated near to the church, was settled on the school. The schoolmaster was to receive some support from rents from shops in the Moot Hall, then held by Richard Thwaites and Thomas Exley. The former had coal mining interests on Barnsley Moor. The school was free to all children in Barnsley and Dodworth whose parents were not worth £200 in land and debtless goods; wealthier people paid half-fees. John Hill may have been one of the first masters.

The prologue to Thomas Keresforth's will, made on 22 October, 1669, even allowing for the standards of the day, suggests that he was a deeply religious character. He described his condition as 'Infirm and weak of body ...' and left instructions for him to be buried 'in the Chancell or Quire or Silkstone where my father was buried' or in St

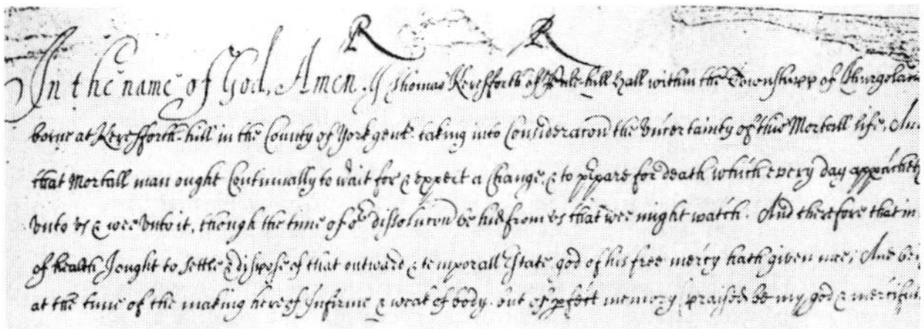

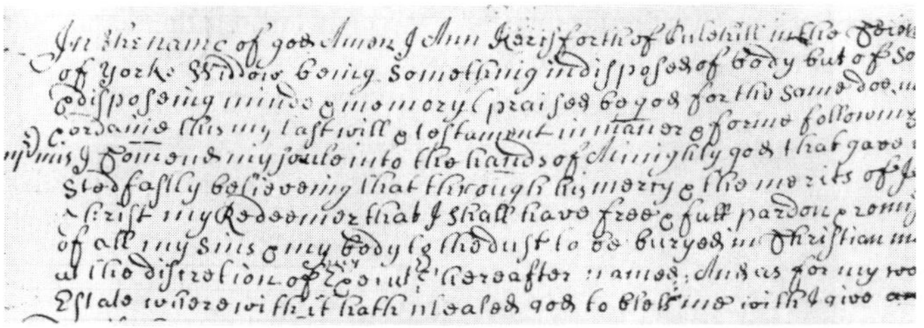

Prologue of the will of Ann Keresforth.

The end of the will, five 'A3' size pages later.

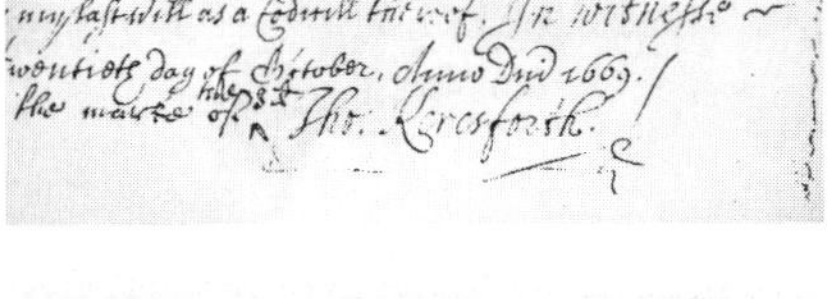

Barnsley Grammar School photographed by Warner Gothard in about 1895.

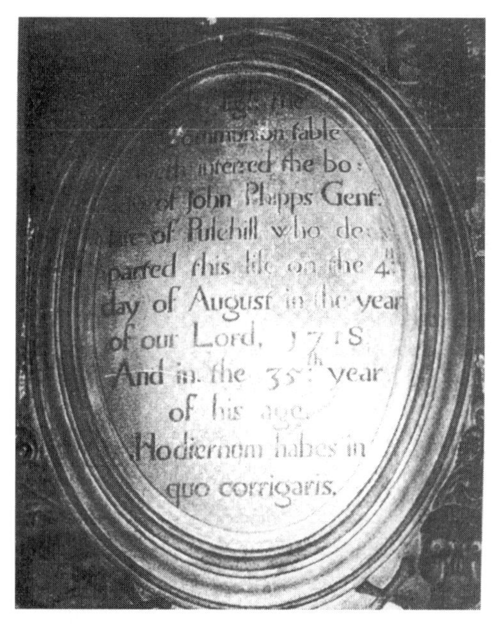

Memorial to John Phipps of Pule Hill in Silkstone Church. Alan Billingham

Memorial to Rev Samuel Phipps, 'above 40 years' Vicar of Silkstone. Alan Billingham

Mary's, Barnsley where his ancestors resided. He was in fact interred in Silkstone church five years later, aged 77.

In his will, revised shortly before his death, he mentioned property and land in Barnsley Thurgoland, Silkstone, Dodworth, Cawthorne and South Hiendley. Some of the property went to the Bower side of the family and to the Browns of Dodworth who were descended from an aunt. His wife, Anne, 'providing she does not marry', inherited his 'Capital Messuage' and cottage at Pule Hill, all the tithes of corn, wood, hay, wool and lamb; and the manor of Thurgoland. Thomas will mainly be remembered, however, as the founder of Barnsley Grammar School.

Some of the last attenders at Barnsley Grammar School, now Cooper Art Gallery. The photograph was taken at the back of the school in 1912 and the pupils are wearing Eton collars.

Anne Keresforth remained a widow for almost thirty years. In her own will, made on 6th February, 1704/5 she referred to herself as 'of Pulehill in the County of Yorke Widdow being something indisposed of body but of sound & disposing minde & memory praised (to) god for the same ...'. She was able to leave £100 to each of the two daughters of Ann Shippen, her neice, and four god-daughters each got a guinea 'to buy a ring'. A small bequest of ten shillings was made to Esther Bamforth, perhaps her servant and the poor people of Thurgoland were not forgotten: £10 was to be paid yearly to 'the poorest Inhabitants ... not having anything in the Common box'.

One of Anne's bequests took the form of a £5 gift to Rebecca Fayram, perhaps a relative. In a deed registered at Wakefield on 1st August, 1706 a Rebecca Fayram, spinster, is stated as being 'of Pulehill, so she was probably living there shortly after the window's death. The Fayrams had mercery shops in Barnsley, so must have been reasonably comfortable.

It seems, however, that the ownership of Pule Hill Hall passed on to the Bower, cousins of Thomas Keresforth, in keeping with the instructions of his will. In an undated deed of about 1680/90, Nathaniel Bower, Thomas's first cousin once removed is said to be of Pule Hill Hall and a 'gentleman'.

In a deed made in November, 1690, Nathanial Bower is referred to as 'deceased' but his widow, Rebecca, appears to have married John Waterhouse 'of Puelhill, gentleman'. By 1701, Waterhouse is referred to as 'of Sheffield', so Rebecca had presumably left Pule Hill, perhaps leaving Rebecca Fayram in occupation.

What is certain is that a family called Phipps lived at Pule Hill not long after Ann Keresforth's death. Samuel Phipps, vicar of Silkstone resided there in 1780.

Such scattered jottings hardly do justice to such an interesting building but perhaps one day its long and interesting past will be revealed in even more detail.

During the late eighteenth century the resident of the hall may not always have cultivated the farm. Lawrence Williams, a later resident, once told the local historian John Burland that the hall was used as a temporary home for Lady Mary Wortley Montague, perhaps when alterations were being made to Wharncliffe Lodge.

"PULE HILL, HIGH FIELD, AND BARNSLEY.

TO BE SOLD BY AUCTION, IN THE FOLLOWING LOTS,

ON *WEDNESDAY, the 27th day of August* next, at the house of Mr. GEORGE SHAW, known by the name of the White Bear Inn, in Barnsley, in the county of York, between the hours of four and eight of the clock in the afternoon, pursuant to such conditions of sale as will be then and there produced.

PULE HILL FARM.

LOT I. All that capital freehold messuage, dwelling-house or tenement, barn, stables, cowhouses, outbuildings, yard, and homestead, situate, standing, and being in the township of Thurgoland, in the said county of York, commonly called or known by the name of Pule Hill Farm. And also all those several closes, pieces, or parcels of land, arable, meadow, or pasture ground, to the said farm and premises belonging, commonly called or known by the several names following (that is to say), the Hall Ing, Little Field, Lower Butts, New Ing, Long Lands, Well Ing, Crabtree Close, Coal-Pit Close, Birk otherwise Birch Field, Grove and North Croft, Chapel Flat, Broad Flat, Great North Croft, Old Field, Rag Lane Closes, and the Long Ing, which said closes and premises contain by estimation ninety-two acres, be the same more or less.

And also all that Spring Wood, or woody piece of ground and soil, commonly called the Pule Hill Spring, situate, standing, lying, and being in Thurgoland aforesaid, containing by estimation nine acres and three roods, be the same more or less.

And likewise all that other small Spring Wood, or piece or parcel of woody ground and soil, commonly called the Rein Spring, situate in Thurgoland aforesaid, containing by estimation two acres, be the same more or less.

HIGH FIELD FARM.

LOT II. All that capital freehold messuage, dwelling house, or tenement, together with the barn, stable, cowhouses, buildings, folder yard, and homestead, situate and being in Thurgoland aforesaid, commonly called or known by the name of High Field Farm. And also all those several closes, pieces, or parcels of land, arable, meadow, or pasture ground, to the same farm and premises belonging, commonly called or known by the several names following (that is to say), the Rough Ing, the Ing, North Croft, the Two Little Closes, the Common Close, Green Close, Nock Close, Great Pond Close, Little Pond Close, High Field Close, Laithe Close, Great Close, Lesser Great Close, and the Wheat Ing, containing together by estimation sixty-four acres, be the same more or less.

☞ The above farms have a right of common on the respective commons called Thurgoland Common, Huthwaite Bank, and Berry Moor, and nearly adjoin the high road from Penistone to Sheffield, and from Thurgoland to Barnsley, and are supposed to contain coal and ironstone, and are free of tythe.

BARNSLEY.

LOT III. All those several freehold messuages, dwelling houses, or tenements, shop, yard, and premises, and the appurtenances, situate, standing, and being in the Church Street, otherwise Kirkgate, in Barnsley, in the said county of York, as the same are now in the several tenures or occupations of William Tooke, Michael Pickering, J. Fletcher, Mrs. Cheetham, and John Crooks.

⁂ A pump is in the yard, which suppplies the premises with water.

For a view of Pule Hill Farm and the woods, apply to Mr. Edward Armitage, the tenant; for a view of High Field Farm, apply to Mr. John Pashley, upon the premises; and for a view of the premises at Barnsley, and for further particulars, apply to Mr. THOMAS HEELIS, attorney-at-law, in Barnsley."

This advertisement, taken from the *Leeds Intelligencer* of Monday, 4 August, 1800, shows that the farm was one of three local properties due to be sold by auction at the *White Bear Inn* (later the *Royal Hotel*) in Barnsley when Mr Edward Armitage was the tenant.

Thomas Heelis, who lived in the Grammar School Yard, was a well-known solicitor. Buried at Monk Bretton, his name survives in a Barnsley Street: Heelis Street, in the area between Park Road and Sheffield Road.

27 JOSEPH BRAMAH, THE INVENTOR

In about 1772 the disabled son of a Stainborough estate worker packed a bag which probably contained a few home-made tools, and walked to London. Thirty years later a series of inventions had made him into a household name.

Joseph Bramah was born on a Stainborough farm in April, 1749 and baptised in the parish church of Silkstone. His father worked as a coachman and servant at Wentworth Castle. Young Joseph would have continued working on his father's tenant farm but for an unusual accident which occurred at the age of sixteen when he badly injured an ankle in a jumping contest at Bolton-upon-Dearne feast. Lameness ruled out active farm work so he was bound apprentice to Thomas Allott, of Stainborough Fold, to be a joiner and cabinet maker. This proved to be the start of Bramah's mechanical interests. In his spare time he demonstrated his skill as a craftsman of note by making two cellos,, a violin, an inlaid tea chest and a caddy.

With his apprenticeship over, Bramah resolved to seek work in London rather than wait a long time for job opportunities at home. It was to be the right decision since he soon found employment with a cabinet maker and after a couple of years was able to start a small business of his own.

Two further accidents contributed to his future success. His mother received fatal injuries when she was thrown from a horse on which she was riding as a pillion passenger when returning from a visit to Barnsley market. The loss of his mother probably made him more determined than ever to make a success of his new business. Shortly afterwards an accident at work resulted in several months of enforced leisure. It proved to be a blessing for he began to put his creative abilities to good effect and an amazing series of ingenious inventions began:

The Water-Closet

Bramah began experimenting in the design of a more efficient water-closet and took out a patent in 1778, describing himself as of 'Cross Court', Carnaby Market, Golden Square, Middlesex, cabinet-maker'. He soon moved to a shop in Denmark Street and registered a further design improvement with the addition of a water-cock which he patented in 1783. The manufacture of the pipes and pumps necessary for the invention took place in Bramah's London works with the help of the village blacksmith of Stainborough who had been sent for to help with the process. With few alterations, and despite numerous pirate claims, the Bramah water-closet continued in widespread use for more than a century.

Bramah's birthplace, Stainborough Lane Farm. From Joseph Bramah. A Century of Invention, 1749–1851 by Ian McNeil, David & Charles, 1968.

Portrait of Joseph Bramah about 1799.

The Lock

Bramah next turned his attention to the invention of a lock which would be more secure than any other then known. After many trials a patent was brought out in 1784 in which he pronounced it 'not to be within the range of art to produce a key or other instrument by which a lock on this principle can be opened'. He was so confident of the device that a notice was displayed in his shop window offering 200 guineas to anyone who succeeded in picking the patent lock. It remained unpicked for almost seventy years until an American called Hobbs mastered it in 1851. Hobbs, was no ordinary character – more like a Paul Daniels of the day, but it took him sixteen days to achieve! Bramah explained the merits of his invention in his *Dissertation on the Construction of Locks*. His design was of national importance and for many years to have a 'Bramah' meant the installation of the best lock on the market. Later locksmiths such as Chubb appreciated Bramah's work. Again Bramah got involved with the manufacturing side of the invention. Henry Maudsley, his foreman and friend at the works, managed to devise ways of making the delicate machine tools necessary for the assembly of the lock.

Steam-Engines

Several patents were taken out for the improvement of the steam engine but Bramah's early ideas were stifled until the Boulton and Watt patent expired. Bramah appeared as a witness in a trial of 1797 when Boulton and Watt objected to a proposed patent for an improved steam engine by Hornblower and Maberley. He went so far as to publish a pamphlet in the form of a letter to the judge complaining about the Watt 'monopoly'. Between 1792 and 1799 a number of successful trials vindicated Bramah's improved designs, especially for more efficient boilers.

Pumping Machines & the Hydraulic Press

In a patent of 1785 Bramah was now describing himself as 'engine maker', of Piccadilly when he was making a variety of improvements in pumps and fire engines. One of Bramah's patent fire-engines was purchased by the Earl of Strafford for use at Wentworth Castle. A revolutionary Beer Pump was patented in 1787 which enabled liquor to be raised from the casks in the cellar to the sale point over the bar. Other modifications appreceated by the brewing trade included a filtering machine, a vent-peg, a method of making flexible pipes and a new type of stop-cock.

Bramah's greatest invention was his Hydraulic Press (1795), a machine 'which gives to a child the strength of a giant'. It was to be used on a number of extraordinary occasions by famous engineers. Robert Stephenson used it to hoist the huge tubes of the Britannia Bridge into their bed, when the weight raised was calculated to be 1,144 tons. Brunel used it to launch the *Great Eastern* steamship. It had a great variety of uses including pressing cloth, extracting oil from hides before tanning, testing cables, uprooting trees, raising buildings, quarrying, drawing piles from dams, making gunpowder, sugar or wax, and packing bales.

The Wood-Planing Machine

In 1802 Bramah took out a patent for a wood-planing machine which was said to have saved a great deal of manual labour and produced straight smooth surfaces on demand. The machine was later adapted for use with metals.

The Printing Machine

Bramah had become a respected and well-known inventor and began to be called upon by individuals and organisations to help solve problems or improve existing operations. A good example of this took place in 1806 when he made a machine which printed the numbers and date lines on bank notes, a process said to be still in use during the 1870s. In 1805 he had patented a new machine for making paper, though it was not adopted by any manufacturer.

Civil Engineering

Bramah continued to produce small-scale inventions such as a method of pen-making which enabled a number of pens to be made out of a single quill but he became increasingly involved in civil engineering projects. In 1812 he brought out a patent for an ambitious scheme to lay water pipes through the main streets of London with the object of providing pressurised water for use in extinguishing fires. He was appointed to design the new waterworks at Norwich (1790–93), which he did with great success despite the scepticism of a rival engineer. Had he

The Great Eastern *was built in Millwall and floated on the Thames in 1858. It could accommodate 4,000 passengers and was the world's largest ship, but it was never a commercial success.*

lived longer it is likely that Bramah would have been involved in further engineering projects since he had ideas about building bridges and canal locks.

Joseph Bramah caught a cold when supervising his hydrostatic press at Holt Forest, Hampshire and died in 1814. He was buried in Paddington Churchyard. A marble tablet, erected by public subscription, was placed in Silkstone Church, on which was placed the following inscription:

> *This stone is inscribed to the memory of Mr. Joseph Bramah, late of Piccadilly and Pimlico, London, and formerly of this parish, who died 9th December, 1814, in the 66th year of his age. By rare genius and eminent perserverance, he advanced himself to considerable eminence as an engineer and machinist, and matured several inventions of the greatest public utility.*

Joseph Bramah did not make a fortune from his remarkable inventions but, like Joseph Locke, deserves wilder recognition.

Isambard Kingdom Brunel (1806–59) photographed in front of the Great Eastern. Science Museum

PART EIGHT: BUSTLING BARNSLEY

28 BULLS & BEARS ON MAY DAY GREEN

May Day Green served as a pleasure ground for many generations of Barnsley folk and on fair days was transformed into a colourful arena, a magnet for visitors from miles around. The cries of street sellers mixed with the music of travelling minstrels and itinerant entertainers but for some there was only one attraction: the gruesome spectacle of bull and bear-baiting.

The process was quite simple. A bull or bear was chained to a stake by the neck or leg and dogs were allowed to attack the virtually defenceless animal, much to the delight of the gathering crowd. When a bull was baited its nose was often blown full of pepper to further arouse it. Specially trained dogs were let loose, each attempting to seize the tethered animal's nose. Sometimes a hole in the ground was dug into which the bull might thrust this vulnerable part of its anatomy. A successful dog was said to have 'pinned the bull'.

There were also sinister variations. Whipping a blinded bear and baiting a pony with an ape tied to its back were not unusual. So much for the romantic view of dancing around the May-pole and lyric drama.

Yet such events were very much a reflection of the society of the time or at least of certain elements within it, though, as we shall see, there were also many Barnsley people who were outraged and sickened by the continuation of this medieval 'sport'.

Our ancestors lived in an age which was often much more humane than ours and yet there was an addiction to bear-baiting and bull-baiting. Queen Elizabeth herself led the way; she had had her own bears and bear-ward since the age of six, providing popular entertainment when foreign ambassadors visited her court. Bull rings and bear rings stood cheek by jowl with theatreland on the disreputable South Bank of London.

Bedraggled and muzzled bears would have been dragged through the streets of Barnsley in order to attract custom for the bloody show to come although of course some bears were of the performing kind, dancing for a few coppers in the market place and green to an excited and half intoxicated crowd.

'Bull-running' also developed. Townspeople, armed with clubs, knives, farm tools etc. chased after a bull until it was absolutely exhausted; then it was killed. Dog fighting and cock fighting, both greatly encouraged by gambling, were often provided as diversions.

Some of the leading citizens of Barnsley could stand these barbaric acts no longer. They joined together to produce a remarkably enlightened public notice in the face of a popular tradition:

Whereas it is become practice with Inn-Keepers and private persons in the Township of Barnsley – without regard to stated pass-times – but at their own diversion to hire and bate Bulls and Bears – which practice has been the cause of much tumult, profaneness and immorality. And whereas – the Bulls have not been as was usual – Game Bulls but poor lame defenceless animals – tied to a stake and worried and torn in a manner too shocking for human nature to reflect on – Now to remedy such outrages done to society and such cruelties to the animals themselves the principal

In the name of entertainment, the cruel sport of bear baiting.

inhabitants do hereby Declare and agree – that they will lodge information against and proceed to prosecute any person or persons who shall hereafter be concerned in leading forth – tying – or exposing to bate any Bull, Bear or other animal – of which agreement the Inhabitants will have public notice.

Barnsley – 6th August, 1783.
John Wilson, John Pickering, Churchwardens. Thor. Hall, John Stocks, Thomas Hawkesworth, Contable. Robert Lodge, Geo. Naylor, Richd. Pickering, Wm. Cardwell, Thos. Taylor, Senr. Edw. Taylor, John Deykin, Joseph Beckett, John Bent, Robert Leatham, Richard Richardson. William Lawton, Constable. Jonas Clarke, Thos. Frudd, H. Clarke, J. Clarke, Geo. Clarke, Foljambe Wood.

The faithful plea of Barnsley's respectable inhabitants would seem to have been only partly successful. Bear and bull-baiting continued to take place on May Day Green and probably at other more private sites around the town for many years afterwards.

There is one record of a local citizen who had sufficient courage to physically try and stop one of the 'performances'. Mr James Cocker went into the midst of the assembled crowd and demanded to know whose property the bear was, but receiving no reply, took out of his pocket a pistol, apparently with the intention of shooting the animal. A man instantly stepped forward and begged him to spare the bear, saying that he would take the animal away and never use him in Barnsley again.

The result was perhaps more effective than the notice!

Bear and bull-baiting was made illegal by an Act of Parliament in 1835 and Barnsley would seem to have been one of the last towns to witness the gruesome spectacle.

According to *Atkinson's Almanack* the last bull bait in Barnsley was on 22 August 1831 (probably Feast Week), when the bull broke loose. On Barnsley Feast Monday, 1823, three bulls and two bears were baited, one bull on May Day Green, one in a small field near to Wesley Street and another at the junction of the roads near Measbrough Dike. Then there was a bear-baiting on Barebones and another on Crow Well Hill where Runcorn's bear was baited.

James Runcorn and his bear came from Sheffield and were really better known to many locals than the inside of St Mary's. The bear had been bought when young by a Barnsley man called Hardisty who sold it to Runcorn. Hardisty was seen after the bait walking up Sheffield Road with the bear on his hind legs walking faithfully behind him and its forepaws resting on each of the old man's shoulders! Runcorn, when visiting the Barnsley Feast would sometimes arrive in the middle of the night and make for Hardisty's house. Hardisty would let him in and no doubt the bear, and a friendship was renewed.

The above story formed part of a detailed letter sent to the editor of the *Barnsley Chronicle* back in 1873. The writer appended further interesting facts about the valiant Mr Cocker. The creature which Cocker threatened to put away was in fact a small black bear, the property of a man who appeared to have been a stranger to all those present on May Day Green:

Mr. Cocker at that time one of the Court Leet constables was by profession a druggist carrying on a business in the shop now occupied by Mr. Edward Horne. He was a post-master, having succeeded to that office on the death of Mr. Charles Greaves. On becoming the owner of the building now the property of Mr. Dandison, in Wellington Street, he removed the post office to that place, for which he received many an inverted blessing from the guards of mail, who had to tramp up Peashill-nook, then a narrow street, which as one of them once said, he never went through on a dark winter's day without expecting to be robbed and murdered.

After introducing the power loom to the town, much to the outrage of the weavers, Cocker departed to London where he kept an 'eating-house' and where he died, in 1850.

Bull and bear-baiting arenas on London's South Bank in Tudor times.

The old bull-stoop was in the centre of the lower part of May Day Green and consisted of the root and a few feet of a tree let into the ground, with an hole in the upper part through which the end of a rope was knotted. The other end of a fifteen foot rope was usually tied around the neck of the bull or bear. Within the memory of the writer the baitings were certainly not confined to fair days but took place on Saturday evenings during the summer:

> *when might be seen men, principally colliers, coming from all the country villages, many leading ugly bull dogs by a string or handkerchief fastened to the dog's collar.*
>
> *As the hour for the sport approached, May Day Green began to fill with those characters, and at the time appointed some of us youngsters who had been keeping a sharp look out, would raise the shout of'* "t bull's coming". *He was a fine looking animal, all white, but sadly disfigured in the face from being bitten by dogs, his nostrils being literally torn out.*

The 'white bull' was apparently the property of a local man who lived in Jumble Lane, behind the *Wellington Inn*. This was Langley or 'Isaac Ellick', a well known bull keeper who was succeeded by a man from Hemsworth named Newhill.

When the bull arrived the rope which was coiled around its neck was unwound:

> *amidst the barking of dogs and the oaths and cursing of the baptised brutes by whom they were held, he was fastened to the stake. He was then, for the purpose of making a ring, led round by the owner, who would then announce the terms of the sport by proclaiming 'One dog, one bull, three slips, and a wind.'*

The owners of the dogs were allowed, for one shilling, to have the privilege of 'sleating' or setting a dog at the bull three times. Any reluctant dog received savage treatment from the owner.

The bull's horns were pointed with steel tips. Sometimes the dog was hurled into the air followed by an anxious attempt to either catch him or break his fall. An apparent 'highlight' was when the dog seized the bull by the nose and held fast, always a praiseworthy feat for the respective owner. Our eye-witness described the scene as follows:

> *I have seen the dogs hold on, the bull in his rage, bellowing in a most horrible manner, and throw his head high in the air without being able to shake them off, and sometimes in his agony he would break the rope by which he was held. Then all was confusion, the bull rushing madly amongst the crowd, and every one trying to get out of his way, many being thrown down and lamed.*

Finally, let us to return to Runcorn and his 'Sheffield bear.' One night the residents of Jumble Lane were startled from their slumbers by piercing female screams. Runcorn and his bear had arrived in town late as usual but had managed to find a bed at Tommy Wike's bakehouse in Jumble Lane. 'Ned' the bear was placed in some shavings in the bakehouse but decided to take a stroll upstairs in the early hours. On entering a room where two

Probably the last bear to be seen in Barnsley's town centre; that of the performing bear. Tasker collection

young women were in bed he mounted his two front paws on to the bedstock and 'took stock' of the two unsuspecting females who presumably knew nothing of the bear's arrival. The resultant screams were said to have been louder 'than ever issued from the throats of human beings.'

Ned the bear was no fool. If he was tramping the road and an empty wagon passed him he would drop down, as if shot, and poor Runcorn had to bargain with the owner to allow him to ride. The relationship with Runcorn came to an end on the morning of 16 May 1824, when the bear, which had been left overnight unmuzzled, attacked him and wounded him so severely that he died the same day. Poor Ned was then shot.

Although banned in England the sport of baiting continued in the frontier towns of the United States but in a variety of forms e.g. dogs against badgers, a chained bull against a grizzly bear.

Next time you are in May Day Green pause and consider you may be near the spot where excited mobs gathered to taunt and occasionally kill noble animals despite the increasing disdain of many Barnsley residents.

29 Goose Pyes, Fat Chickens and Fine Cheeses

Long before the Barnsley Chop gained widespread fame many Barnsley people were noted for the making of goose pies. Mr Henry Rayney, a London apothecary, with family connections at Tyers Hill, in Darfield parish, and grandson of the draper benefactor of Worsbrough Grammar School, wrote to local attorney Mr Henry Carrington on 19 September 1727 with a very special request:

> *Pray buy me three goose pyes at Barnsley of a groat a piece, not those that has a quarter of a goose in small pieces, as Timothy tells me, and one pye bigger, these I desire may be purchased on Mich. day, and sent up in a box by the carr., and I will return the money with thanks or will have no pyes. It being purely to show people here what good things Yorkshire produces and what sort of goose pyes is made.*

Michaelmas Day, 29 September, more correctly the day of St Michael and All Angels was observed as a feast by the Church of England and was widely marked by the eating of a goose at dinner. Fairs were often held on saints' days when traders and merchants set up stalls to try and tempt visitors to part with money perhaps intended as an offering or for the journey home. The feasting on goose pie coincided with Barnsley's most ancient fair, traditionally held on the Wednesday before Michaelmas Day.

The town's market charter, granted by King Henry III in 1249, gave to the Prior and Convent of Pontefract, for ever 'one market every seven days on Wednesday in their town of Barnsley, and that they have one fair day lasting for four days, viz., the eve of Saint Michael's day and two days hereafter ...'

The site of the fair gave its name to 'Fairfield', an open piece of land stretching from modern Sackville Street towards St Mary's Church and adjacent to 'Churchfields', one of the main townfields of Barnsley.

Soon there were three more annual fairs, held in October, May and February. The February fair occupied land to the east of the town on a site later occupied by the gasworks on Pontefract Road and also at the bottom of 'Swinhills' (Queens Road).

Fairs were of tremendous social and economic importance. Into the town would come livestock and farm produce. Some products were brought in on foot from nearby farms and villages. Other goods, including livestock, arrived from considerable distances. Drovers brought in flocks of sheep and cattle, dry goods in carts and wagons and on packhorses.

The three great Barnsley fairs were noted for horned cattle, swine and corn but by the seventeenth century Barnsley had specialist markets for malt and cloth. The Michaelmas Fair continued its reputation for goose pies and also for cheeses. Two pewterers, mentioned in David Hey's book *Packmen, Carriers and Packhorse Roads* (Leicester UP, 1980), arrived in 1485 all the way from York. The May fair was held on Barnsley Common and May-Day Green.

A country woman carrying live geese to market. British Museum

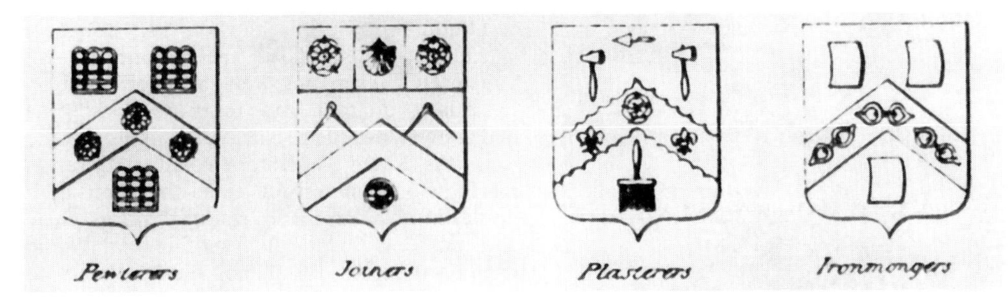

Arms of four of the Trade Companies of London.

When the Duke of Leeds purchased the manor of Barnsley in 1735 he also gained the rights of tolls and rents from the fairs and markets. However, his patronage also included a number of maintenance duties and expenses. His annual accounts are preserved in the Yorkshire Archaeological Library, Leeds and demonstrate how important a landlord could be in the success or failure of towns.

One of the Duke's first acts was to erect a fine public bakehouse to replace the old ovens which were pulled down. He did this with considerable care, viewing ovens at Wakefield, Sheffield, Rotherham and Doncaster 'and Inquiring for a proper person to build ours'. The Duke employed a variety of Barnsley craftsmen who would have been no doubt pleased for the work. Joseph Smith was paid £1.7s.8d. for slating and pointing with lime.

Leonard Rusby and John Horn received more than £6 for further slating. The glazier got £3. The bricklayer and plasterer submitted a bill for £12, as did the carpenter and joiner. 'Old Brown' hewed some flags (1s.6d.), Isaac Crossley provided windowstones and flags (£2.18s.11d.), John Birkhead made bricks (£6.10s.11d.), Timothy Rhodes, blacksmith, did some of the ironwork (11s.7d.), Ezra Morton built 'the great oven' (£12.2s.6d.), Sam Hough made the locks (15s.7d.) and there were numerous payments to labourers and for timber, for the leading of goods and to the masons. The workers were occasionally rewarded in 'ale' and 'beef'.

The building must have caused widespread interest, giving the market place a new lease of life under the new owner and brought a good proportion of the community together working on a common project.

The Duke's 'disbursements' included paying wages to tollmen who went around the markets and fairs collecting from stallholders and pedlars. He also employed a 'scavenger' to clear away all the rubbish. He paid a stall-setter to erect the stalls and had to keep them well-maintained. In return, tolls were paid to the Duke for the sale of beasts on market and fair days, and from horse and cheese sales and rents of stands used by pewterers and tinners. In addition he received annual income from about fifty stall rents.

The Duke was not slow to realise the value of advertising the Michaelmas Fair. His accounts for 1752 show payments to the *Leeds Mercury, York Courant* and even the *London Evening Post*, underlining the considerable distances that people would travel.

Merchandise ranging from pins and packthread to candles and cloth would be carried and 'cried' through the main streets on market and fair days. All kinds of food would be offered. Some vendors would have loud or melodic voices, others would place emphasis on particular words: 'Buy my fat chickens!', 'Buy a dish of great eels!' and so on.

Pin seller and thread lace sellers from the Cries of London *(1711).* Courtesy of Syndics of University of Cambridge Library

Second-hand clothes dealer from the Cries of London (1711). Syndics of University of Cambridge Library

There would be hawkers of tobacco, spectacles, dolls, ballad sheets, buttons, rat poison etc., competing with the 'shows' put on by quack doctors and tooth-pullers. Some pedlars would rattle pots and pans, others would ring bells. Shrewd operators would try to tempt residents or their servants to let them into their homes in order to mend, sharpen, sweep, clean and pick (e.g. corns!) At May fair there would have been scores of itinerant street-sellers with an atmosphere enhanced by the sound and colour of impromptu entertainments: puppet shows, performances from strolling musicians and players, booths of fortune-tellers and freaks, keepers of strange animals.

The cruel spectacle of bear/bull baiting and cock-fighting attracted large crowds whilst alehouses and inns did a roaring trade.

The poorest and least successful of all the street sellers were children from poor families or orphans trying to earn three or four pennies each day. Street urchins could be girls in thin dresses, fingers aching in the cold, selling violets or barefoot boys in rags begging for cast off fruit. It was a pitiable existence made even worse if they were disabled.

When William Hutton, the Birmingham historian, visited Barnsley market place on a miserable day back in 1808 he described it as 'a market in confusion'. Yet markets were 'unplanned' and not necessarily places where the well-to-do went shopping. They were, more importantly, an integral part of the lives of most ordinary Barnsley folk.

A hectic cock fighting scene depicted by William Hogarth.

30 THE MARKET PLACE

The ancient Market Place of Barnsley was the commercial and social heart of the town, the very reason for its existence. The removal of the stalls from Market Hill in modern times was surely a great mistake; more than seven centuries of trade and a wealth of character was lost.

The original market occupied a remarkably small area. At the top was the Moot Hall with its attached row of small shops and tenements; at the bottom of the hill was the open Sough Dyke, crossed by a wooden bridge. The upper part of the Market Place, according to Warburton, was seven poles ($38\frac{1}{2}$ yards) wide and only five poles at the bottom ($27\frac{1}{2}$ yards). In this space were held the market stalls and the corn market. The butchers' market was held at the entrance to Westgate or Shambles Street, under and near to the gateways *Cock Inn* and *Old Horns Inn* (site of the *Lord Nelson/The Shambles*). The hill, as we have seen, was also the venue for both mobile public floggings as well as the place for stationary disgrace, via pillory and stocks.

The Market Place was also the scene of great social gatherings.

On May Day, up to about 1790, milkmaids 'decked with flowers' and 'carrying soured milk pails' paraded, no doubt with a mixture of pride and Barnsley humour. It was also an unofficial venue for playing football, though one would hope that sides 'changed ends' to allow for the hill! On August 17 1790, a football match caused all the traders to close their shops. Another event also caused some traders to conduct business 'by side doors and back entrances'. This was the annual hiring of farm labour (men and women), traditionally known as Statutes Day. Such events no doubt attracted large crowds.

Crowds were nothing new to the hill. National events were celebrated there, especially coronations. When Queen Victoria was crowned, a great meal was cooked and catering resembling the Denby Dale Pie took place; every man (but no women?) received a quart of porter to go with his roast beef. In 1856, it was estimated that nearly 8,000 children were assembled on the hill, singing hymns to celebrate the end of the Crimean War. If correct, such numbers would be equivalent to the entire field of the first London Marathon of 1981. A similar sized crowd of children is said to have mustered a year earlier, at the fall of Sebastopol when a huge bonfire was lit. Bonfires and fireworks also lit up Market Hill in 1900, commemorating the relief of Mafeking and the entry into Pretoria.

BARNSLEY MARKET PLACE IN 1785

(Courtesy of E. G. Tasker)

Lodge's Almanack for 1901/2 provides a marvellous description of Barnsley Market Place in 1785. One of the tenants of the little shops under the Moot Hall was Joseph Smith, bookseller, who, according to his own advertisement sold 'all sorts of books on divinity, history, law, mathematicks, musick, classicks etc.' Perhaps it was a place of some refuge, especially when the adjacent butter market was in full cry. The first brick building adjoining the Moot Hall was the town gaol and then there was William Crossland's

Barnsley Market Place in about 1895. From a Warner Gothard Photograph

house: he was the 'stall-setter' and toll collector. Next was John Hyde's shop, later occupied by confectioner Thomas Peat. This shop looked down on what is now the Arcade, but then called Broadgates where the fish market was held. The last of the tenements attached to the venerable hall was occupied by a Miss Ratcliffe but it must have been a very noisy place to live.

A broad space separated the 'Moot Hall Row' from a short row of three more tenements; one of them was occupied by barber Tattersall whose trade – and banter – was increased on market days. 'Tommy' Morton, a tinker, came next. When his premises were pulled down he protested by taking up his mattress and 'domiciled himself' in the Jury Room of the Moot Hall where he remained until he was 'half-starved' and then removed to the Workhouse. Morton was a Quaker, and his wife, who predeceased him, was laid to rest in the Burton Burial Ground. Poor Tommy could not bear the thought of himself being buried a pauper, so managed to save five pounds, and lodged it in the safe of Mr. Richard Dearman, who received instructions (duly executed) that Tom was to lay next to his wife at Burton.

The last tenement was probably the most notorious of the row; in it resided Samuel Truelove, blacksmith. At the corner was a well which supplied water for the hill and for Church Street. Old Sam, born in about 1730, refused to leave his premises when the row was due for demolition. He apparently received a great deal of ridicule and perhaps good natured 'leg pulling' because of his stance. Sam threatened to shoot all-comers who dared touch his house; he threatened the workmen and a crowd gathered. Jack Fish, rag gatherer, of Hoyland Swaine, and therefore not afraid of heights, climbed up on to the roof of Truelove's house and shop, onlookers watching with increasing glee. Sam mustered his blunderbuss, fired but missed and the crowd jeered. Primed again, Sam took a more determined aim and pulled the trigger. This time he was on target; Jack fell, rolled down the slates, his clothes were spiked near the gutter but his body fell on to the ground – dead, his back containing about fifty shot. Banker Foljambe Wood was said to have rushed across to the assailant, saying, 'You old villain! Do you know what you have done? You have taken the life of yonder poor man! I will have you bound hand and foot and sent to your task'.

Truelove was placed on trial at the next assizes, in July, 1788 but was only found guilty of manslaughter, fined £20 and imprisoned for two years. He returned to Barnsley as a poor cripple and died a few years later.

'The Tragedy of Old Smithy' however, lived on in the memories of many Barnsley folk, perhaps helped by the following lines:

A poor honest man, John Fish was his name,
About his own business, to Barnsley he came;
But little he thought it would be his sad lot,
By a blood thirsty smith to be wantonly shot.

Peasehill Nook (Peel Square) around 1895. Warner Gothard

31 Inns & Innkeepers

A high proportion of innkeepers and shopkeepers was a feature of market towns and Barnsley was no exception. During the first half of the eighteenth century twelve innkeepers were involved in land and property transactions in the town, and after mercers or drapers they were the most important occupational group. A survey of other extant records reveal at least a further ten names.

The growth of hostelries in Barnsley during the eighteenth century was only partly due to better documentary sources but rather reflected the increasing importance of the town as a communication centre with a good hinterland.

It is not easy to identify the sites of the early inns. Names of the inn signs occasionally changed, residential and commercial buildings were sometimes adapted for service as inns or even had shared usage and the changes were complicated where a particular family was associated with several establishments.

However, a number of clear features emerge. The larger inns and posting houses were on the main streets amid the hub of traffic and trade. They were sited in the Market Place, on Kirkgate (Church Street) and Westgate (Shambles Street). They were ideally positioned to deal with visitors arriving via the main thoroughfares of the town.

Innkeepers of Barnsley were often wealthy inhabitants. Their variety of duties made them key members of the community. One family – the Hawksworths – appear frequently in records and serve as a most interesting example.

Thomas Hawksworth, kept the *Old Horns* for many years until his death in 1737. The hostelry was well-sited on Shambles Street and later became *The Lord Nelson*, later replaced by *The Shambles*. He was landlord in 1714 at the same time that Josiah Hawksworth occupied the *Boot and Shoe* on Kirkgate. After Thomas died, his widow continued to keep the premises going and was determined to let folk know that business would be as usual, despite contrary rumour:

> *August 1st 1737, whereas it hath been falsely and maliciously reported that the house of the late Thomas Hawksworth of Barnsley hath been shut up and business given over: this is to certify that the said house is kept on by Margaret, widow of Thomas Hawksworth where Gentlemen, Ladies and others may meet with the same good usage as usual by their humble servant Margaret Hawksworth.*

Margaret died in 1739 and was probably replaced by Sampson Brown, the inn then being used as one of the venues for Barnsley racegoers. It was about this time that the diarist John Hobson reported how local attorney Henry Carrington died shortly after consuming a barrel of oysters at the *Horns*.

Hawksworth's probate inventory survives, providing a marvellous view of an important Barnsley inn. The ground floor consisted of what would seem to have been a substantial kitchen containing a large number of cooking utensils, including a chafing dish or food warmer, 38 pewter dishes, 8 dozen plates,

Formerly near the Old Horns, *The* Lord Nelson *in Shambles Street closed in 1972. It was replaced by a new public house called* The Shambles *but in 1992 re-named the* Lord Nelson *in respect of its predecessor.* Tasker collection

This could have been a typical scene in any of Barnsley's inns. From a painting by George Morland. (1792). Christies

pudding, pastry and stew pans and two tea kettles. Such an array was clearly not meant solely for his own use but for the preparation and serving of meals to guests.

Next door was the Brewhouse containing all the equipment necessary to brew ale on a considerable scale, the most important item being the 'Brewing Lead with Copper' which stood near to a 'Grate' malt chest or 'ark'.

Nearby were the principal storeplaces for the kind of dry produce one would expect at an important hostelry which had farming interests: Mill Chamber, Corn Chamber and Meal Chamber.

The appraisers then entered the main living quarters: the low parlour, used as a bedroom, comfortably furnished, lit by a 'lanthorn' where Thomas may have worked on one of three desks. In the main room or 'House' were two 'long settles', a form, five tables, several chairs, a long case clock, an hour glass and, interestingly, (perhaps to entertain and attract) three bird cages. The birds were not identified or valued! This was the main social room of the inn which led to a smaller Upper Parlour containing four tables and 12 chairs; the walls were even enhanced by 11 maps, a picture and a stagshead.

Two connecting butteries came next, approached via a passage which also housed a bed, warming pan, and 'close stool' (commode) – every little space was valuable on market days!

Upstairs could be found seven 'chambers' used for family and guests. The first three: the 'Gate House Chamber' (probably overlooking the street) 'Mr. Oates Room', 'Blew Chamber', 'Green Room' and 'Great Chamber' were rather grand affairs each having feather beds and well furnished. The Great Chamber had 15 chairs, maps and a picture and even window curtains, the height of luxury for early eighteenth century Barnsley. Some of these rooms may have been permanently occupied.

In contrast, the little chamber contained three beds – less affluent guests paid less but shared a room, or even a bed! The end chamber, over the butteries, was also finely furnished, including window curtains. The adjacent 'Lad's passage', the servant's room, was frugal in comparison.

There were two cellars. The upper one contained 29 half-hogsheads, 10 hogsheads, and 13 small casks (all empty) representing the recent use of about 1,400 gallons of real ale – quite a turnover! The other cellar contained the actual stock of ale which may have been run down if Hawksworth had had a long illness, but contained 4? hogsheads, about 240 gallons. The ale was valued at £8. There was also what would seem to have been a huge stock of wine, valued at £69.

The innkeeper also had silver tankards, spoons and cups and a good stock of bed linen. Thomas was also very much a farmer, having six horses, a cow, seven pigs, a stock of hay and crops of barley, wheat, peas and beans along with the usual range of implements and tools. Interestingly, he also had some butchers' stalls – these were originally called 'shambles', hence the name eventually given to the street which, at the corner with the market place was the place where butchers displayed their meat, perhaps at times with blood running down the hill. Abraham Hawksworth, probably Thomas' brother, died a year later and was a butcher by trade, but true to family tradition, kept a cellar full of ale.

Thomas Hawksworth's personal property was valued at almost £340, making him one of the leading citizens of the town and one with high social rank. His will, for example, included bequests to two gentlemen with whom he was obviously on good terms; Henry Edmunds of Worsbrough Hall and John Kent of Kimberworth; also one of his sureties was a cleric from Nostell.

Another Morland painting: Travellers resting by an inn fire (1792). Christies

Another interesting Barnsley hostelry was the *George Inn*. This was near the top of the east side of the Market Place, opposite the Moot Hall and reached by a yard which later was a routeway towards the Public Hall. Part of it was later used as premises for a chemist and tobacconist. Yet another of the Hawksworths, John, occupied it in the mid 1750s. John Nicholson kept it at the time of the Barnsley Races of 1774. The churchwardens accounts show how he provided fourteen shillings of wine for communion but two penneth of ale was issued to the parish clerk for fetching the wine to St. Mary's Church!

Several mail coaches stopped at this famous hostelry, especially the London, Birmingham, Derby, Sheffield and Leeds coaches, calling daily at 9 a.m. The return coaches arrived every evening, the fare was £1. 9s. (quite expensive).

The property was sold in 1798 by Joseph Hawksworth and passed to the Clarkes, another well known family of drapers and innkeepers, and eventually owned by Miss Frances Day, milliner, from an old Monk Bretton family.

The passage leading into George Yard was used as a butter market.

A lovely advertisement described the *George* in 1787 in words which would do justice to any modern estate agent:

> *All that capital and good accustomed inn, situated in the centre of town. The premises have been much enlarged and improved, are in complete repair, and contain numerous well proportioned apartments etc., which have been lately fitted up in a most genteel manner. There is good stabling for near fifty horses, a very commodious yard and all convenient offices. (Leeds Intelligencer, December 18, 1787).*

Francis Roper (1696–1780), innkeeper, was an important citizen of Barnsley and was commemorated on a plaque in St Mary's. With his wife, Margaret, who lived until 1809, he kept the *White Bear Inn* on Kirkgate. Another branch of the family were grocers.

Francis and Margaret became well known figures in the town, kept busy by the demands of the mail and other duties. The Ropers were frequently involved in land and property agreements

The Coach and Horses Hotel *at the bottom of Market Hill; built in 1857, it replaced an earlier inn of the same name but was converted into a bank in 1912.* Tasker collection

The Royal Hotel, *formerly* The White Bear, *one of the town's premier posting houses.* Tasker collection

during the latter half of the eighteenth century and must have been very proud of their new and impressive hostelry.

The Duchess of Kent and Princess Victoria passed through Barnsley in 1835 and the landlady of the *Bear* – yet another Hawksworth – supplied them with new post horses for their royal carriages. One result was a change of name to the *Royal Hotel*, which ended confusion with the *Old White Bear* of Shambles Street, a site now ocupied by Barnsley Central Library. The 'Sarah Hawkesworth Room' unveiled in 1985, paid tribute to this interesting Barnsley landlady.

A much older inn occupied a piece of land which became known as 'Guest's Yard', now the Arcade. Here was *Broadgates*, an inn associated with the Clarke family. When Joseph Clarke of Barnsley, yeoman, died in 1759, he left the substantial sum of £500 to John Clarke of *Broadgates*, innholder.

The latter was probably the son of John Clarke the elder, who died in 1737 and had substantial property interests in Barnsley. Under the gateway, fish was sold on market days. The kitchen of the inn was apparently intact prior to the creation of the arcade and when demolished revealed an oak beam which bore the date 1667.

The old town house of the Wood family, situated near the bottom of Market Hill was converted into the *King's Head Hotel* in about 1775. It became renowned for 'Barnsley Chops' and a local conundrum: 'Why was the executioner of Charles I like a visitor to a noted Yorkshire Hotel?' Answer: "Because he had a chop at the King's Head."

The premises were occupied by the Johnson family and it soon became a famous posting house, with mail coaches calling daily.

At the foot of the hill (there was no Eldon Street) stood the *Cross Daggers*, another famous Barnsley inn, tenanted by John Clarke in 1764. Clarke's widow, Martha, was commonly known as 'Matty-at-the-well' or 'Matty O'Daggers'. The inn may have closed after the establishment of the *King's Head*.

The *Three Cranes Inn*, Sowbridge Street was mentioned in a deed of 1722 when the Clarkes were innkeepers. Towards the end of the century it was kept by Thomas Howden, licensed victualler and carpenter.

The King's Head Hotel *on a royal occasion. The National Westminster bank now occupies the site.* Tasker collection

Another early inn was the *Black Bull*, Church Street, kept by Cornelius Wood in 1716. *The Packhorse* and the *Red Lion* appear in deeds during the 1750s. *The Six Ringers* occupied the site of the later *White Hart*. Cock fighting was held there during the Races of 1774.

The *Old Angel Inn* occupied premises on the lower west side of the market place later occupied by William Horsfield and was purchased by Mr Foljambe Wood, Barnsley's formidable early banker in 1782.

The *Old White Bear* on Shambles Street was kept for many years by William Crabtree but was due to be sold according to a Leeds newspaper advertisement of 1st July 1788:

A pair of King's Head *beer glasses. (Courtesy of Mr and Mrs Findlow, Royston).* Alan Billingham

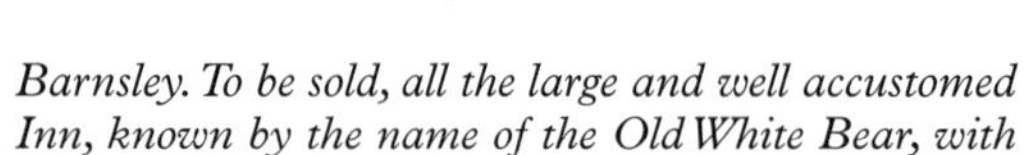

Barnsley. To be sold, all the large and well accustomed Inn, known by the name of the Old White Bear, with

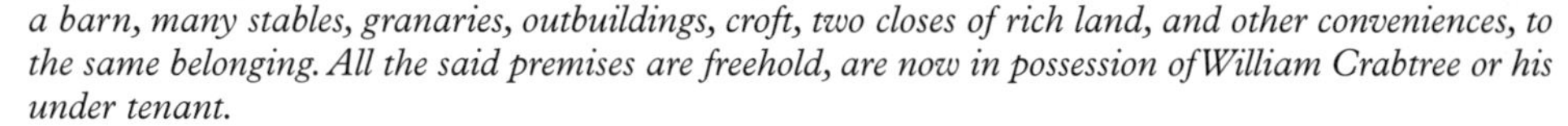

a barn, many stables, granaries, outbuildings, croft, two closes of rich land, and other conveniences, to the same belonging. All the said premises are freehold, are now in possession of William Crabtree or his under tenant.

There are other early inns whose histories remain fairly obscure and more well known ones which could be elaborated on in more detail.

The inns of Barnsley, especially the larger hostelries, were far more than dispensers of ale or providers of good food and accommodation.

When they linked up with carriers and coaches they were lifelines for the commercial development of Barnsley. At other times they were great meeting places for private or public where business was done and decisions made. They even had legal functions, especially with the decay of the old Moot Hall, and served as unofficial banks.

The pleasing facade of the East side of Market Hill as it appeared in the nineteenth century.

An alehouse keeper, from a drawing of about 1650.

It is no wonder that their keepers were so important citizens. Let us, however, finally remember them as places of entertainment, perhaps a fitting way to end a book about life in Barnsley before the Industrial Revolution:

> *At Barnsley, on Thursday evening there was a free ball at the White Bear Inn, which was respectfully attended, and on Friday evening the town was elegantly illuminated, the bells and bonfires were lighted. The whole concluded by the gentlemen assembled at the Bear parading the streets and singing (to the strains of) a band of music 'God Save the King'.* [Leeds Mercury – March 17th, 1789.]

Bibliography

1. Documentary Sources
Borthwick Institute of Historical Research, York.
Exchequer Wills and Inventories (Deanery of Doncaster).
Registered Wills.
Ecclesiastical Court Records (Cause Papers).

Sheffield Archives
Wood Brothers Records (Glass).
Wharncliffe Muniments: Deeds & Barnsley Colliery Papers (Courtesy of the Earl of Wharncliffe).
Elmhirst Papers.
Newman and Bond Collection (Maps).
Barnsley Cordwainers Records (formerly in S. Yorks Record Office). S.I.R.12.

West Yorkshire Archive Service Headquarters (Registry of Deeds), Wakefield.
Quarter Session Records.
Deeds (1703–1760).

Yorkshire Archaeological Society Archives, Leeds.
M.B. Weinstock: Notebook of John Mence MSS 748 (circa 1950).
Duke of Leeds Papers.

City of Wakefield Library Headquarters
Hearth Tax Returns (1672).

Hereford & Worcester Record Office
Memo Book of John Mence 2 X496.5 BA 9360 C? Box 2, Courtesy of Worcester County Solicitor.

The National Archives, London
Exchequer & Chancery Court Records

2. Libraries
Barnsley: Local Studies and Archives
Elliott B. Barnsley: 'The Anatomy of a Yorkshire Market Town and its neighbourhood c1660–c1760', M.Phil thesis,
University of Sheffield, 1990.
E.G. Bayford Bequest.
Papers, collections, MSS relating to E.G. Bayford, J.H. Burland, E. Hoyle, G. England, J. Wilkinson and E.G. Tasker.
Local maps
Lodge's Almanack
Newspaper cuttings

Friends Library, Euston, London
Quaker Historical Society Journal.
Advice from library staff (1972).

Barnsley Meeting House Library, Huddersfield Road.
Miscellaneous Papers relating to Burton and Barnsley Meetings.
Quaker Diaries (printed).

3. Printed Works

Ashurst, D. Excavations at Gawber Glassworks, near Barnsley, *Post Medieval Archaeology*, 4 (1970).
Ashurst, D. *The History of South Yorkshire Glass*, J R Collis Publications (n.d)
Baines, E. *Baine's Yorkshire*, David & Charles reprint (1822/1969).
Betjeman, J. and Vaisey, D. *Victorian and Edwardian Oxford from Old Photographs*, (1971).
Bigland, J. A. *A Topographical and Historical Description of York*, (1812).
Burland, J. H. Market Hill and its People a Hundred Years Ago, *Barnsley Chronicle*, 20 November, 1866.
Clarke, P. *The English Alehouse: A Social History, 1200–1830* (1986).
Crossley, D. W. and Ashurst, D. Excavations at Rockley Smithies, a Water-Powered Bloomery of the sixteenth and seventeenth centuries, *Post Medieval Archaeology*, 2 (1968).
Defoe, D. *A Tour Through the Whole Island of Great Britain*, Everyman edition (1962).
Dodsworth, R. *Glass and Glassmaking* (1982).
Elliott, B. John Foster of Woolley: An early eighteenth century Coalmaster *South Yorkshire Historian*, W.E.A., 3 (1976).
Elliott, B. The Early Quakers of Monk Bretton, 1657–1700: A study of Dissent in a South Yorkshire Village, *Transactions of the Hunter Archaeological Society*, X (1977).
Elliott, B. *Royston: People of an Ancient Parish*, 2 vols (1985).
Elliott, B. Aspects of Medical Care in Barnsley during the seventeenth and eighteenth centuries, *Old West Riding*, 6, No.1 (1986).
Elliott, B. Lime, Liquor and Leathermen: Oak Bark Tanning, the Forgotten Rural Industry of South Yorkshire, *Hallamshire Historian*, 2, No.1 (1987/88).
Elmhirst, E. *A Peculiar Inheritance*, private printing (1951).
Farrar, H. *The Book of Pontefract* (1986).
Goodchild, J. *The Coal Kings of Yorkshire* (1978).
Goodchild, J. *Golden Threads: The Barnsley Linen Industry in the Eighteenth and Nineteenth Century* (1983).
Hey, D. G. *The Making of South Yorkshire* (1979).
Hey, D. G. *Yorkshire from A.D. 1000* (1986).
Hibbert, C. *The English, A Social History* (1987).
Hunter, J. *South Yorkshire*, 2 vols (1823/31).
Inglis, B. *A History of Medicine* (1965).
Jackson, R. *The History of the Town and Township of Barnsley, in Yorkshire from an Early Period* (1858).
Jenkins, G. *The Craft Industries* (1972).
Latham, R. (ed.) *The Illustrated Pepys* (1983).
Lobban, R. D. *Doctors* (1976).
Miller, E. *History and Antiquities of Doncaster* (1804).
Pevsner, Sir N. *The Buildings of England: The West Riding* (1967).
Redmonds, G. *Huddersfield and District under the Stuarts: Seventy Years of Law and Disorder* (1985).
Sheffield Trades Historical Society *Wortley Forge Guide*
Sigsworth, E. and Brady, V. (Ed's) *The Ledger of William Elmhirst, Surgeon and Apothecary, 1769–1773*, Humberside College of Education (1987).
Smith, A. H. *The Place-Names of the West Riding of Yorkshire*, Part One (1961).
Smith, D. J. *Aspects of Life in Old Cawthorne, South Yorkshire* (1987).
Spufford, M. *The Great Reclothing of Rural England.*
Surtees Society *Four Yorkshire Diaries*, LXV (1875).
Tasker, E. G. *Barnsley Streets*, 9 vols. (1974)
Thompson, E. P. *The Making of the Working Class* (1968).
Walker, J. W. An Historical and Architectural Description of the Priory of St. Mary Magdalene of Monk Bretton in the West Riding of Yorkshire, *Yorkshire Archaeological Society*, Extra vol V (1926).
Wilkinson, J. *Worsbrough: Its Historical Associations and Rural Attractions* (1872).
Wilkinson, J. *Worthies, Families and Celebrities of Barnsley and the District* (1883).
Wakefield Historical Publications: *Samuel Buck's Yorkshire Sketch-Book* (1979).

ACKNOWLEDGEMENTS
New research has gone into the making of the book but I am also indebted to Rowland Jackson, Joseph Wilkinson and other former historians of Barnsley listed in the Bibliography. The late Edward Tasker has been most kind to loan material; his unselfish work on nineteenth century Barnsley, and his monumental collection of photographs, will be appreciated by future generations of family and local historians. I am very fortunate at having the help of Kenneth Hawley for explaining some of the technicalties of wiremaking and also Denis Ashurst who has been willing to share his research and knowledge of local glassmaking.

Many thanks are due to achivists and librarians who have been so helpful over many years, especially at the Borthwick Institute of Historical Research, Sheffield City Archives, West Yorkshire Archive Service at the Registry of Deeds and Yorkshire Archaeological Society Archives. Maurice Hepworth, librarian at Barnsley Local Studies has also been most helpful and so as John Goodchild, Principal Archivist and Local Studies Officer at Wakefield M D Library Headquarters. To Sylvia Thomas, Archivist to the Joint Committee in the YAS Library, Leeds, for her help in locating the original Mence Diary. Quaker records have been obtained from Barnsley Friends Library (Mr Dyer was kind enough to allow access), Ackworth School and Friends House, London.

Quotes from Wharncliffe Muniments and the 'Barnsley Collieries' map (114) is by kind perrmission of The Earl of Wharncliffe (Sheffield Record Office); and the photographs relating to Wood Bros. Glassworks are also part of Sheffield Archives (WBR7). Elmhirst family papers (A O Elmhirst EM 888) Alfred O Elmhirst deserves great credit for his many years of campaigning on local historical features and issues; and for depositing family papers in Sheffield archives. I am grateful to the director of Libraries and Information Services for use of the above and for the kind help of archivists David Postles and Richard Childs.

Several people were kind enough to let me visit their homes: Mr. and Mrs R Barr, and Mr and Mrs T Carr of Cawthorne (for tanning industry); Mrs. Hilary Smith allowed access to the old nail forge at Hoylandswaine; Mr and Mrs Findlow of Royston, for the *King's Head* glasses; Mrs. Holmes of Banks Hall Residential Home, Cawthorne allowed photographs to be taken; and Malcolm Lister has not only provided photographs of Priory Mill but his enthusiasm has also encouraged my long-term interest in this unique building.

Brian Murray has been most kind to allow access to Cannon Hall Museum and its rich source of Barnsley exhibits. The staff and trustees of Cawthorne Victoria Jubilee Museum have also been most kind and their excellent work is much appreciated. I am indebted to Calderdale Industrial Museum, Halifax (wire-making), Sheffield Trades Historial Society (Wortley Forge) and Broadfield House Museum, West Midlands, especially its Keeper, Roger Dodsworth, for photographic material. Also Mr George Smith, Warden of St Mary's Church, Worsbrough for allowing us to photograph the Rockley Monument.

Thanks are also due to Norma Ledbury and Josie Oliver for occasional reprographic and typing help, and Lady Victoria Leatham of Burghley House, near Stamford for her kind help in connection with the Leathams of Barnsley.

Picture Acknowledgements

INDEX

PLACE-NAMES